British Tank Production and the War Economy, 1934–1945

British Tank Production and the War Economy, 1934–1945

Benjamin Coombs

BLOOMSBURY
LONDON • NEW DELHI • NEW YORK • SYDNEY

Bloomsbury Academic

An imprint of Bloomsbury Publishing Plc

50 Bedford Square	1385 Broadway
London	New York
WC1B 3DP	NY 10018
UK	USA

www.bloomsbury.com

First published 2013

British Library Cataloguing-in-Publication Data
A catalogue record for this book is available from the British Library.

ISBN: HB: 978-1-4725-0504-0
ePDF: 978-1-4725-1069-3
ePub: 978-1-4725-1282-6

Library of Congress Cataloguing-in-Publication Data
A catalog record for this book is available from the Library of Congress.

Design by Newgen Knowledge Works (P) Ltd., Chennai, India
Printed and bound in Great Britain

Contents

Acknowledgements

I would like to thank the following who have helped me in the completion of this book. First and foremost I am indebted to Professor Mark Connelly and Dr Timothy Bowman, for their continued advice and support. Professors David Welch and David Edgerton are thanked for their comments and recommendations during the examination of my original thesis. The University of Kent and Mr Paul Dyer receive my special thanks for awarding me the Alumni and Dyer scholarships. I am also grateful for the Royal Historical Society for providing me with the travel grants towards my research expenses within the United Kingdom and in Canada. I would like to thank the staff at Bloomsbury Publishing, particularly Claire Lipscomb and Rhodri Mogford, for their guidance and assistance.

My thanks go to the assistance provided by the staff at the various archives consulted. First, the National Archives in Kew, the Library and Archives Canada in Ottawa and the National Archives of Australia in Canberra. Secondly, the Bodleian Library in Oxford, the Cambridge University Library, the Liddell Hart Centre for Military Archives at King's College London, the Churchill College Archives in Cambridge, the Nuffield College Library in Oxford, the Modern Records Centre at the University of Warwick and the Museum of English Rural Life at the University of Reading. Thirdly, the Birmingham Archives and Heritage Service in the Birmingham Central Library, the Gloucestershire Archives in Gloucester and the Staffordshire Record Office in Stafford. Finally, the British Commercial Vehicle Museum in Leyland and the Heritage Motor Centre Motor Museum in Gaydon. Notwithstanding this help, any errors of fact or interpretation remain my responsibility.

A final word of thanks goes to my parents for their unfailing support and encouragement towards my continuing studies.

List of Tables

List of Figures

Abbreviations

AEC	Associated Equipment Company
AFV	Armoured Fighting Vehicles
ARP	Air Raid Precautions
BAH	Birmingham Archives and Heritage
BAS	British Army Staff
BCVM	British Commercial Vehicle Museum
BLO	Bodleian Library, Oxford
BPC	British Purchasing Commission
BSM	British Supply Mission
CAFV	Chairman, Armoured Fighting Vehicles
CCA	Churchill College Archives
CGMP	Controller-General of Munitions Production
CMH	Canadian Military Headquarters
CUL	Cambridge University Library
DAFV	Director of Armoured Fighting Vehicles
DCIGS	Deputy Chief of the Imperial General Staff
DD	Duplex Drive
DDGOF	Deputy Director-General of Ordnance Factories
DGAFV	Director-General of Armoured Fighting Vehicles
DGAR	Director-General of Army Requirements
DGFVP	Director-General of Fighting Vehicles Production
DGMP	Director-General of Munitions Production
DGP	Director-General of Programmes
DGTT	Director-General of Tanks and Transport
DND	Department of National Defence
GAG	Gloucestershire Archives, Gloucester
GMC	General Motors Corporation

HMC	Heritage Motor Centre
HMSO	His/Her Majesty's Stationery Office
hp	Horsepower
LAC	Library and Archives Canada
MOA	Mass Observation Archive
MP	Member of Parliament
MRC	Modern Records Centre
NAA	National Archives of Australia
NCL	Nuffield College Library
SP	Self-Propelled
SRO	Staffordshire Record Office
TNA	The National Archives

Introduction

The official history of *British War Production* for the Second World War accurately describes tank production as a 'highly-specialised industrial art without parallel in peace-time industry and without any special affinity with any branch of civilian engineering'.[1] The introduction of the tank during the First World War meant that the government and military authorities had to decide upon the tactical requirements for this new weapon and the numbers to be produced. As a result, industry had to overcome the issues of design, development and production to meet these objectives. The interaction between the government, the military and industry for the emerging tank programme almost one hundred years ago remains just as important today. These issues include tank designs that aim to find the required balance between firepower and overall size, armour protection and gross weight, and speed and manoeuvrability. The tactical and operational requirements of the General Staff when attempting to achieve this balance must fully understand the realistic capabilities of industry. Tanks will never be invulnerable to all forms of attack, so the enemy is always at liberty to test and exploit any weaknesses. The fighting compartment must be designed to permit tank crews to operate at peak efficiency in terms of battlefield performance and endurance. The number of tanks made available need to be sufficient for operations to have a reasonable chance of success. The issue of mechanical reliability is paramount if the tanks are to perform the different roles assigned to them. The availability of spare parts is essential to maintain the vehicles in the field during operations or behind the lines in base workshops. Finally, tanks have the potential to both strike fear into the enemy and provide inspiration and enhance the morale of friendly troops. These different issues will be discussed in this book from rearmament until the end of the Second World War, as part of an examination of British tank production and the war economy as a whole.

While the subject of armoured warfare has received continued interest by historians, a scholarly analysis of the British tank industry for the period before and during the Second World War has so far received insufficient attention. In 1960, Richard Ogorkiewicz provided a detailed study of the development and use of armour, although the available archival material has since greatly expanded.[2] Later, Peter Chamberlain and Chris Ellis completed a comprehensive review of Allied tank specifications by identifying the particular nuances between the various models.[3] British official papers were considered by David Fletcher in his two-part study and by Peter Beale during the late 1980s and 1990s. However, this limited research methodology produced mostly negative and incomplete arguments relating to British tank production, with the latter author lacking objectivity as well.[4] More recently, John Buckley has provided an academic and more positive account of the British tank programme in relation to the background and combat actions of the Normandy campaign.[5]

The broader themes relating to the emergence and evolution of armoured warfare have been considered by J. P. Harris, F. H. Toase et al., Patrick Wright and Robert Citino.[6] While these studies provide a useful history of the tank since the initial deployment during the First World War, they do not provide a detailed analysis of the pressures upon industry to provide this equipment. Some of the manufacturing issues relating to British strategy, the economy and arms production during the Second World War have been highlighted by the recent scholarship of Stephen Broadberry and Peter Howlett, David Edgerton, and George Peden.[7] With regard to British industry during wartime, some of the experiences of factory workers have been presented by Penny Summerfield and Richard Croucher, with Helen Jones providing an account of the methods used to undertake air raid precautions.[8]

This book will consider the different influences upon the British tank programme and the effect that these had upon specific examples from industry from 1934 until 1945. The requirements, design, production and use of British tanks, before and during the Second World War, will be discussed as part of an overall study of British war planning and the economy. To provide a global perspective, this analysis will be discussed with comparative examples from the war industries of the United States, Germany, Canada and Australia. This book will consider the personal papers and company records in university, community and vehicle museum archives, in addition to the official material released by the national archives of Britain, Canada and Australia.

Each of the nations considered in this book had to overcome or minimize a number of shared common pressures that hindered the ability to commence and maintain a programme of war production. While they differed in frequency and severity, these included the internal availability of industrial capacity, labour, raw materials and finance, and the external threat and reality of enemy attack and blockade. Furthermore, the production of equipment and munitions for the army, navy and air force had to be prioritized to reflect the different strategic realities faced by each nation.[9] This meant that Britain and the United States prioritized aircraft production, whereas the Continental powers of Germany and the Soviet Union emphasized a greater proportion of ground equipment.[10] When comparing industrial effectiveness, the quality of Allied production improved during the war as the strategic situation stabilized and munitions programmes became standardized and mutually beneficial, such as with Lend-Lease and aid to the Soviet Union. In contrast, the quality of later German production deteriorated with the disruption caused by Allied bombing, and because factories could no longer pursue the earlier rigorous standards of workmanship as they became more reliant upon foreign labour for manpower.[11]

Specific condemnation of the British war industry by Correlli Barnett has been repeatedly disputed by later scholarship. Sebastian Ritchie has demonstrated that contrary to the pessimistic opinion of Barnett and official historian Professor Postan,

British aircraft production was more efficient than German industry.[12] George Peden rightfully argues that while Barnett's criticisms of some early British tanks are justified, Barnett underestimates the design and development problems that new tank firms had to overcome before they became effective.[13] The details of this transition will be illustrated further in this book. Contrary to Barnett, post-war industry did not decline because Britain focused upon the promise of improved welfare through the 'social miracle of New Jerusalem', rather than the potential 'economic miracle' of transforming industry.[14] In keeping with the central theme of this book, historians have instead emphasized the achievements of British industry during the war. Furthermore, historians have highlighted that post-war Britain was affected by an acute housing shortage due to German bombing and that welfare expenditure and industrial regeneration were not exclusive options.[15]

Contrary to the arguments of J. F. C. Fuller and Basil Liddell Hart, the British interwar army was not opposed to incorporating the tank but instead failed to organize the armoured divisions for greater combined arms co-operation similar to the German Panzer divisions.[16] With regard to the main tank arm during the war, unlike the United States, Germany and the Soviet Union which concentrated upon Medium tanks, Britain divided production into Infantry and Cruiser tanks with supposedly complementary but otherwise different combat roles and capabilities.[17] David French argues that the differences in tactical ability between the Infantry and Cruiser tanks unintentionally impeded British armoured doctrine for most of the war. What was needed was a more balanced formation of infantry and tank units for greater combined arms co-operation.[18] When Britain despatched an expeditionary force to the Continent in 1939, Brian Bond emphasizes that while no longer dependent upon horses, the army was motorized rather than being fully mechanized, as civilian transport had to be requisitioned upon mobilization.[19] Over the course of the war, the motorization of the Allied armies expanded and became increasingly mechanized. In contrast, Richard DiNardo and Austin Bay have shown that the quality of German fighting efficiency was hampered by the predominantly horse-drawn army throughout the war, reflecting the unmechanized nature of German society.[20]

When examining the transformation of tank design into mass production, there are a number of key factors that need to be recognized before the reliability of the finished equipment can be assessed. To begin with, the pressures of increased production during rearmament or sudden changes in the strategic situation resulted in some tanks being ordered straight off the 'drawing-board', without the necessary and elaborate trials.[21] Secondly, tank components that tested satisfactorily on the factory bench could perform very differently when used operationally and under the stress of battle.[22] Thirdly, the expectations upon the civilian firms transferred to the complexities of tank production must be realistic, as any experience in mass production and the assembly of heavy vehicles could not overcome the difficulties alone. In essence, these firms were faced with the sudden demand to produce tanks en masse requiring the assembly of many thousands of separate parts.[23] Fourthly, the military necessity for greater and uninterrupted output could override the requirement to introduce modifications to improve the quality or modernize the vehicles under production.[24] Finally, the emphasis upon quantity provided the army with tanks for training and fighting, and gave the tank firms production experience so that improved components and better assembly techniques could be incorporated into the later tank programmes.[25]

An important consideration for tank armament was that the size of the gun was dependent upon the width of the turret ring. British tank design before the war was partly constrained by the requirement to keep the tank width within the limits of the railway gauge for transportation. British tank designs were also limited in weight for bridge crossing and shipping overseas, and in height for having the lowest silhouette possible.[26] The decision to situate the turret and upper hull between the tracks on British tank design for greater cross-country manoeuvrability and for the lower height had a greater significance on restricting the width of the turret ring for most of the war. This was different to American, German and Soviet tank design which positioned the turret ring to extend over the tracks to incorporate larger tank guns. British designers took advantage of the wider turret ring on the Sherman tank to mount the 17-pounder gun and produce the Firefly tank.[27] In addition to the position of the turret, German tank designers increased armour protection and firepower due to the wider gauge of Continental railways and because most of the heaviest tanks were not sent overseas in large numbers. However, the tactical advantages of the Panther and Tiger tanks could not improve Germany's deteriorating strategic situation from 1943, because of the limitations in available numbers, operational range and mechanical reliability.[28] On the Eastern Front, the combat advances of the heavy German tanks were further mitigated when Soviet designers improved the armament on the T-34 and introduced the Joseph Stalin series of tanks.[29]

Each chapter in this book will focus upon a particular feature necessary to examine the British tank industry. The first two chapters review the relationship between government and industry. Chapter 1 will highlight the requirement and production of tanks and other munitions from disarmament after the First World War through to the period of rearmament. This will include the greater centralized control of the government, the expansion of industrial capacity and Britain's strategic reality. Tank development was intrinsically linked to experimentation at Vickers-Armstrongs and technical advances in the motor and metallurgical industries. The orders for the latest Light tank provided the army with workable vehicles by 1939, while awaiting the new Infantry and Cruiser tanks. The period of rearmament meant that industry benefited from increased sales and employment. The effects of bombing were recognized by industry with air raid precautions starting from April 1938.

Chapter 2 will review the relationship between government and industry during wartime. The necessity for aircraft production meant that the tank programme was given a lower industrial priority until November 1941. A new Tank Board was formed with each new Minister of Supply with the fifth and final board becoming an executive authority in keeping with the increasing centralization of British wartime planning. The tank industry was mostly located in the Midlands and the north of England. Government policy relating to the cost and ownership of the increased industrial capacity changed throughout the war, and reimbursement was provided for ongoing air raid precautions and factory dispersal.

The military requirements for tank production will be examined in Chapter 3 for the ability of industry to meet the priorities of the General Staff. This will highlight the changing terms of reference for each Tank Board and the production of the Meteor tank engine for greater operational mobility and increased armour protection. The General Staff relied upon Lend-Lease tanks from the United States for the balance of requirements. Finally, the post-war tank programme included the state retaining some control over production of the successful Centurion tank with the creation of a Royal Tank Arsenal.

The effects of tank production upon the experience of the factory workers will be discussed in Chapter 4, including a consideration of public opinion and propaganda efforts to encourage greater output. The different methods used to overcome the shortages in skilled labour and the reasons for leaving the workplace beyond the call-up for the armed forces will be examined. The entrance of women into industry resulted in greater welfare facilities, the ability for firms to work without pause and offered new skills such as welding, albeit with the risk to health due to the poor system of factory ventilation. The impact upon output by the necessity of taking worker holidays and by industrial action will be measured.

A technical review of tank production will be carried out in Chapter 5 to show how industry increased productivity by becoming more standardized, specialized and simplified. Tank firms overcame the delays caused by shortages of tank components and the problems of poor workmanship and inspection. The later production tanks required less maintenance and repair and received a greater supply of spare parts. Continuation orders for obsolete tanks were necessary to prevent an unacceptable break in production and interruption to manpower. Ultimately, sustainable quality production was achieved by using a smaller number of tank designs among fewer tank firms, with a reduction in tank assembly man-hours using specialist jigs and equipment.

The international influences upon British production at home and the Allied war effort overseas will be considered during Chapter 6. This will include the benefits and problems of receiving assistance from North American industry, including the production of the Valentine tank in Canada to meet continued Soviet requests. The production of British tanks in the United States proved impossible, although tank components were supplied. British cash orders for American tanks supported the expansion of industrial capacity in the United States until superseded by Lend-Lease. There was extensive co-operation and collaboration between the Western Allies towards tank policy and design. While the delivery of large numbers of Sherman tanks from 1943 permitted British industry to transfer some capacity to locomotive production, Britain became too dependent upon the United States. When Lend-Lease tank deliveries ceased at the end of 1944, Britain had the same fear of quantitative deficiency for 1945, as they had experienced following the defeat of France in 1940.

Overall this book demonstrates how the British tank programme achieved the 'synthesis of the tactical and production plans', which Minister of Production Oliver Lyttelton described as essential for successful production in war.[30] The demands of the 'user' and 'supplier' were eventually met by the formation of tank policy on a joint basis between the General Staff and Ministry of Supply. Many of the firms introduced to war production found that the design and assembly of tanks was a 'unique industrial process' that required 'years of specialised experience'.[31] As a result, the British army had to wait until the second half of the war to be provided with the desired mass production of reliable and battleworthy tanks. This book has not identified any specific 'learning curve' which George Peden suggests might have existed to account for the improvement in the quality of tank production.[32] Rather, this book will demonstrate the manner in which British industry successfully transformed to produce quality tanks at a sustainably high rate of output to meet the operational requirements of reliability and mobility to mutually support the Allied war effort.

Government and Industry during Disarmament and Rearmament

This chapter will examine the relationship between the government and industry during the interwar period to establish the background and development of tank production prior to the start of the Second World War. The period from 1919 is often characterized by the 'Ten Year Rule' in which the British Cabinet decided that Britain would not become involved in a major war or require an expeditionary force for 10 years.[1] The actual effects of this decision upon the development of the armed forces must also consider the actual timing of Treasury control over the services and strategic policy during this period.[2] The period of rearmament discussed in this chapter relates to the five years from 1934 to the end of 1938. It could be said that rearmament began from 1932 with the abandonment of the 'Ten Year Rule', however the Cabinet received a five-year programme of increased defence expenditure from the Defence Requirements Sub-Committee in February 1934.[3] Apart from contextualizing the five years under review, the events of 1939 will be examined in the following chapters to recognize that while Britain was still at peace for much of the year, the nation had moved much closer to a position of total war.

This chapter will begin by highlighting both the expansion of industry during the First World War to meet the increasing requirements for tanks and aircraft and the peacetime contraction and concentration among fewer firms to meet the different strategic obligations. The extent of government influence to direct the armaments industry continued to expand during the interwar period to reflect the growing mechanization of the army, and give the War Office greater organizational strength when dealing with industry. The capabilities of industry upon beginning rearmament were supported by technical advances within the motor industry and the benefits of experimentation in metallurgy generally. To meet the limited demand for tanks from the War Office and the export market prior to rearmament, Vickers-Armstrongs had focused upon developing a series of standardized designs and components. Once rearmament began, the production for aircraft and anti-aircraft defence received priority ahead of other army programmes in accordance with Britain's strategic reality. A range of civilian firms were introduced to war production from 1936 to fulfil the orders for the latest types of aircraft and tanks. Government policy towards retaining control of the expanding industrial capacity among private firms was based upon financing new 'shadow' factories for aircraft production and new plant and equipment for other production, although the firm could own some of the new machinery for a percentage of the cost. The effect of rearmament upon industrial activity and levels of employment was demonstrated by the production diversity of Vickers-Armstrongs and the introduction of tank production at Vulcan Foundry. Some firms were deliberately excluded from rearmament work due to concerns about the internal economy and exports. Finally, industry unilaterally instigated a series of costly air raid precautions in response to the political events occurring in Europe during 1938.

Military requirements after the First World War

The first battlefield use of the tank on 15 September 1916 demonstrated both the potential for future deployment and the range of mechanical and ergonomic difficulties to be overcome if tanks were to be used again with a greater prospect of success. The original order for 100 Mark I tanks on 16 February 1916 involved 25 from the tank designers and agricultural machinery firm, William Foster in Lincoln, and 75 from railway carriage firm, Metropolitan Carriage Wagon and Finance in Birmingham. The bullet-proof plate was provided by shipbuilders Cammell-Laird in Sheffield and William Beardmore in Glasgow, and engineering and armaments firm, Vickers Limited in Sheffield.[4] The problems of mechanical breakdown before and during the advance on 15 September meant that only 21 tanks out of the 48 available reached German positions. The tank crews were subjected to appalling conditions of heat, noise, poor ventilation, restricted outside vision and immense physical exertion to operate. However, there were examples of the unsuspecting German defenders retreating or surrendering upon the first sight of the tank, although others maintained their positions and fought. This mixed performance still encouraged General Douglas Haig to order 1,000 new tanks despite the shortages in raw materials, particularly in the case of steel, and against the greater priority for petrol engines given to aircraft.[5]

The success achieved at Cambrai during November 1917 was because the assault occurred over unshelled terrain, the attackers had the element of surprise and used better tactics to overcome the trench lines with greater numbers of the latest Mark IV tank. However, the acclaim was short-lived due to the inability to hold ground with the absence of infantry and artillery support, while remaining vulnerable to enemy artillery.[6] Tanks were not war-winning weapons in their own right and as demonstrated at Cambrai and the battles at Hamel and Amiens during 1918, the effective use of tanks in battle relied upon reconnaissance whenever possible and close co-operation and training with infantry.[7]

The enthusiasm that Winston Churchill showed towards the tank by setting up the Landships Committee in February 1915 was later repeated as the Minister of Munitions. During June 1918, Churchill suggested that the Tank Corps should have 7,000 tanks, although this would have taken 12 months to achieve with the existing Tank Corps establishment at 1,080. To illustrate the type of expansion required, British industry produced 2,619 tanks between 1916 and 1918.[8] Part of the planned increase in tank production would have been met by the planned Allied Tank Factory at Chateauroux in central France under an Anglo-American agreement in January 1918. This had the potential of 1,200 tanks per month, however the Armistice in November 1918 occurred before the delivery of any tanks.[9]

By comparison, the performance of British aircraft during the First World War increased with the transformation of industry from a technologically undeveloped state to become an essential part of the war effort.[10] The role of aircraft during the war included the effective co-operation with artillery, the use of reconnaissance photographs to produce accurate maps, and the fixing of machine guns and bombs for aerial and ground operations.[11] To demonstrate the expansion of the aircraft industry for these operational requirements, the number of firms involved in aircraft construction grew from an estimated 200 before 1914, to 771 in November 1917, and to 1,529 by October 1918.[12] In relation to production and against an average attrition rate of 670 aircraft per month during 1918, the number of front line aircraft available increased from 113 aircraft in August 1914 to 3,300 by November 1918.[13]

After the First World War, Britain and France became the principal powers in Europe with Germany under disarmament restrictions and the United States withdrawing their interest by rejecting the Treaty of Versailles. France wanted to secure against future German aggression, while Britain aimed to restore the balance of power in Europe by preventing the dominance of one nation over another.[14] With British military requirements following the First World War based upon colonial policing and the League of Nations' mandates, the development of tanks and aircraft were restricted to experimentation and not advancement through major conflicts.[15] To meet these strategic obligations during disarmament, the War Office still wanted an army bigger than 1913 with some mechanized units, the Air Ministry wanted a permanent air force comparable to the wartime strength, and the Admiralty wanted the largest navy in the world.[16] The problem for the War Office and Air Ministry was that ongoing technical advances meant that tanks and aircraft needed to be continually improved, while warships remained effective for much longer.[17]

During the early 1920s, Britain did not have the military strength to meet the different strategic obligations. Over the course of the decade the Treasury gained control of service estimates and policies so that Britain had a small regular armed forces with reserve elements and modern weapons and equipment, if these reduced overall expenditure. Army estimates came under Treasury control from 1922, while the Royal Air Force increased the number of new squadrons and the Royal Navy introduced new big gun cruisers, until the Treasury had full control over the three services in 1928.[18] Rather than the Treasury hindering rearmament during the late 1930s, the strategic demands of protecting British cities and home and overseas ports were met by deliberately investing in the air force and navy at the expense of the army. When the amounts spent by Britain fell behind the rearmament efforts of other countries, this was because expenditure had increased at a faster rate in those countries and not because of spending cuts in Britain.[19]

The design and production of tanks following the First World War until the expansion of General Staff requirements with rearmament was limited to Vickers-Armstrongs and the state owned Royal Ordnance Factory at Woolwich. As a result, the British army became dependent upon a variety of Light and Medium tanks during the 1920s and 1930s, until the separate Infantry and Cruiser types were introduced late into rearmament as discussed in greater detail below.[20] For the aircraft industry, the overall reduction in post-war civilian and military demand and an excess profits tax meant that only 13 firms were working on aircraft production during 1920, while many other firms went into liquidation.[21]

Government influence upon the peacetime armaments industry

The task of supplying the British army was the joint responsibility of the Master-General of the Ordnance representing the 'supplier' and the Chief of the Imperial General Staff for the 'user'.[22] Each head of the army advanced the progress of mechanization in the years approaching and during rearmament. Between 1926 and 1933, Field Marshal Sir George Milne attempted to advance the mechanization of the army, but was limited by financial stringency.[23] From 1933 to 1936, Field Marshal Sir Archibald Montgomery-Massingberd was not a 'blinkered reactionary' as claimed by Basil Liddell Hart, but actually wanted the British army to be the most highly mechanized in the world.[24] For 1936 and 1937, Field Marshal Sir Cyril Deverell wanted to appoint the Inspector of Cavalry, Major-General Blakiston-Houston, as the commander of the Mobile Division, but was prevented by the influence and interference of Liddell Hart.[25] Finally during 1938, Lord Gort noted that if the 'Air Defence of Great Britain' received complete priority through the production of fighter aircraft and anti-aircraft measures as discussed later, Britain would be unable to send a Field Force to the Continent.[26]

Rather than following the United States by abolishing the Tank Corps at the end of the First World War, the position of a tank arm within the British army was secured from 1923 with the creation of the Royal Tank Corps and the experimentation of equipment.[27] The War Office continued the mechanization of the army in 1927 with the formation of the Director of Mechanization and the establishment of the Mechanical Warfare Board. The board was headed by the Master-General of the Ordnance, Lieutenant-General Sir Webb Gillman, who had centralized control over the research, design, supply, inspection and repair of all types of army vehicles. The board had the Director of Mechanization and officers from the Mechanization Directorate, the Royal Tank Corps, the Ordnance Committee and the Design Department at Woolwich, together with the important representation from leading civil and mechanical engineering institutions. The board also directed the Mechanical Warfare Experimental Establishment at Farnborough to instigate vehicle trials.[28]

The start of rearmament during 1934 brought an important change in the perception and organization for tank research and development with the replacement of the Mechanical Warfare Board by the new Mechanization Board. Similarly, the Mechanical Warfare Experimental Establishment became the Mechanization

Experimental Establishment.[29] While the removal of the term 'Warfare' suggested a position of disarmament, the government was actually increasing defence expenditure under the policy of rearmament. The board was divided into two main committees for Armoured Fighting Vehicles and Mechanical Transport Vehicles and carried out research and development towards the design of all mechanized army vehicles. This was done by liaising with the mechanical engineering industry to benefit from the latest advancements and commercial production.[30] The civilian scientists and engineers on the Mechanization Board were given an executive function within their field, which had previously been denied to them under the Mechanical Warfare Board.[31] The transfer of tank experts from the Superintendent of Design to the Mechanization Board meant that the board did not introduce any new designs and only vetted and suggested modifications to the designs submitted by tank manufacturers. This lack of official instigation of design continued until November 1943 when the Centurion tank was proposed, although the Mechanization Board provided direct support to Vulcan Foundry for the design of the Matilda tank and to Vauxhall Motors for the Churchill tank.[32]

The appointment of Sir Thomas Inskip as the new Minister for the Co-ordination of Defence during March 1936 was to provide an oversight of strategy by deputizing for Prime Minister Chamberlain as chairman of the Committee of Imperial Defence. Inskip also replaced the President of the Board of Trade on the Principal Supply Officers Committee which was responsible for co-ordinating the allocation of industrial capacity.[33] The selection of Inskip caused some to doubt whether the government was serious about defence with the claim that nothing had actually changed in respect of policy.[34]

A further organizational change was announced during July 1936 when the Secretary of State for War, Duff Cooper, appointed engineer Vice-Admiral Sir Harold Brown as the new Director-General of Munitions Production to co-ordinate and expedite the production of army equipment.[35] The reason for selecting a naval officer to meet the demands of the War Office, instead of an army officer as expected, was because Brown had the prerequisite experience of working with the engineering industry.[36] This appointment helped the War Office to counter the disadvantage of having ordinary cost accountants, while the Admiralty and Air Ministry used technical cost accounting which better understood the production processes. The progress of the War Office munitions programme was also affected by having to use inexperienced firms, while the Admiralty and Air Ministry employed manufacturers that had civilian markets for similar products before rearmament.[37] The Master-General of the Ordnance, Lieutenant-General Sir Hugh Elles, was still responsible for deciding on the specific requirement, research, design and inspection of equipment before being supplied to the army. Brown was responsible for the production and expansion of army contracts, including placing orders for building supplies, the preparation of plans and monitoring the progress.[38] Within this new organization, the production of munitions under Brown was still dependent upon the General Staff specifying their demands in a timely manner.[39]

By the end of 1937, the Secretary of State for War, Leslie Hore-Belisha, reorganized the design and production arrangement to coincide with the retirement of Lieutenant-General Elles. The responsibilities of the Master-General of the

Ordnance were amalgamated with the duties of the Director-General of Munitions Production. The office under Brown was formed to meet the demands of rearmament and did not prevent the role of Master-General of the Ordnance from being 'resuscitated' sometime later.[40] The purpose of this reorganization was to bring the research, design, experimentation, production and inspection under one authority and presumably with the outbreak of war, production would receive priority over all other considerations. Greater demarcation was established under the Director of Mechanization with a Deputy Director for Tanks and Vehicles and another one for Engineering and Signals.[41]

Control of the air programme went through a number of similar changes with the creation of the Air Ministry and Royal Air Force during the latter stages of the First World War. The post-war aircraft programme was maintained by the Air Council which included the Secretary of State for Air as President and the Chief of the Air Staff.[42] The Air Ministry subcontracted some work from relatively successful firms, like Fairey, Gloster, Bristol and Vickers Aviation, to less prosperous firms in an effort to keep them from dissolving and maintain a sizeable industrial base. By 1927, it was noted that any significant increase in demand would need the involvement of firms from outside the aircraft industry, as seen later with the 'shadow' firms from 1936. A reduction of the aircraft industry was under consideration to remove the smaller firms and require others to seek amalgamation with another larger aircraft firm. Despite having weaker firms, the Air Council decided during 1931 not to reduce the aircraft industry and instead maintained the somewhat wasteful competition of design resources among the many firms.[43]

When a new type of aircraft was required the Air Staff provided the specification necessary for the Air Ministry to instruct the appropriate firms to produce a prototype. The Air Ministry remained cautious and suppressed industrial initiative before rearmament by selecting biplane instead of monoplane designs and wooden instead of metal construction.[44] As a result, industry had to overcome the problems of monoplane designs privately until orders were placed during rearmament. Production policy remained the sole responsibility of the Air Council until 1938 when the Air Council Committee on Supply was given the authority to accelerate the aircraft programme and decide where government expenditure for expanding the aircraft industry should be allocated.[45]

Industrial capabilities upon rearmament

The decision to commence rearmament from the mid-1930s had different effects upon the economies of the various powers concerned. Germany had the initiative by being the aggressor in the coming war and devoted the most resources to the pre-war programme. This was achieved by using an underemployed economy and concentrating production upon particular military equipment. The Soviet Union allocated a similar amount of effort to create a mass army, although the defence industry was at a lower technical level and the resources for the civilian sector were reduced. French rearmament was limited in both absolute terms and relative to the economy, whereas the preparations of the United States were negligible. The extent of British rearmament was smaller than Germany or the Soviet Union and constrained by maintaining financial stability through economic status quo for much of the period. Once a larger programme had been approved, Britain and her allies had to provide their armed forces with the means to fight in a variety of theatres because Germany had the advantage of deciding when and where to attack.[46]

Once rearmament had commenced, the official history contends that the British motor industry was unsuitable for both tank development and assembly, despite the obvious connection to the production of vehicles, engines and gear boxes.[47] The different complexities of civilian vehicle and tank production provide some justification for this opinion, however the quality of mechanized components for the British tank programme was dependent upon design and development within the motor industry. Furthermore, the decision of the British government to tax vehicles based upon their unladen weight, meant that manufacturers were forced to design commercial vehicles within this limitation and thus produce smaller engines.[48] Finally, the British motor industry was introduced to aircraft production from 1936 with the establishment of 'shadow' factories.

A demonstration of design progress or stagnation by motor manufacturers was displayed during the annual motor exhibitions. During 1934 the Mechanization Board reported a lack of serious developments in the design of commercial vehicles. Part of the reason for this inactivity was attributed to the absence of the Commercial Motor Transport Exhibition in London, and when the Scottish Motor Exhibition in Glasgow was attended, any progression in vehicle design was minimal.[49] The lack of economic activity from the Depression was another cause for the decline in new designs, until the revival of trade during 1935 increased the level of motor industry work.[50] During 1936, the Mechanization Board reported that the motor firms were satisfied with the existing designs and only introduced refinements to detail.[51] By 1937, the cessation of new design work was due to the increased activity on the production of armoured vehicles, although the greater amounts of money spent by other nations meant that Britain's lead in tank research and development had reduced.[52]

The impact of rearmament upon the motor industry during 1938 was also reflected in the poor level of global trade and recession similar to that experienced up until 1935, with the reduction in the development of motor vehicle and component design and research. The Mechanization Board was uncertain whether the downturn in motor vehicle sales was due to the threat of war during 1938, or because of a 'normal industrial cycle'.[53] In any event, AEC noted that the reduction in vehicle work resulted in the loss of 200 workers in May 1938, with the prospect of losing a further 500 workers by August unless other work, presumably rearmament related, was obtained instead.[54]

In relation to the other industries, Professor F. W. Harbord reported to the Mechanization Board during 1934 that the processes of working with metals or metallurgy had displayed improvements and experimentation of general practice, albeit without any great metallurgical advances. These activities were nonetheless very important for industry in the fields of welding and casting and to understand the different properties of various alloys. The technique of electric welding had become more common and skilled with parts of high pressure boilers transferring from riveted to welded construction, and welded railway track could now withstand the changes of expansion and contraction in temperate climates.[55]

The use of alloy cast iron, instead of ordinary cast iron, expanded during this period by incorporating nickel, chromium and molybdenum to double the life-span of the engine cylinder liners.[56] The experimentation with these three elements continued during the 1930s to produce better quality armoured plate when combined with steel.[57] In an example during 1936, the English Steel Corporation incorporated a higher percentage of chromium-molybdenum to produce 'Hykro' steel tank armour that was less prone to flake and produced a wider range of tensile strength than with other alloy combinations.[58] The quality of this type of armour on British tanks was appreciated by Soviet tank crews during the defence of Moscow in November 1941. Essentially, unlike the turret on the Soviet T-34 tank, the turret on British tanks did not shatter upon being hit resulting in greater crew survivability.[59]

The Ford Motor Company successfully experimented with a mixture of cast iron and steel alloyed with copper, chromium and silicon to form cast crankshafts instead of using steel forgings. Legitimate concern was raised with the use of castings with each component being a separate unit, whereby defects would be hard to detect during mass production.[60] Alloy cast irons also lacked the flexibility of steel castings. While these fears were justified, they would be overcome once the manufacturing processes had been standardized into routine foundry practice. Moreover, the benefits of alloy cast iron during wartime were appreciated with an anticipated higher and cheaper rate of output when compared to forgings, and would release greater amounts of steel to fulfil other requirements.[61]

War orders during rearmament

Prior to rearmament, the Royal Air Force was meant to be a cheaper and more versatile alternative to the army for colonial control and could potentially attack enemy targets on the Continent and defend Britain from similar attack in the event of a European war. The Royal Navy had maintained its strength, although the ability to influence events during wartime would be limited to the long-term effects of blockade while defending the British mainland and other overseas interests. The small army would take time to expand before enough men and equipment became available to have a decisive influence on the battlefield.[62] The onset of rearmament maintained this arrangement so that the army received a lower priority and funding when compared to the Royal Air Force, anti-aircraft equipment and the Royal Navy.

The decision by Chamberlain to dramatically increase the strength of air power at the expense of limiting the other defence programmes was meant to discourage Germany.[63] However rather than deterring Adolf Hitler, the impact of British rearmament actually brought forward the decision to attack.[64] The Royal Navy remained unaffected by the priority given to air defence with the existing Admiralty programme giving Britain superiority in large vessels at the outbreak of war when compared to other nations.[65] The availability of equipment for the Continental Field Force, especially in tanks, was affected by the Cabinet policy from 1936 to 1939 to instruct the War Office to concentrate upon anti-aircraft defences.[66] As a result, the majority of industrial capacity for army equipment produced anti-aircraft guns and reserves of ammunition for the defence of Britain, and not tanks or artillery for the Field Force.[67] While this strategy left Britain more vulnerable following the loss of equipment after the defeat of France, the justification was nonetheless realistic by recognizing that any Field Force sent abroad would be very small by Continental standards.[68]

When put into context, the deliberate decision to make the army a 'Cinderella service' by prioritizing air power, air defence and control of the seas was correct, as it responded to Britain's strategic reality. This was the strategic situation that put Britain as a European power vulnerable to adversaries on the continent, while also holding the position as an imperial power with overseas possessions that needed protection. As a result, Britain lacked the resources to completely guard against the sheer number and variety of dangers.[69] The Chamberlain government responded to this situation in 1937 by correctly prioritizing Fighter Command and the system of air defence based around radar.[70] To sum up, Britain responded to this strategic reality by adopting a policy that defended against each threat in the order that the island nation would come under attack. This meant that first priority was given to meet the danger from the air. If the air force was overcome then the naval programme was aimed at preventing the seaborne invasion across the channel. If that failed, then the army equipment would be used to engage the various landings on British soil from the sea and air. The essence of this policy was to prevent the second and third threat by increasing the strength and capability of successfully defending against the first.

The greater priority given to the aircraft programme during rearmament was carried out by the approval of four expansion schemes from 1934 until 1940 with consecutive increases in requirements. The first scheme A from 1934 was meant to provide just over 1,250 aircraft by 1939. Scheme C introduced in 1935 was more ambitious with the intention of producing 3,800 aircraft by 1937. While the next scheme F in 1936 could not provide the Royal Air Force with war capability by 1939, the planned total production had risen to 8,000. The final scheme L from 1938 was designed to provide 12,000 aircraft across 1939 and 1940. The number of aircraft produced over this period was less than planned, although deliveries did increase from 2,828 in 1938 to 7,940 in 1939. The reasons for this impressive and seemingly sudden growth in output was the culmination of better state-industry planning, the new 'shadow' factories discussed below, the greater use of subcontractors, and improvements to design and production methods. This was demonstrated under the 1936 scheme F which replaced light bombers with monoplane medium bombers like the Fairey Battle, the Bristol Blenheim, the Handley Page Hampden and the Vickers Wellington, together with orders for the first Hawker Hurricane and Supermarine Spitfire fighters.[71]

Before new tank designs and tank firms were introduced during rearmament, Vickers-Armstrongs had front-loaded their experimental work on tanks in the years before and even during the Depression. As a result, by 1932 Vickers had produced a series of standardized tank models and components that could be successfully marketed around the world. To benefit from this work, tank designer John Carden proposed to cut the expenditure relating to new models for a period of two years, thereby saving an estimated £13,000 per year.[72] Rather than cutting development expenditure altogether, it was decided that new design work should instead be fixed at the beginning of each year.[73] The particular benefit to Vickers by concentrating upon standardized production was that the overall quality of the components would improve through continued testing and ongoing modification.[74] When compared against financial stringency and negligible demand during the pre-rearmament period, it is commendable that Vickers maintained any form of new tank development at all.

Despite these positive indications on tank design, the problem was a shortfall in demand from the War Office. During 1933, the Master-General of the Ordnance, Lieutenant-General Sir Ronald Charles, confirmed that the requirement for tanks was limited to 18 Light tanks at £1,500 each, despite Vickers having sufficient capacity to manufacture more.[75] During 1934, the War Office indicated the desire to increase deliveries of the Vickers 3-man Light Mark V tank, but not at the expense of enhanced labour costs.[76] Therefore, financial limitations meant that increased activity in the tank programme was restricted to the earlier completion of an existing contract, rather than the creation of a new tank order.

Until an increase in new orders was received, Vickers maintained their supply of tanks to foreign markets to utilize their standardized designs and available capacity. From 1934 until the end of 1936 Vickers received orders for a variety of tanks and tractors from Belgium, Holland, Switzerland, Poland, Lithuania, Finland, India and China.[77] Vickers was not given *carte blanche* authority to supply their tanks for export as the vehicles needed to be approved by the War Office beforehand. In one example, the Vickers Command Tank, which had been on the 'free list' since April 1936, was placed back onto the War Office 'secret list' during March 1938. The reason was an apparent similarity with the Light Mark VI B tank, which was under production for the British army. Given the context of the time, the War Office did not want to reveal current tank attributes to foreign authorities. Vickers persuaded the War Office that the only similarities were the positioning of the engine, transmission and cooling system and four months later Lord Gort approved the release of the Command Tank from the 'secret list'.[78]

The slow introduction of new firms to the production of tanks during rearmament can be partly attributed to the absence of long-term requirements from the War Office. Vice-Admiral Brown informed the Secretary of State for War throughout 1936 and 1937 that General Staff orders, such as for tanks, small arms ammunition and gun barrel forgings, had to be substantial enough or be coupled with continuation orders for firms to accept the commercial risks and expense.[79] When the number of War Office orders increased in 1938, many were still not large enough for the firms to create the level of industrial capacity required to make the contract economically feasible.[80] This was an issue of administrative understanding by simultaneously educating industrialists to understand military requirements and the War Office to understand large-scale industrial processes.[81] Prior to the enlargement of the aircraft programme and the 'shadow' factories during 1936, the Air Ministry encountered the different problem of persuading the aircraft industry to fully expand their capacity despite providing sizable orders under scheme C. With the expectation of reduced orders when rearmament was due to finish in 1942, the firms wanted to avoid repeating the situation after the end of the First World War when the sudden cancellation of military requirements caused surplus capacity and a number of bankruptcies.[82]

The number and size of tank orders between 1934 and 1936 were limited in both the models being considered and the introduction of new manufacturers. Overall, the numbers of tanks used by the army in 1936, whether as a result of the legacy of pre-rearmament production or via new orders, was 375 tanks divided into 209 Light and 166 Medium. From this total, 304 were considered obsolete leaving only 69 Light Mark V and VI tanks that were of any use to the army and these were still deficient in armament.[83] When reviewing the industrial situation, Vickers continued to be the sole commercial organization capable of receiving new tank orders from the War Office during 1934 and 1935. This situation helped the new Mechanization Board which could effectively leave Vickers alone because this firm designed all the vehicles and any problems would be dealt with internally.[84]

Despite the death of Sir John Carden during 1935, the War Office could expect a reasonable rate of delivery from Vickers given their experience, the ready facilities and commercial drive. This was demonstrated by the order of 28 Light Mark IV tanks placed during June 1934, which was shared equally between Vickers and the Royal Ordnance Factory in Woolwich.[85] The difference in productivity between Vickers and the state factory was striking with Vickers delivering all 14 of their vehicles to service units in time for the annual training during 1935. On the other hand, the Woolwich factory eventually delivered 12 of their order during May 1936 and the remaining 2 later in October, which was 15 months after Vickers. While the performance and reliability of the tanks from either source were deemed 'satisfactory', the different delivery times meant that state factories did not receive any further tank orders when War Office requirements expanded.[86] The reason for the difference in output was because the Woolwich factory had to give priority to work from the Admiralty and Air Ministry instead of the War Office.[87]

The remaining tank orders from the War Office during 1934 and 1935 were all placed with Vickers and remained small in quantity, such as the requirement for 22 Light Mark V and separate orders for 10 and 41 of the latest Light Mark VI tanks.[88] Following the decision by the Cabinet early in 1936 to begin a 'serious' programme of rearmament, the War Office increased the size of new orders. This was shown at the end of the year when Vickers received an order for 100 Light Mark VI tanks which was the best vehicle available to be produced in large numbers at this time.[89] Locomotive manufacturer Vulcan Foundry became the first new commercial firm to start tank production with an initial order for 10 Light Mark VI tanks in January 1936 and another contract for 97 tanks during November.[90] The larger order reflected the 'serious' attempt by the War Office to expand the tank programme at the end of 1936, while also showing that Vulcan Foundry now had the production facilities and experience to accept a greater level of tank work.

As more commercial firms were introduced to tank and aircraft production, the organizational relationship between the service departments and industry was based around a group of assembly firms headed by a parent. This leading firm would support the dependent firms by usually designing and building the prototype, obtaining the required machine tools and equipment, controlling the ordering and supply of materials, establishing the level of production among the group and managing the ongoing or ad-hoc obstacles to maintain the required rate of output.[91] The policy of using parent firms to supervise the production groups instead of ministry officials was strongly advocated by industry. The success of this arrangement was first shown in the aircraft industry, when the new 'shadow' factories benefited from the close liaison with the parent firms by observing assembly techniques, discussing production problems and by receiving direct training.[92]

The largest expansion of tank orders occurred during 1937 and 1938 with new designs and manufacturers. Three new firms became involved for the production of the Light Mark VI B, which were North British Locomotive and agricultural vehicle engineers, Ruston & Hornsby and John Fowler. Vickers and Vulcan Foundry also received additional orders during 1937 and 1938 for this Light tank, in addition to receiving orders for the new Infantry and Cruiser tanks. Vickers held the parentage of four new tank designs with the Cruiser Mark I and Mark II, the Infantry Mark I and the Tetrarch Light tank. Vickers was joined by shipbuilders Harland & Wolff for the Cruiser Mark I, and by railway carriage constructors Birmingham Railway Carriage & Wagon and Metropolitan-Cammell for the Mark II. Vickers was the only manufacturer of the Infantry Mark I and the Tetrarch order was later transferred to Metropolitan-Cammell.[93] Vulcan Foundry became the parent of the new Infantry Mark II, more commonly known as the Matilda tank, alongside Ruston & Hornsby, John Fowler and new tank firm London, Midland and Scottish Railway.[94] The order for 65 Cruiser Mark III tanks in January 1938 was given to parent firm Mechanization & Aero because of a lack of capacity at any other existing armaments firm.[95]

The new Infantry and Cruiser classes of tank resulted from the inability to produce a suitable all-purpose Medium tank. As a result, Infantry tanks were meant to provide close support to unmechanized infantry and were typically formed into army tank brigades. Cruiser tanks were used for mobile operations as part of an armoured brigade.[96] The decision to divide the development and industrial resources to produce the different Light, Infantry and Cruiser classes placed a strain on the available capacity. This was shown with Vickers-Armstrongs who were producing all three types of tank, and despite the introduction of new firms the tank programme still had the lowest priority among the three services. As a result, when the aircraft programme expanded under schemes F and L with thousands of aircraft expected each year from 1936 onwards, the number of tanks ordered during 1937 was only 526 with another 1,147 during 1938.[97] On a more positive note, with the exception of the Light Mark VI B, most of the other tanks on order were the latest Infantry and Cruiser designs which were comparable to the German Panzer tanks in terms of fighting ability. However, British Infantry and Cruiser tanks would not be produced in sufficient numbers by 1939 or before Germany attacked in the West during 1940 and were generally inferior to German tanks in mechanical reliability.[98] Ultimately, a British Expeditionary Force of greater strength and mechanization would still not have prevented the defeat of France. This was because the German advance was tactically and operationally superior with the close co-operation of arms and concentration of the Panzer units at the decisive areas.[99]

British numerical inferiority at the start of 1940 can be illustrated by a comparison to the relative size and strength of the French and German tank programmes. As a result of the tank orders placed from 1936 when Britain was under a period of 'serious' rearmament, British industry produced 1,462 tanks until the end of 1939. The vast majority of these were variants of the Light Mark VI, while only 280 tanks were of the early Infantry and Cruiser type.[100] Furthermore, the increase in the production of Light tanks did not quicken the mechanization of cavalry regiments, resulting in many units having insufficient time to adequately train with the new equipment before the start of hostilities in 1940.[101] Over the same four-year period from 1936, French industry delivered 2,411 tanks, including many of the highly regarded Char B1, B1-Bis and Somua S35 types.[102] German industry produced a similar number of 2,481 tanks of the Panzer Mark I to IV range, although 78 per cent of these were the insufficiently armed and armoured Mark I and IIs. On the other hand, these smaller tanks had the operational mobility and reliability to assist in the success of the 1940 campaign once the fighting had begun.[103]

Increasing industrial capacity

To meet the growing demands of rearmament, service departments created 'war potential' by providing civilian firms with the capabilities and understanding of armaments production in readiness for a complete transfer at the outbreak of war.[104] At the start of rearmament the War Office programme was limited by the lack of industrial capacity for guns, shells and tanks with only three national ordnance factories at Woolwich, Waltham and Enfield retained after the First World War. While ten new Royal Ordnance Factories were authorized between 1936 and 1939, much of this capacity was dedicated to the strategic priority of producing anti-aircraft equipment, rather than providing equipment for the field army.[105]

As already indicated the Air Ministry created a series of 'shadow' factories from 1936 by introducing firms from outside the established industry to meet the increased requirements of the aircraft programme under scheme F. The decision to employ the motor industry at the outset was meant to be a prompt way of producing the required number of aircraft within the 1936 to 1939 time limit set by the Air Ministry. While valuable experience was gained in design and production, the difficulties in setting up the 'shadow' factories affected both the quantity and quality of aircraft available at the outbreak of war.[106] The initial 'shadow' schemes included Standard Motors, Daimler, Rootes, Austin Motors and Rover Company with new factories that were financed and owned by the government and managed by the firms for an agency fee.[107] A second 'shadow' scheme introduced in 1938 included new factories at Metropolitan-Vickers and English Electric to meet the increased industrial capacity required under scheme L. These new factories were now managed by the traditional aircraft firms.[108]

In response to the increased demands for war production, the steel industry completed a general expansion during 1935 by incorporating modern by-product facilities, the rebuilding of blast furnaces and the installation of new plant for the total cost of £20 million.[109] The War Office made plans for new factory locations during rearmament, but was unable to begin construction because the limited labour resources available meant that priority was given to new aircraft factories.[110] Therefore, the new firms receiving tank orders had to use existing factories until new capacity was created at the works when the tank programme expanded during 1939 and 1940, as described in the next chapter. The transfer of production from one tank design to another still meant that the assembly firm obtained new jigs and machine tools when changing over, for example, when Ruston & Hornsby switched production from the Light Mark VI B to the new Matilda in late 1938.[111]

Existing armaments firm Vickers-Armstrongs and steel producer English Steel received a large expansion of capacity during 1936 to meet the growing demands of the War Office and Admiralty once a policy of 'serious' rearmament had begun. For example, the Barrow works received machine tools worth £240,000 for the production of gun mountings and field equipment for the army and a further £240,500 to produce heavy naval guns for the Admiralty. The works at Elswick received mountings for heavy naval guns for £50,500, alongside a new tank shop for £47,000 and machine tools for £129,000 for the production of guns, breech mechanisms and cartridge cases. The Crayford works received new machine tools for £20,000 to increase machine gun output and a further £70,000 for Admiralty requirements. Finally, English Steel received additional plant for Admiralty requirements of armour plate, bullet-proof plate and gun forgings for over £1 million.[112]

This investment provides a useful record of the production diversity of Vickers-Armstrongs and shows that the existing capacity could have been expanded earlier had the firm received an increased demand for munitions before 1936. The increase in the demand for machine tools and equipment to supply the rearmament programme affected the similar requirements for machinery from those firms still involved in manufacturing civilian products. For example, during May 1939 Rover was compelled to sanction new machinery for their Tyseley car plant four months ahead of schedule due to the anticipated delays in delivery.[113]

The amount reimbursed by the Treasury in relation to industrial expansion reflected government policy towards the financial impact upon industry and preventing undue enhancement. The recommendations of the Robinson Committee during 1936 stated that the government should pay the entire cost of new factories, thereby ensuring that the potential for war production remained under direct state ownership.[114] In respect of English Steel and the additional plant for naval armour plate above, the Admiralty reimbursed the total expenditure eventually adjusted to £1,056,000.[115] It was agreed that at the end of the emergency production the government would reinstate the original facilities displaced by the expansion and maintain any additional plant retained.[116] In respect of the additional machine tools relating to the Barrow, Elswick and Crayford works, the government agreed to reimburse 60 per cent of the cost back to Vickers.[117] The reason for not receiving a full repayment was because Vickers obtained complete ownership of the new facilities for 40 per cent of the value.[118] The policy of providing reimbursement to industry, but also ensuring that the firm did not unduly benefit from the larger plant facilities and brand new machine tools, continued throughout war as examined in greater detail in the next chapter.

The effect of rearmament upon industrial activity

The production of Light, Infantry and Cruiser tanks at Vickers-Armstrongs needs to be compared against the other activities of this armaments firm by the total sales recorded from 1933 until 1938 inclusive. This will show the situation just before rearmament in comparison to the period before the increase in sales during 1939 with the approach and outbreak of war. To begin with, the total value of sales across all areas increased from £6.6 million in 1933 to £17.7 million in 1938. The sales relating to the production of tanks and tractors more than doubled from £441,000 to £911,000, including a large increase in 1938 to reflect the new Infantry and Cruiser tank orders. The expansion in tank orders was part of an overall and even greater increase for all land armaments from £1.3 million to £3.4 million. The sales for naval armaments doubled from £2.1 million to £4.1 million, while the sales for naval and merchant shipbuilding rose from £2 million to £3.7 million. The decision to transfer all Wellington bomber production to Vickers-Armstrongs at the end of 1938 contributed to the sudden increase in aircraft sales from a mere £29,000 in 1937 to £3.9 million in 1938.[119]

In order to meet the production demands from these sales, the number of workers employed at Vickers-Armstrongs grew by three-and-a-half times from 1933 until 1938 including those from the Supermarine and Weybridge aircraft factories.[120] As for Vulcan Foundry, while the orders for Light tanks were received during 1936 and work continued on the two Matilda tank prototypes during 1937, the number of employees fell during a time when the rate of unemployment also declined. Conversely, when the unemployment rate increased during the 1938 recession, the level of employment at Vulcan Foundry also increased. This indicates that the firm had transformed to meet the demands of the large orders for the Matilda tank placed during that year.[121]

When considering the limitations on time, industrial capacity and priority, the development of the Matilda tank should be considered a resounding success. As highlighted in the introductory chapter, the pressures of rearmament resulted in the practice of ordering tanks straight off the 'drawing-board', although not in the case of the Matilda tank developed by Vulcan Foundry. The official history suggests that Matilda tank development took four years from the General Staff specification in 1934 to being approved for production in 1938, and a total of five years until the first delivery in September 1939. This history does qualify these assertions by stating that the figures are 'rough and ready and should not be pressed too far'.[122] Despite this caveat, the suggestions are misleading as the 1934 specification related to the general requirement for an Infantry tank, which became the Infantry Mark I, rather than directly relating to the later Matilda tank.

Vulcan Foundry received instructions for the construction of two pilots in November 1936 with only two draughtsmen under employment by May 1937, although the Mechanization Board did provide assistance. Despite the official history stating that the total number of draughtsmen had 'only' quadrupled to eight by November 1937, the first prototype was delivered for testing during April 1938.[123] The prototype tank was subjected to performance trials and completed over 1,000 miles in six weeks. Problems were identified with the cooling and gear box but otherwise nothing which was considered to be insurmountable.[124] This opinion was expressed directly to Vulcan Foundry by the Director of Mechanization, Major-General Alexander Davidson, who stated that the success of the prototype was based upon sound design and good workmanship.[125]

This was a highly impressive introduction to tank design and development for Vulcan Foundry as demonstrated by the order for 130 Matilda tanks across May and June 1938, and the involvement of three more assembly firms during August 1938. John Fowler and Ruston & Hornsby received orders for 40 tanks each, and London, Midland and Scottish with an order for just 10 vehicles in recognition of their introduction to tank assembly and the requirement to gain some experience before accepting anything larger.[126] Therefore and contrary to the claims of the official history, the time between the November 1936 specification and the May 1938 production order was 18 months and not 4, and less than 3 years instead of 5 for the first Matilda tank delivery in September 1939. The order for 130 Matilda tanks with Vulcan Foundry was divided equally between May and June 1938. Both of these orders were valued at £1,170,000 each, with corresponding increases in the company's order book.[127] To put these orders into context with the other production activity at Vulcan Foundry during 1938, the value of locomotive work on the books had peaked at £745,000 during April and May, whereas government orders during 1938 increased from £822,000 in January to £3,150,000 in December.[128]

The unit cost price of the 130 Matilda tanks with Vulcan Foundry was £18,000, which was three times the £6,000 for the Infantry Mark I. This reflected the greater complexity and weight of the second over the first, and the increase in costs of involving a new manufacturer like Vulcan Foundry, over an experienced tank firm like Vickers-Armstrongs. The estimated cost of the remaining tanks under design or production between 1936 and 1939 are shown in Table 1.1, together with the costs of aircraft. The Light tanks were the least expensive to produce and fighter planes remained below the cost of either Infantry or Cruiser tanks. The single-engine medium bombers were comparable to the cost of Cruiser tanks across the period. The greater cost of the Matilda tank was mirrored by the increased cost required for the later twin-engine medium bombers. The heavy bombers were the most expensive by a sizeable margin.

In addition to those firms introduced to tank production or other armaments work, there were still large firms who had not received any munitions orders as late as 1938 and two years into 'serious' rearmament. This delay was partly caused by the government adopting a 'business as usual' approach by not allowing the demands of rearmament to disrupt the economic status quo. As such, service departments were not encouraged to let their demands displace normal commercial production.[129] This policy hindered rearmament efforts in respect of gun production, as non-interference with normal trade meant that the Director-General of Munitions Production could not place all the orders that had been authorized.[130] By March 1938, the Secretary of State for Air, Lord Swinton, asked the government to give the demands of rearmament some priority over normal civilian production.[131] While defence contracts had some priority over exports, firms still had to be encouraged to transfer their skilled labour to armaments work while lucrative civilian contracts remained available.[132]

Table 1.1 Estimated cost price of British tanks and aircraft, 1936 to 1939

Year	Type	Tank	Price	Type	Aircraft	Price
1936	Light	Light	£3,250			
1937	Infantry	Mark I	£6,000	Fighter	Gladiator	£5,300
	Cruiser	Mark I	£12,710	Medium	Battle	£11,250
				Medium	Blenheim	£13,500
				Heavy	Whitley	£30,000
1938	Light	Light	£4,000			
	Infantry	Matilda	£18,000			
	Cruiser	Mark II	£12,950			
	Cruiser	Mark III	£12,000			
1939	Infantry	Valentine	£14,900	Fighter	Spitfire	£8,000
	Cruiser	Mark IV	£13,800	Fighter	Defiant	£10,500
	Cruiser	Covenanter	£12,000	Medium	Wellington	£18,500
	Cruiser	Crusader	£13,700	Medium	Hampden	£20,000
				Heavy	Halifax	£42,000

Sources: The National Archives, CAB 24/272, 'Defence Expenditure in Future Years', 22 October 1937, p. 18; M. M. Postan, D. Hay and J. D. Scott, *Design and Development of Weapons: Studies in Government and Industrial Organisation* (London: HMSO and Longmans, Green, 1964), pp. 360–1; G. C. Peden, *British Rearmament and the Treasury: 1932–1939* (Edinburgh: Scottish Academic Press, 1979), p. 199n.

This late transfer to rearmament work was experienced by English Electric who had not received any significant government munitions contracts until 1938. When the company attempted to secure armament contracts during April 1938, they were informed that government policy had prevented their involvement to date as they were already occupied with supplying overseas and domestic markets.[133] Upon pursuing the matter further into July, English Electric considered manufacturing 75 aircraft frames if this did not interfere with their normal business, and that a reasonable guarantee could be provided that further contracts would follow.[134] It was therefore English Electric who had approached the government to become involved in rearmament work, while being suitably diligent not to allow munitions work to affect their usual business. This attitude was reflected in the sales book for October 1938. Within six months of the initial rearmament enquiry the firm had orders totalling £5,300,000 of ordinary business for the year to date compared to other defence orders at only £390,000.[135] This was a measured and steady introduction by English Electric into rearmament work that avoided displacing the existing capacity or labour for supplying the civilian markets. It also suggests how many other firms could have become involved in armaments production much earlier had the government not deliberately excluded them.

Air raid precautions

Following the warning by Stanley Baldwin during 1932 that the 'bomber will always get through',[136] industry took unilateral action in response to the threat of air attack as the situation on the Continent deteriorated during 1938. The crippling of factory output was a key war aim for any belligerent which Gloucester Railway Carriage & Wagon Company recognized after the annexation of Austria or *Anschluss* in April 1938, when they began to consider taking air raid precautions.[137] During August, the managing director of Metropolitan-Cammell announced to the board that the existing precautions at all works required a further £2,000 to ensure that they were fully up-to-date.[138] The possible consequences of European leaders failing to reach agreement at the Munich conference during September 1938 was understood by industry, together with continued uncertainty regarding the prospect of war until the outbreak a year later. For Gloucester Railway at the time of the 'Munich Crisis', the firm was satisfied that the existing measures could be swiftly enacted in the event of a national emergency.[139] During October, AEC reported that the planned system of air raid precautions would cost an estimated £6,000.[140] Similarly, English Electric recognized in October that important company information such as drawings, accounts and other records needed to be duplicated to protect against the effects of bombing.[141] By February 1939, Gloucester Railway revised their position and decided to spend an extra £2,000 on air raid shelters to protect the workforce which were completed in April.[142] At the end of August 1939 and in recognition of the situation in Europe, the board of Gloucester Railway authorized the managing director to take whatever precautionary measures were deemed necessary.[143]

The factories of Vickers-Armstrongs, being the only firm dedicated to armaments production, were an obvious and well-established target in respect of air attack. Vickers responded to this threat by increasing the expenditure on air raid precautions from £95,000 during 1938 to £400,000 during 1939. In respect of protecting individual locations, the Barrow works increased from £25,000 to £88,500 over these two years. Elswick received a similar increase from £24,000 to £70,000, and the amount spent on Dartford grew from £14,500 to £37,500. Part of the increase in expenditure during 1939 can also be attributed to the £96,000 spent on protecting the Supermarine and Weybridge aircraft factories.[144] These locations were not recorded during 1938 because Supermarine and Vickers Aviation were not absorbed into Vickers-Armstrongs until October 1938, as part of the concentration of Wellington bomber production as discussed above in respect of sales.[145]

In the absence of a monthly or quarterly breakdown of these costs, the majority of the 1939 expenditure at Vickers-Armstrongs might have related to the last three months of the year when war was declared. However, the board agreed at the beginning of 1939 that each factory should proceed with individual air raid schemes which could be activated within 48 hours of an emergency.[146] Therefore, the majority of the precautions and costs involved during 1939 would have taken place in the eight months prior to the outbreak of war. In addition to the precautions to existing premises, Vickers went one stage further by purchasing neighbouring premises to meet the concerns of air attack. During April 1939 the firm purchased property from London, Midland and Scottish Railway for the sum of £5,500 where the employees at the Barrow works could be evacuated during an air raid.[147] A similar purchase was made again just after the outbreak of war, when the firm purchased premises near the Weybridge works for the sum of £2,750.[148]

The attitude of Rover towards taking air raid precautions revealed the understandable fear that firms had regarding government policy and the extent of centralized control in the event of war. During November 1938, Rover was advised by the Air Ministry to take various precautionary measures which the Board sanctioned for £2,000. The concern was whether this expenditure would benefit the shareholders, as it was feared that a wartime government would take control of the factories, and the shareholders' interests would be lost.[149] Despite these legitimate concerns, by the end of 1940 Rover had spent over £50,000 on air raid precautions since 1938, and as discussed in the next chapter the government now provided industry with a grant towards part of the costs incurred.[150]

Conclusion

The contraction of the armaments industry following the First World War reflected the reduction in military requirements and the gradual control of the Treasury over service estimates and policies during the 1920s. The Air Ministry and Air Council maintained an industrial base by keeping a number of firms involved with aircraft work, although the requirement for monoplane and metal construction did not occur until rearmament. While the War Office only had Vickers-Armstrongs and the Woolwich Royal Ordnance Factory for tank design and production, the mechanization of the army was supported by each Chief of the Imperial General Staff and important experimentation and training was carried out.

The mechanization of the army before rearmament improved with the appointment of a dedicated Director of Mechanization and the formation of the Mechanical Warfare Board, which included the expertise from the civil and mechanical engineering industries. The organization transformed into the Mechanization Board in 1934 upon rearmament, where the involvement of these scientists and engineers extended to an executive role. The policy of 'serious' rearmament during 1936 introduced Vice-Admiral Sir Harold Brown as the Director-General of Munitions Production because of his experience in dealing with the engineering industry. Brown obtained full control of the War Office programme for the remainder of rearmament with the dissolution of the Master-General of the Ordnance. The research and development of tank production at the start of rearmament was intrinsically linked to the activities of the British motor industry, the investment by Vickers-Armstrongs into standardized designs, and technical advances and alloy experimentation in metallurgy.

The decision to give the Royal Air Force, anti-aircraft requirements, and the Royal Navy a higher priority than the production of other army equipment was correct as it mirrored the strategic reality of Britain. This meant that the existing aircraft industry received a number of enlargement schemes which were supported by the involvement of motor firms into the 'shadow' industry. A number of new civilian firms were also introduced into the tank programme to meet the mass production of the latest Light Mark VI tank and for the production of the first Infantry and Cruiser tanks.

By funding the expansion of industrial capacity, the government retained control over the pace and purpose of the new 'shadow' and Royal Ordnance factories, and the new plant and machinery for other firms. Vickers-Armstrongs already had the capacity for more armaments work before the government pursued a policy of 'serious' rearmament from 1936 and owned the new equipment for part of the cost. The high demand for machine tools for the rearmament programme affected those industries still needing similar tools for the production of goods for the civilian markets.

The effect of rearmament upon individual firms saw Vickers-Armstrongs receive a large increase in sales and employment, assisted by the transfer of aircraft work from Vickers Aviation and Supermarine. The successful development of the Matilda tank by Vulcan Foundry demonstrated the ability to provide a pilot tank ready for production in 18 months, and deliver the first production tank 3 years after the original instruction. The order for new tanks provided Vulcan Foundry with a welcome increase in sales following a period of stagnation in the core locomotive business and a gradual increase in employment after a period of decline. The example of English Electric highlights that some firms were deliberately excluded from munitions work until very late into rearmament, as the government did not want to affect domestic consumption and the export market.

The response of industry towards the threat of air attack reflected the rise in tensions on the Continent with various precautionary measures carried out. These efforts ranged from the construction of shelters, the duplication of important documents and purchasing adjacent premises for evacuation. In addition to the potential loss of workers and physical damage to factories caused by bombing, Rover Company had concerns about the level of centralized control that might be placed upon commercial industry in the event of war.

Government and Industry during Wartime

British industry went through a variety of changes as a result of the different political and economic priorities and pressures brought about by the Second World War. During the First World War and against the typical position of laissez-faire liberalism, the state had assumed more control over the different facets of the British economy than ever before.[1] The extent of state influence over the British economy during the Second World War increased even further with greater controls over prices and quantities, controls over the supply of labour and scarce resources, new taxes, restrictions on capital and with the curtailment of exports. While business generally supported the temporary centralization of economic power, there were concerns that this might become permanent or result in the nationalization of private companies.[2] The change from rearmament under peacetime conditions to a state of continuous total war for six years meant that industry underwent a series of physical and organizational transformations. These changes were repeated in the war industries of other nations, depending upon the relationship between the government and industry, the priorities for each of their service departments, and whether the factory locations supported the concentration or dispersal of production.

To illustrate these types of changes, this chapter will identify the greater involvement of industrialists to senior positions within the British government upon the outbreak of war. The priority system for all three services emphasized the dominant position of aircraft production and anti-aircraft defence until November 1941, when the tank programme was given an equal status. The strengthening involvement of senior industrialists into key positions of authority will be examined by the case example of the five different Tank Boards, alongside the other changes that occurred in war planning and centralized organization. The ability of British industry to supply the tank components and carry out the final assembly were located in the larger manufacturing regions of the country and supported by the simplification of the parent system. The government continued to fund the expansion of industrial capacity necessary for greater war production, while industry made a contribution towards these costs so that each firm did not unduly benefit from the larger facilities and modern plant and equipment. The final effect upon British industry discussed in this chapter will be the response to the threat and reality of enemy bombing with a range of air raid precautions, although the wholesale dispersal of production facilities was rejected.

Government and industry

The planning for war production in Britain was carried out by specialist ministries under the War Cabinet instead of being directed by central planners.[3] The extent of state control upon war production increased during August 1939 with the creation of the Ministry of Supply which gave absolute priority to defence matters at the expense of the free-market civil economy.[4] The Ministry of Supply became solely responsible for meeting the needs of the army once the shipbuilding programme remained with the Admiralty and following the appointment of Lord Beaverbrook to the new Ministry of Aircraft Production in May 1940.[5] The autonomous nature of the Ministry of Aircraft Production meant that the requirements of the air programme were better co-ordinated with the industrial and strategic planning of the government, compared to the prior arrangement under the Air Ministry.[6]

By comparison, the organization for supplying the different branches of the armed forces in the United States was different. The General Staff dealt with planning, whereas the War Department issued official instructions to all subordinate commands of the Army Ground Force, the Army Air Force and the Army Service Force within the United States and overseas. The procurement of the various requirements occasionally merged with the Ordnance Department obtaining tanks, artillery guns and fire control equipment for the army, and the guns, ammunition and high explosive bombs for the air force.[7] Under the full authority delegated by the War Department, the Tank Automotive Center in Detroit became the administrator of armoured fighting vehicles and artillery production.[8] The political difficulties relating to controlling the supply of equipment to the armed forces were eventually overcome, which provided the War and Navy departments with unrestricted access to the industrial and technological capacity and creativity of the United States.[9]

The outbreak of war in September 1939 emphasized the need for increased war production and the greater involvement of leaders of industry to fulfil the requirements of the services. Since January 1939, a group of industrialists and officials from the Air Ministry had already established a committee to supervise the distribution of light alloys. After the outbreak of war, a system of voluntary control within the light alloy industry organized the priority and planning for the different alloy requirements while co-operating with the Air Ministry.[10] In April 1940 and a month before the end of Neville Chamberlain's government, the managing director of Vickers-Armstrongs, Sir Charles Craven, became the Civil Member of the Air Council for Development and Production bringing his experience of aircraft and general armaments manufacturing.[11]

At the Ministry of Supply, Vice-Admiral Sir Harold Brown, as the Director-General of Munitions Production discussed in the previous chapter, retained the responsibility for gun and shell production, but had a number of other areas transferred to new authorities.[12] Lord Weir became the Director-General of Explosives with his experience in aircraft production during rearmament and chairmanship of a number of firms.[13] Experienced businessmen Lord Woolton became the Director-General of Equipment and Stores for the army and Sir Andrew Duncan became the controller of iron and steel.[14] The organizational capabilities of Duncan were shown in 1934 when he was appointed the independent chairman of the Iron and Steel Federation. Duncan was later appointed to Chamberlain's cabinet as President of the Board of Trade in January 1940, and was Minister of Supply from October 1940 until June 1941 and again from February 1942 until July 1945 with the end of Churchill's government.[15]

The responsibility for tank production was given to the President of the Federation of British Industries, Peter Bennett, as the new Director-General of Tanks and Transport. By the middle of June 1940, Bennett had resigned from tanks and transport and was replaced by another industrialist and general manager from the Birmingham Small Arms Company, Geoffrey Burton.[16] The controversial mixture of civilian and military personnel that had existed since the formation of the Ministry of Supply could have been exacerbated by the decision to introduce members of industry with production experience. In essence, the senior military personnel within the ministry could have taken offence at being bypassed with industrialists for the co-ordination and control of war production. As a result, the Director of Mechanization and the army members on the Mechanization Board received assurances that the restructuring was not an indictment of them as military officers or as ministry officials, but instead a realization of the need to involve business leaders with production experience.[17]

Priority of armaments production

After Germany threatened Western Europe with the invasion and occupation of Norway and Denmark, the Chiefs of Staff Committee reported on 4 May 1940 that aircraft and air defence production should be accelerated, even at the expense of delaying the long-term programme.[18] With the fighting escalating to France and Flanders, the precedence for the aircraft industry was formalized with the 'Priority of Production Directive' that provided firms with the order in which their efforts should be directed for each of the services. This gave top or 1 (a) priority to the production of fighters, bombers and anti-aircraft equipment, while army equipment such as tanks, field artillery, anti-tank guns and machine guns were positioned at the lower 1 (b) priority. Admiralty requirements that could be completed within the year to May 1941 also received priority except when this work interfered with aircraft or tank production.[19] As examined during the previous chapter, this priority situation reflected the strategic reality of Britain during the early stages of the war, with air defence and attack receiving priority over land weapons and the navy.

The official history rightfully contends that despite being essential to deal with the immediate demands of 1940, this strict priority system made war planning extremely difficult as it gave no consideration for the production and labour requirements over the longer term.[20] For individual firms like AEC, the more pressing concern during July 1940 related to the continued shortage of materials which had prevented the firm from achieving the planned 24-hour shift work seven-days-a-week. This meant that despite the majority of AEC contracts being classified as 1 (a), the new priority system would not produce an increased output as this firm was unable to run one night-shift per week until the materials position improved.[21]

The possibility of raising tank production to 1 (a) status was considered by the Production Council during July 1940, which highlighted the conflict with aircraft production in the availability of alloy steel and drop stampings. Given that Prime Minister Churchill had placed a great deal of importance on expanding the tank programme, the council agreed to raise tank production to 1 (a) priority in principle, although an amended directive was not issued to industry.[22] The delay permitted the Production Council to investigate the consequences of giving the tank programme a higher priority and reported that a fourfold increase in tank production would have little effect upon general industry as aircraft and tanks were produced by different firms. The capacity for an increase in armour plate was deemed adequate following the reduction of the capital ship programme for the Royal Navy. The main concern was the impact upon drop stampings and that a greater priority for tank production would adversely affect both the aircraft and anti-aircraft programmes.[23]

The prospect of weakening Britain's air defence while the Battle of Britain was being fought overhead was clearly unacceptable and hence unlikely. Furthermore, winning this battle would forestall the threat of invasion and thus no longer require Priority 1 (b) equipment to be used on British soil. Churchill confirmed this overriding position to the Minister of Aircraft Production Beaverbrook, when he stated that 'if it came to a choice between hampering Air Production or Tank production, I would sacrifice the Tank'.[24] The possibility of increasing the priority for tanks was further weakened when the Air Ministry used 26 per cent of drop stamping capacity each week compared to 32 per cent by the Ministry of Supply, especially when the majority of this was used for unarmed wheeled vehicles. Churchill suggested that tanks be given 1 (a) status except when the requirements conflicted with the aircraft industry, but Beaverbrook rejected this proposal as a reduction in aircraft output would result through the redirection of resources. In an attempt to redistribute drop stamping capacity more appropriately, the War Cabinet agreed to relegate motor cars and lorries for all the services to Priority 2, however tank production remained at 1 (b).[25] The distribution of steel under these changing priorities for these different programmes was carried out by the Raw Materials Department of the Ministry of Supply, after the independent Materials Committee had decided upon the appropriate allocation. This committee ensured that the demands upon steel requirements were justified and resolved any interdepartmental disputes.[26]

In November 1940 the DGTT, Geoffrey Burton, declared that the lack of 1 (a) priority would not affect existing production tanks like the Matilda and Valentine, as much as it would the tanks entering production, such as the Covenanter, Crusader and Churchill.[27] The situation changed by March 1941, when the executive second Tank Board discussed below, stated that unless tank engines were given 1 (a) priority, Valentine production could be limited to 100 instead of the anticipated 130 tanks per month until August.[28] While the production figures across the 4 months to the end of July 1941 averaged at 120 per month, the lower priority status certainly had some effect.[29]

By July 1941, the arguments against lifting tank priority to 1 (a) remained, although the role of Beaverbrook had now reversed with him arguing in favour of the change as the new Minister of Supply.[30] With improvements in the capacity for drop stampings, agreement was reached to give tank and tank spares priority 1 (a) status, under a scheme that was reminiscent of the one that Beaverbrook had rejected under the pressures of August 1940. Rather than issuing a new directive to industry, manufacturers were advised of the change in priority but with the caveat that aircraft production took precedence in the case of conflict. The reason for not superseding the June 1940 directive was to prevent the suspected 'psychological impetus' of contractors overproducing well-supplied tank components, at the expense of items that were in high demand.[31] This changed on 14 November 1941 with a new Priority of Production Directive that gave 1 (a) priority to aircraft, anti-aircraft weapons, tanks, anti-tank guns, small arms and ammunition for all types. The new 1 (b) priority included field artillery, mortars and other anti-tank weapons not included under 1 (a). The understanding behind this new priority system was to achieve the delivery of all top priority items, but to prevent the production of these items expanding beyond requirements and thus hampering the output of lower priority items.[32]

Similar fluctuations occurred with the priority of German war production as a result of the strength of Germany's front line position, the competition between the different services, the introduction of new ministerial leadership and changes in the decision making by Adolf Hitler. For example, the production priorities at the start of hostilities in France and Flanders during May 1940 were to provide weapons for stationary warfare to overcome static defences similar to the First World War, with tanks listed as the penultimate priority.[33] The combined effects of the Battle of Britain, the Blitz, the political necessity to assist the Italians in the Balkans and with the defence of German occupied Europe, the Luftwaffe attacked the Soviet Union in June 1941 with a smaller force than 12 months before.[34] In the days before the start of Operation Barbarossa, Hitler enlarged the aircraft programme at the expense of army equipment based upon the ideological and analytical miscalculation of Soviet military capabilities.[35] When Albert Speer became Minister for Munitions in January 1942 after the death of Fritz Todt, the management of armaments production improved resulting in the better use of resources and increased output. The so-called miracle carried out by Speer was only achieved at the expense and exploitation of the human and material resources in the occupied territories, and that Speer only gained control of the navy programme in January 1943 and the air programme in August 1944.[36]

Industrialists on the five Tank Boards

The Mechanization Board discussed in the previous chapter was replaced at the end of July 1940 by the Directorate of Tank Design to coincide with the earlier introduction of the Tank Board in June.[37] Historians have noted that the role of the Tank Board had a limited advisory role until it became effective from September 1942, and that the membership frequently changed throughout the war.[38] While accurate, this does not take into account that each Minister of Supply brought about the changes that resulted in five different Tank Boards. Furthermore, the reasons behind the transfer of individual members on each board needs explanation, in particular how the industrialists became more influential with the authority to take executive decisions to meet the requirements of the General Staff.

The first Tank Board operated from 24 June until 25 November 1940. The idea of a Tank Board was recommended to Prime Minister Chamberlain in April 1940, when members from both Houses of Parliament expressed their dissatisfaction with the monopoly that Peter Bennett had over tank production.[39] The creation of the first advisory Tank Board was agreed at the Military Co-ordination Committee on 6 May 1940 to include members from the Ministry of Supply and War Office, but without any additional experience from industry.[40] This had already been shown when the former Secretary of State for Air, Lord Swinton, was rejected as chairman of the new Tank Board because this might have interfered with his duties as chairman of the Danubian Company.[41] While the changes in personnel with the new Churchill government brought about greater determination and clarity to the British war effort, the authority and function of the first Tank Board remained unchanged.[42] With the departure of Leslie Burgin as Minister of Supply in favour of Herbert Morrison, the Ministry continued to regard the Tank Board as a 'lightning conductor' to secure consultation and agreement with the War Office, but without any executive power.[43] There was improvement regarding the chairman of the first board with the appointment of Sir Alexander Roger from the Birmingham Small Arms Company, who also brought his experience as Director-General of Trench Warfare Supply from the First World War.[44] Roger continued as chairman for five meetings before departing to head the new mission to India.[45]

Herbert Morrison continued with the understanding that more members from industry should be incorporated into the first Tank Board. This included the chief engineer from the London Passenger Transport Board, Albert Durrant, the managing director of tank firm Birmingham Railway Carriage & Wagon Company, Harry Moyses, and a member from the General Council of the Trades Union Congress, G. W. Thomson. These independent members were joined from the Ministry of Supply by the new DGTT, Geoffrey Burton, and the Director of Mechanization, Brigadier John Crawford.[46] Separate from any Tank Board role, the chief mechanical engineer from the London Passenger Transport Board, William Graff-Baker, was given the responsibility for tank production that included the planning, material control and the study of capacity.[47] Lieutenant-Colonel William Blagden was added to the board at the first meeting to act as a liaison between the Ministry of Supply and the War Office.[48]

The War Office members on the first Tank Board were Major-General Vyvyan Pope as the Director of Armoured Fighting Vehicles and Brigadier Douglas Pratt.[49] Pope gained his experience in the Royal Tank Corps and the War Office during the 1920s and 1930s. Pope continued in the Royal Armoured Corps until he was assigned to Lord Gort's staff in France following the German offensive in May 1940.[50] Pratt had experience of tanks during the First World War as a company commander at the Battle of Cambrai and during 1940 in command of 1st Army Tank Brigade in France.[51] While the War Office positions were important they lacked the seniority that would have been provided by a member linked to the Chief of the Imperial General Staff. The War Office membership on the first Tank Board was reduced to just Major-General Pope after three meetings, because Brigadier Pratt was sent to the United States as part of the Dewar Tank Mission and his place on the board remained vacant.[52] Rather than suggesting a lack of seriousness by the War Office, it was more likely a consequence of the board's advisory nature and that the evacuations from France provided more immediate concerns.

The formation of the first Tank Board against the deteriorating military situation in Europe was similarly repeated by the Canadian government. For the greater co-ordination on tank policy between the 'user' and 'supplier' branches, a Joint Committee on Tank Development was created. The role of Canadian industry in supporting the British war effort will be discussed in Chapter 6, including the importance of supplying Valentine tanks on behalf of British political obligations to the Soviet Union. The level of interest in European affairs by the Canadian Cabinet War Committee was shown when they met eight times during May 1940 following the German offensive, compared to six times since December 1939, and none during the Norwegian campaign.[53] During August 1940, the Minister for National Defence, Colonel James Ralston, suggested to the Minister of Munitions and Supply, Clarence Howe, that the two departments combine their resources with the creation of a joint tank committee.[54] Howe fully supported the proposal by stating that the committee would support the existing discussions between the officials from both departments on the issues of tank production.[55] The joint committee continued for 25 meetings until December 1941, when it was terminated and replaced by the Army Engineering Design Branch. This new organization discussed the issues raised by the joint committee, and expedited matters with direct contact with the army authorities and the Production Branch.[56]

While the Joint Committee on Tank Development was a shared venture, the Canadian official history notes that after the defeat of France the Department of Munitions and Supply was moved into 'the forefront of the war effort and much in the limelight', when compared to the Department of National Defence. According to the official history, part of the reason for this situation was because the Canadian armed forces only received a small proportion of the equipment produced in Canada.[57] This was the result of underlying organizational reasons that gave the Department of Munitions and Supply more responsibility for war production and thus an actual or perceived greater contribution towards Canada's war effort. The role of the Department of Munitions and Supply was highlighted by the new Chief of the General Staff Lieutenant-General Kenneth Stuart in December 1941, when approving the abolition of the Joint Committee on Tank Development. In essence, as of July 1941 the Department of Munitions and Supply became responsible for the Army Engineering Design Branch under the direction of an 'experienced and qualified engineer', who was ultimately accountable to Minister Howe. In order to maintain the liaison with other branches, an 'Inter-departmental Advisory Committee on Army Engineering Design' was set up to include a representative from the General Staff, the Master-General of the Ordnance and the Quartermaster General. The committee chairman was the Director-General of Army Engineering Design, who likewise reported to Minister Howe on matters relating to engineering designs and industrial production for the army.[58]

Following the termination of the first Tank Board in November 1940, the next Minister of Supply, Sir Andrew Duncan, set up a second Tank Board which functioned between 17 January and 11 July 1941. The organizational structure of this board followed the suggestion of Duncan's friend and advisor, Lord Weir. In November 1940, Weir argued that the board should have members of 'recognised and authoritative technical and industrial' understanding.[59] As a result, Duncan began by making the logical choice of appointing Sir James Lithgow as the Tank Board chairman and the new Controller-General of Mechanical Equipment.[60] Apart from being another friend to Duncan, Lithgow had the experience as chairman of steel manufacturer William Beardmore and in February 1940 became the Controller of Merchant Shipping and Repairs at the Admiralty.[61] The technical role from industry expanded once again to include Geoffrey Burton as the new Director-General of Supply for mechanical equipment, alongside James Weir from engineering firm G. & J. Weir Limited, as the new Director-General of Design and Development.[62] Independent member Harry Moyses from Birmingham Railway remained on the board and was joined by Commander E. R. Micklem from Vickers-Armstrongs.[63]

The War Office representation on the second Tank Board also increased in authority with Major-General Gordon Macready as the Assistant Chief of the Imperial General Staff, Major-General Kenneth Stewart as Inspector Royal Armoured Corps and Major-General Pope as before.[64] Macready was a General Staff Officer from 1934 until becoming Deputy Director of Staff Duties at the War Office from 1936. In 1938 he became Chief of the British Military Mission to the Egyptian Army and was later appointed Assistant Chief of the Imperial General Staff in October 1940.[65] Major-General Stewart brought the experience based upon a history of service with the Royal Tank Corps during the interwar period, including that of a Senior Instructor.[66]

At this point during the war the Ministry of Aircraft Production had undergone a number of reorganizations between July 1940 and 1941, including the replacement of Lord Beaverbrook by John Moore-Brabazon in May 1941. The new Minister was complemented by the creation of an Aircraft Supply Council that supervised the affairs of the Ministry with membership from leading production, research, development, financial and North American supply staff. Having previously held the position of chairman of the Air Supply Board, Sir Charles Craven from Vickers-Armstrongs returned as the Controller-General for aircraft production. The reorganization during 1941 abandoned the priority system of material allocation under Beaverbrook and created the Directorate of Materials Production to ensure that industrial output specialized in the right types of material.[67]

As before, a change of direction and Tank Board membership followed the introduction of Lord Beaverbrook as the new Minister of Supply at the end of June 1941, with Duncan returning to the Board of Trade. The third Tank Board operated from 1 August 1941 until 17 February 1942 with less representation from industry with Lithgow, Weir, Moyses and Micklem all departing. These changes were probably the result of Beaverbrook's general dislike of committees and individual resignations, similar to when Lord Weir left the Ministry of Supply upon the arrival of Beaverbrook.[68] Geoffrey Burton continued on the third Tank Board having been elevated to chairman, while two new industrialists were incorporated to fulfil senior positions relating to the design and production of tanks respectively. These were Oliver Lucas from motor component firm Lucas & Company, as the Controller-General of Research and Development, and George Usher from steam and electricity equipment manufacturers International Combustion, as the Director-General of Tank Supply.[69] Finally, William Robotham from Rolls-Royce was added as the Chief Engineer Tank Design to advise Lucas on all engineering matters and approve the final tank designs before being passed to Usher for allocation to an appropriate production group.[70]

The War Office representatives continued in seniority with Major-General Macready as before and Major-General Ronald Weeks as his deputy. Major-General Pope remained until his accidental death outside Cairo before the Crusader offensive in November 1941 and was replaced by Major-General Alexander Richardson.[71] Richardson was previously a member of the Royal Tank Corps and gained further experience with mechanized equipment between 1928 and 1930, when he commanded the Mechanical Warfare Experimental Establishment under the Mechanical Warfare Board discussed in the previous chapter.[72]

With the return of Duncan as Minister of Supply in February 1942, it is not surprising that Lord Weir would return given their extremely close working relationship, this time as chairman of the fourth Tank Board from 7 May to 4 August 1942. However, when taking into account the experience of the previous tank boards, this fourth organization was confused and disjointed. During March, Prime Minister Churchill was sceptical about placing Weir as the head of fourth Tank Board as Churchill considered him no longer effective.[73] Weir later stated as much following his resignation as chairman in August, when he said to Duncan that he never wanted a full-time and demanding executive responsibility.[74] This limitation was reflected in the Ministry's policy upon appointing Weir as chairman, which stipulated that he had no executive function or authority. The fourth board was still supported by Lucas and Usher and now with the chairman of the Supply Council Sir William Rootes from vehicle manufacturer and aircraft 'shadow' firm, Rootes Group.[75] Upon the departure of 'dynamic salesman' William Rootes to the Ministry of Supply, airframe and aero-engine production at Rootes Group continued under the direction of his 'sage administrator' brother Reginald.[76]

The General Staff representation on this fourth Tank Board expanded even further to include new areas of the War Office relating to mechanical equipment. Lieutenant-General Macready was sent to the United States during June 1942 to become the Chief of the British Army Staff.[77] Macready was replaced by Major-General Daril Watson, with Major-General Richardson remaining on the board as before. Major-General Weeks was added to the board as Director-General of Army Equipment and later as Deputy Chief of the Imperial General Staff, a post which he held until June 1945.[78] Finally, Major-General Eric Rowcroft was added to the board as the Director of Mechanical Engineering with his experience as Inspector of Tanks at the War Office between 1932 and 1936, and he eventually became a full Member of the Institution of Mechanical Engineers.[79] This meant that while the fourth Tank Board was made up of members of senior authority from both the Ministry of Supply and War Office, it was without a chairman who could make executive decisions based upon the different priorities of those members.

The resignation of Lord Weir resulted in the comprehensive restructuring of the different tank departments into the Armoured Fighting Vehicle Division, which included the fifth and final Tank Board from 16 September 1942 until 24 April 1945.[80] Commander Micklem returned from Vickers-Armstrongs to become the executive chairman of both the new division and the fifth board, while remaining available to consult on company affairs that were not connected to his duties at the Ministry.[81] George Usher returned to International Combustion and was replaced on the board by Archibald Boyd from tank firm Metropolitan-Cammell.[82] Boyd fulfilled the role as Director-General of Fighting Vehicles Production on a 12-months secondment which was due to conclude in September 1943.[83] When the time came, Minister of Supply Duncan was reluctant to release Boyd back to Metropolitan-Cammell, until the intervention of part-owners Vickers Limited resulted in Boyd returning in December 1943.[84] Lucas continued on the fifth Tank Board until September 1943 when he left to chair a tank mission to the United States. Lucas was replaced by engineer and general manager from C. A. Parsons, Claude Gibb, who was previously the Director-General of Weapons and Instruments Production.[85] When Boyd returned to Metropolitan-Cammell during December 1943, Gibb was given the all-encompassing responsibility for both the design and production branches, as Director-General of Armoured Fighting Vehicles.[86]

The War Office members on the fifth Tank Board maintained the focus upon combining General Staff seniority and recent combat experience. Lieutenant-General Weeks continued alongside Major-General Watson, until he was replaced late in 1942 by Major-General John Evetts who had commanded the 6th Infantry Division in North Africa during 1941.[87] Evetts was later replaced by Major-General Vyvyan Evelegh who had earned his reputation as commander of the 78th Infantry Division in North Africa, Sicily and Italy and then commanded the 6th Armoured Division from Cassino to Florence.[88] Major-General Richardson had continued since the third Tank Board until replaced by Major-General Raymond Briggs as Director, Royal Armoured Corps.[89] Briggs had fought in the North African campaign and rose to command the 2nd Armoured Brigade early in 1942 and then the 1st Armoured Division into 1943 before entering the War Office and joining the fifth Tank Board.[90] The major discussions carried out by the fifth board were complemented by the creation of the Armoured Fighting Vehicle Liaison Committee which had senior Tank Board members from the Ministry of Supply and War Office to make the executive decisions of a minor nature relating to the tank programme.[91]

The strength and success of the Armoured Fighting Vehicle Division and the fifth Tank Board was part of the increased centralization of British war planning from 1942 to manage the different production programmes more effectively. This included the greater control over capital and industry, the conscription of men and women for war work, the central direction of labour and a system of rationing to regulate civilian consumption.[92] Furthermore, in addition to the return of Duncan to the Ministry of Supply during February 1942, the Ministry of Production was created under Oliver Lyttelton, following the two-week appointment of Beaverbrook.[93] This new ministerial responsibility replaced the earlier Production Council and later Production Executive, and provided a member of the War Cabinet to negotiate with the United States on behalf of the different supply and service departments.[94] Similarly, a closer relationship between industry and official procurement occurred in the United States from 1942, when 'integration committees' were created to bring manufacturers together to eliminate bottlenecks and increase the rate of production. A total of 27 committees were formed by April 1943 with some continuing until the end of the war, while others were disbanded once the problems had been resolved.[95]

Location of industry

The geographical distribution of the tank industry supported the greater capacity for manufacturing in the northern Home Counties, the Midlands and in the north of England where London, Midland and Scottish Railway carried out tank assembly at Crewe and Horwich. With the exception of Vickers, the firms represented a wide range of civilian work, including private, commercial and agricultural vehicles, railway carriages and locomotives, shipbuilding and engineering.[96] While there may have been political reasons behind the locations of particular orders, this was not always necessarily the case. For example, the North British Locomotive Company received their tank contracts during the late 1930s when the Clydeside region had high unemployment and presumably the labour capacity.[97] Similarly, the decision to give Harland & Wolff the Churchill tank prototype during November 1939 was not to provide the Belfast area with tank work, but because they were the only firm that had the required amount of unused machinery available.[98]

As discussed in the previous chapter, the production of tanks and aircraft in Britain were controlled by a parent system under the firm that typically had the greater administrative and design capacity. Experienced armaments firm Vickers-Armstrongs in Newcastle-upon-Tyne had the parentage of the Light Mark VI tank, the Cruiser Mark I and II tanks, the Infantry Mark I tank and the Valentine tank. Locomotive manufacturers Vulcan Foundry in Newton-le-Willows and London, Midland and Scottish in Crewe were the parents for the Matilda and Covenanter tanks respectively. The Nuffield Organisation with Mechanization & Aero in Birmingham had the parentage of the Cruiser Marks III and IV, the Crusader tank and later the Cavalier tank. Motor firm Vauxhall Motors in Luton continued as the parent of the Churchill tank throughout the war, while commercial vehicle firm Leyland Motors became the parent of the consecutive Centaur, Cromwell and Comet tanks.[99] The possible transfer of Centurion tank development from the government controlled Royal Ordnance Factories to the private organization of Leyland Motors was offered by Commander Micklem during May 1944. Leyland Motors declined because they had insufficient design capacity for at least six months, and that it would have given their design staff the 'wrong impression' as they were working on preparing the Comet tank for production.[100]

Leyland Motors required an extensive organization to administer the responsibilities as parent of the Centaur, Cromwell and Comet programmes during the second half of the war. These included the full-time duties of Group Engineering Controller, Group Production Co-ordinator, Plant Consultant, Foundries Consultant and the co-ordination of material control and inspection.[101] A number of firms expecting to produce the Centaur tank, such as Fodens, Ruston-Bucyrus and West's Gas were under the parentage of Mechanization & Aero, as a continuation of the organization that had produced the Crusader tank. This could have meant a great deal of unnecessary confusion and duplication of effort with each dependent firm communicating their demands separately to Mechanization & Aero and Leyland Motors. This concern was resolved during a General Policy Meeting at the Ministry of Supply during May 1943, following which Mechanization & Aero retained their parent status over the dependent firms under the overall parentage of Leyland Motors. Therefore, each dependent firm would continue to request and receive information and materials from Mechanization & Aero as their parent, who in turn passed these requirements to Leyland Motors for action.[102] While this arrangement was never used with the reduction of the Centaur contract and the transfer of Fodens, Ruston-Bucyrus and West's Gas to other war work as discussed in Chapters 4 and 5, the parent system was now organized to prevent any future duplication.

The different material requirements for each tank under production during April 1941 illustrates the diversification of industry to support the completion of the tank programme. With the exception of an increased involvement in Scotland, the regional division of these orders was similar to that identified for tank assembly, with particular importance given to the Midlands and the North East. In respect of individual component contractors, parent firms Mechanization & Aero and Vauxhall Motors supplied engines and suspensions to the tank programmes they were co-ordinating, thereby making them jointly responsible for organizing and providing some of the material requirements. A number of contractors supplied different components to different tank programmes from the same location. For example, Leyland Motors provided engines for the separate Covenanter and Matilda programmes and Harland & Wolff supplied steering units for Matilda tanks and gun mountings for Valentine tanks. Self-Changing Gear in Coventry provided gear boxes for Matilda production and steering units for the Covenanter and Churchill tanks. Finally, Clyde Alloy Steel in Motherwell and the English Steel Corporation in Sheffield provided armour plate for all of these early tank programmes.[103]

The supply of engines and gear boxes were provided by a small number of firms for each tank programme, whereas the Matilda was dependent upon seven sources to supply steering and final drive units. The Matilda and the Valentine programmes had only one or two track contractors when compared to the Covenanter, Crusader and Churchill tanks which were supplied from eleven to fourteen firms. The Valentine programme was also only dependent upon three sources for the supply for armour and bullet-proof plate, while the other programmes required between six and ten contractors. Many British tank programmes also received a supply of tank components from North America, as discussed in Chapter 6. When including gun mountings and suspensions, the Valentine programme required the total supply from sixteen British firms compared to the Crusader programme that relied upon forty suppliers. Part of the reason for this increase in the number of firms was because the Valentine contracts had been allocated much earlier using the industrial capacity available, which could not be used on the later Crusader programme.[104] As a result, new capacity was generated by incorporating a larger number of new and smaller firms in Britain that were not involved in tank or component production, such as with the expansion of the Crusader programme.

Increasing industrial capacity

The British government programme of industrial expansion from 1936 to 1945 provided capital assistance to support the increase in war production, which the official history calculates at £1,000 million. A quarter of this cost went to directly operated government establishments, such as Royal Ordnance Factories, with a further quarter going to government factories operated by commercial firms on an agency basis, such as the 'shadow' aircraft factories. The remaining half provided individual firms with new building extensions and new plant and equipment to meet the demands of each production order.[105] A total of 170 agency factories in the aircraft, chemicals and explosives industries were authorized by 1942, together with 40 Royal Ordnance Factories and the expansion of dockyard capacity by incorporating privately owned facilities.[106] Germany underwent a similar expansion of capital investment for war production from 1936 to 1945, although the full extent of this industrial capacity was not used until late into the war.[107]

The policy of the British government towards the costs of this industrial expansion was driven by the avoidance of enhancing the firm at taxpayers' expense, although the particular agreements fluctuated over the course of the war. During July 1940, Metropolitan-Cammell received a direct grant from the Ministry of Supply of 80 per cent of the £182,000 total cost to supply machine tools for the production of the new Valentine tank.[108] By August, Mechanization & Aero incurred the entire £192,000 for the installation of additional plant and equipment at their Birmingham works for Ministry of Supply work, under an agreement that the Ministry would reimburse the firm within three years.[109] In October, Gloucester Railway Carriage & Wagon Company received a 60 per cent contribution from the Ministry towards the £25,680 required for the expansion of drop stamping capacity at the works. The firm retained the ownership of the new plant for an annual cost representing the interest on the amount provided by the Ministry and the level of depreciation on the equipment.[110] From 1941, firms such as Morris Commercial Cars, Mechanization & Aero and Nuffield Exports were provided with a full reimbursement for the cost of the new plant on a variety of Ministry of Supply contracts. In each instance the Ministry retained the ownership until the end of the agreement, at which point the firm negotiated the cost of retaining the equipment for future company requirements.[111]

The cost of new building work for the contracts with Morris Commercial Cars and Nuffield Exports from 1942 until the end of 1944 was met by the Ministry in full, together with an agreement that the firm would pay the Ministry at the end of the contract an amount which reflected the increased value of the buildings.[112] Birmingham Railway reached such an agreement with the Ministry in November 1946, resulting in the firm paying 44 per cent of the value of the original building work, and 32 per cent of the original cost to retain the additional plant and equipment.[113] Similarly, English Electric purchased much of the plant it had operated during the war for aircraft production at Preston and tank production at Stafford.[114] When an end to the war appeared more likely in April 1945, the agreement with Mechanization & Aero for new building work avoided these post-war negotiations with the firm receiving immediate ownership at a cost of 50 per cent of the value.[115] The difference between this cost and the 44 per cent agreed by Birmingham Railway reflected the increased depreciation and hence this firm received a lower degree of enhancement.

Having placed the contract and agreed the level of industrial capacity required there were a number of difficulties to overcome before production commenced. The first order for 151 Covenanter tanks with Leyland Motors in September 1939 required the construction of a new 'B/X Factory' to meet the requirement of 24 tanks per month, and the expectation of deliveries commencing in July 1940. By December 1939, three-quarters of the steel work had been completed, although heavy snow caused stoppages with material and labour shortages until February 1940. By March, no more than 75 per cent of the walls and floor had been completed and the building remained unfinished in June when the first deliveries were due the following month.[116] When the Covenanter order increased to 251 tanks in June 1940, Leyland Motors could not promise the optimistic July 1941 completion date, nor the delivery of 33 tanks per month.[117] By August 1940, progress under the tank contract was hampered by ongoing vehicle modifications and shortages of 'free issue' items, such as armour plate and final drives discussed in Chapter 5. The first production model was now expected during September 1940, although continuing shortages and the effects of bombing at the end of 1940 delayed the first tank for three months until December.[118] As a result of these interruptions, Leyland Motors delivered the 251th Covenanter tank during February 1942, which was seven months after the July 1941 forecast.[119]

Following the inability to secure Crusader production in the United States during 1940, discussed later in Chapter 6, the Crusader programme expanded in November from three tank firms to eight with an increased capacity from twenty to sixty tanks per week. As a result, three of these new firms and four additional firms became component contractors by collectively providing turrets, suspension units, engines and gear boxes towards the planned production of over two thousand Crusader tanks under the new programme. This further illustrated the diversification of industry to support the war effort. For example, Morris Engines provided engines, gear boxes and steering units. Wolseley Motors provided suspension units, while Ruston-Bucyrus and M. G. Cars provided turrets and assembled the finished tank.[120] The expansion scheme was successful when seven out of the eight assembly firms reached or well exceeded their maximum monthly forecast after approximately fourteen months of production. While the average monthly output after reaching the target did fall below requirements in five out of the eight firms, the programme was later enhanced by the addition of Morris Industries Exports during mid-1942.[121]

In comparison with the United States, Congress increased the spending on defence from $5 billion during 1939 and 1940 to $20 billion during 1941 in light of the events following the defeat of France. The attack on Pearl Harbor resulted in even greater defence spending to $75 billion in 1943 and $82 billion for 1944 and 1945 as the armed forces and industrial capacity expanded.[122] Similar to the practice adopted in Britain, the United States used the locomotive and motor firms to expand war production. American industry achieved this on a much grander scale given the greater experience in mass production, the larger reserves of manpower and industrial capacity, and not being exposed to enemy bombing.[123] These expansion schemes included the new $21 million Chrysler Tank Arsenal following the defeat of France, and the $37 million General Motors Fisher Tank Arsenal authorized during November 1941 in response to President Roosevelt's demand for increased tank output.[124] Together with the production from Cadillac, by March 1942 these 3 motor firms had the combined potential capacity of 3,000 tanks per month and eventually delivered over half of the total 88,410 tanks produced by the United States during the war.[125] The relatively small output of nearly 1,700 tanks by Ford was because the firm produced thousands of tons of armoured plate each month, together with bomber aircraft at their Willow Run plant at an eventual rate of one plane every hour.[126] This greater productive ability during the war resulted in the United States producing nearly three-and-a-half times as many tanks as Britain and four times as many as Germany between 1940 and 1945.[127] In respect of aircraft, the United States produced two-and-a-half times as many as Britain and nearly three times more than Germany.[128]

In contrast to Britain and the United States, the motor industry in Germany was both ill-prepared and incapable of producing tanks and other military vehicles in large numbers. The German military suspected that mass production techniques would not provide satisfactory equipment towards the required standard of quality. As a result, the industrial capacity within the motor firms was not fully converted to war production as carried out in Britain and the United States. For example, when Daimler-Benz was working at 95 per cent of total capacity in 1939, only 65 per cent of this level was allocated for military purposes. Later in 1944 when the maximum production capacity was being employed at Daimler-Benz, the extent of military work still accounted for 93 per cent. A serious consequence of not fully employing the motor industry for war production earlier, was that the Panzer units had to rely upon unsuitable civilian and captured equipment for the motorized transportation of artillery, fuel, ammunition and men.[129]

Air raid precautions, bombing and factory dispersal

The programme of air raid precautions started by industry during 1938 discussed in Chapter 1, continued during 1939 with the government now providing financial assistance for the costs incurred. During January 1939, the board of Austin Motors decided to replace their inadequate system of covered trenches by installing tunnels to protect the workers. The board provided the authorities with full details in case the government provided a contribution towards the costs incurred.[130] In March 1939 both Austin Motors and Rover Company noted that the government had announced an 'Exchequer grant' equivalent to the 27.5 per cent standard rate of income tax towards the costs of air raid precautions.[131] Among other reasons, the grant was meant to accelerate the level of precautions undertaken, following the concern that a number of employers had been procrastinating.[132] Leyland Motors delayed vital air raid precautions until August 1939, despite having appointed 'A.R.P. Officers' at the different works since September 1938. This delay resulted in no more than 70 per cent of the trenches necessary to accommodate all personnel at each factory at the outbreak of war, although inexpensive precautions had been carried out such as marking out evacuation routes.[133]

To put these efforts into perspective, armaments firm Vickers-Armstrongs spent nearly £400,000 during 1939 on completing air raid precautions across their factory locations and another £440,000 in 1940.[134] The importance of steel production, drop stampings, castings and armoured plate for all three services was reflected by the £100,000 spent by the English Steel Corporation from 1938 to 1939.[135] Austin Motors sanctioned £103,000 during 1939 and 1940, and the six firms under the Nuffield Organisation incurred nearly £135,000 for the same period.[136] Between 1939 and 1944, the ongoing requirement to maintain the blackout at Morris Motors was 45 per cent of the total cost of their air raid precautions. The cost of shelters totalled 21 per cent over the same period, while the 5 per cent for providing sandbags was mostly incurred during 1939. The remaining expenditure went towards securing vital pieces of plant, employee training and protective clothing and equipment.[137]

The effect that bombing had upon factory output was particularly acute when damage to the roof compromised the ability to maintain blackout discipline, especially during the longer winter nights. In the example of West's Gas producing the Crusader tank, the bomb damage sustained during December 1940 suspended night work for several weeks and permitted only 7 hours of work per day until repairs were completed.[138] This was a serious situation given the requirement for increased output with the loss of equipment following the defeat of France. In response to this situation, the Nuffield Organisation on behalf of the parent firm Mechanization & Aero, decided to create a reserve stock of roofing material at all factories so that similar delays could be avoided in the future.[139] The bombing delayed the first Crusader tank delivered from West's Gas until January 1941 instead of December 1940, which had been achieved by the similar sized production capacity of Fodens.[140]

To avoid unnecessary work stoppages during the bombing, a voluntary roof spotter system was employed to warn of imminent attack upon specific areas, allowing production to continue after the public siren had sounded. Some firms and government authorities jointly funded and operated schemes linked to the Royal Observer Corps to gain detailed information on bomber positions for use in conjunction with the roof spotters.[141] Leyland Motors reported that this system had been successful during the first four months of 1941. Despite losing 38 hours on the night-shift due to spotter warnings, this was less than 3 per cent of the total night-shift hours worked.[142]

The Allied bombing campaign against Germany shows how industry could still operate under relentless aerial attack. Between 1940 and 1945, the Allies dropped 2 million tons of bombs on Germany with the industrial and transport facilities accounting for 40 per cent of this campaign, compared to 30 per cent allocated to urban areas. While strategic bombing was meant to dislocate the economy and undermine the morale of the people, German war production continued and expanded regardless.[143] The daylight bombing raids on industry by the United States during 1943 did not cause significant disruption, although some success was achieved in August when the ME-262 jet plane factory in Regensburg was severely damaged. The bombing campaign did result in the greater emphasis upon anti-aircraft defences. In August 1944, 39,000 guns and 1 million men were assigned to protect German targets, rather than this equipment and manpower being deployed against the Allied armies on the different fronts.[144] German industry continued to produce armaments during 1944 despite the shortage of manpower and against heavy air and ground assault. As a result, the German war effort ran out of fuel and trained soldiers and airmen to fight on the front line, before running out of new tanks and aircraft.[145]

The dispersal of production was used by the government and industry to limit the interruptions caused by bombing, albeit at the expense of achieving greater output. In essence, while dispersing industry was deemed essential to avoid the consequences of bombing, this was incompatible with the requirement for a large increase in the scale of production.[146] Unlike Britain and Germany, the long-term and efficient mass production of North America was achieved through the concentration of large factories that were safely outside enemy bombing range.[147] In the Soviet Union, the concentration of production was the result of war on the Eastern Front, which compelled the relocation of industry away from the western and southern regions to hundreds of miles eastwards to the Urals and western Siberia.[148] For Britain, the threat of bombing meant that the large factory approach could not be adopted for the risk of sustaining an industrial disaster and because the government preferred the subcontracting of production, particularly in the aircraft industry.[149]

While the dispersal of industry meant that Britain could not take advantage of greater economies of scale with larger production facilities, it was altogether logical given the acute possibility of air attack. The size of the individual firm also contributed to the increased resilience to the consequences of bombing as shown by English Electric from February 1940. This firm considered themselves less vulnerable than other firms because they had spread production across their four factory locations in Stafford, Rugby, Bradford and Preston.[150] In December 1940, Minister of Supply Duncan identified the extent of government policy towards the distribution of British production by rejecting the complete dispersal of industry. This assessment was based upon the realization that no area was safer than any other, the transfer of labour would disrupt production and worker morale, and it was detrimental to disperse vital industry outside of well-defended areas. A localized form of dispersal was accepted when specialist production was too concentrated in any one place.[151]

The dispersal of aircraft production under Beaverbrook represented 23 per cent of the productive floor space within the airframe industry by December 1941. As a direct influence upon output between 1940 and 1943, dispersal increased the number of non-productive workers when compared to the number of productive workers at the Weybridge factory of Vickers-Armstrongs.[152] Dispersal also complicated the management of production when Supermarine was divided between 66 different locations in 3 separate counties following the bombing raids of 1940.[153] Vickers had detailed discussions with the ministries of aircraft production and supply during 1941 in respect of reimbursing the firm for the cost of dispersal. The ministries paid the costs of relocating the 'Crown plant' and the employees to the new premises, together with any new buildings, plant and equipment and air raid shelters. Ongoing expenses such as rent, rates, insurance and maintenance of the new premises were recoverable by Vickers as overheads. The ministries disputed the reimbursement of dismantling and installing Vickers' own plant at the new premises, and then the later reinstallation back at Vickers' works once the period of dispersal had ended.[154]

Up to the end of April 1941, the total cost to Vickers in carrying out this dispersal was estimated at a substantial £680,000, with £414,000 having been spent to date and £205,000 recovered from the Ministry concerned.[155] An alternative form of factory dispersal was the relocation to underground shelters; however, these were uncommon due to the particular costs and intensive preparations required.[156] Germany had similar problems despite successfully distributing the production of the Panzer Mark III during 1941 across four factory locations in Nuremburg, Brunswick and two in Berlin.[157] Early in 1944, Adolf Hitler demanded the construction of 'six gigantic underground shelters' in response to the Allied bombing, but these would have replaced other construction projects and were never started.[158]

Conclusion

The relationship between government and industry grew closer in response to the demands for increased war production. This was achieved by transferring greater control of the war programmes from the military to leaders from industry, while simultaneously not offending the existing military personnel within the new ministries. The co-ordination of industrial activity was managed by the Priority of Production Directive that met Britain's strategic reality by giving aircraft equipment the correct dominance over the tank programme until late 1941. This hierarchy was fully endorsed by Prime Minister Churchill who was willing to sacrifice the tank programme in order to maintain the high production of aircraft. By comparison, German war production similarly fluctuated in accordance with the changing situation on the battlefront, the whims of Adolf Hitler and the different priorities of the services, until Albert Speer gained complete control of all munitions production from August 1944.

The centralized control of British tank design and production fluctuated with the changes in direction brought about by each new Minister of Supply. Similar changes occurred in the Ministry of Aircraft Production following the replacement of Lord Beaverbrook with John Moore-Brabazon. The consecutive changes in the organizational arrangement for each of the five Tank Boards increased the number of industrialists taking senior positions of authority to meet the demands of the General Staff. The War Office representation similarly changed from a few knowledgeable officers to senior members of the General Staff making executive decisions based upon their recent command and battle experience. While these changes caused some disruption as new members were introduced, it is unrealistic to expect an interdepartmental organization not to change in composition from its creation in June 1940 until April 1945. The likelihood of military promotion, the transfer of members to 'missions' overseas, and that firms needed the return of their directors remained a possibility. As a result, the successive changes in membership on each board resulted in strengthening the function and effectiveness of the executive fifth Tank Board from late 1942 until April 1945, as part of the increasingly centralized control of the war and the economy as a whole.

The majority of firms connected to the British tank programme were concentrated in the northern Home Counties, the Midlands and the north of England, with an increased involvement in Scotland for the production of tank components. The number of subcontractors to provide the necessary armour plate, engines, gear boxes and tracks for each tank model varied given the differences in design. However, production of the Covenanter, Crusader and Churchill tanks used a greater number of smaller firms that were new to war production on this scale, as many of the other contractors were already fully involved on the earlier Matilda and Valentine tank programmes.

British industry went through continuous factory expansion in floor space and new plant and equipment to meet the demands of the tank programme. Government financial support towards the cost of these extensions frequently changed during the war, although it remained focused upon not permitting the firm to benefit at taxpayers' expense. The United States and Germany similarly increased the capital investment for industrial expansion throughout the war. However, in contrast to Britain and the United States, the maximum industrial capacity in Germany remained underdeveloped until late into the war with an even lower proportion of the German motor industry actually dedicated to war production.

The effects of bombing upon industry delayed production especially when the blackout was compromised in the winter. The government provided some reimbursement for the costs incurred by industry to put in place air raid precautions prior to the outbreak of war and for maintaining camouflage and shelters for the remainder of hostilities. The consequences of bombing meant that British industry could not concentrate production among large facilities. As a result, the government supported and paid for the partial dispersal of war production, accepting that this would limit overall output.

Unlike Britain and Germany, the United States and the Soviet Union concentrated industry to produce vast quantities of munitions without the risk of enemy bombing. The ability of German industry to maintain output against persistent Allied bombing is testament to the difficulties of disrupting war production and to the successful dispersal of industry. While the relocation of industry to underground facilities was desired by Britain and Germany, this was ultimately unfeasible due to the costs and effort required.

3

General Staff Requirements and
Industrial Capabilities

Having considered the relationship between the British government and industry in relation to centralized control and productive capacity, this chapter will discuss how British industry met General Staff requirements for the wartime tank programme. The mass production of the Light Mark VI B tank was maintained during 1939, while orders for the new Infantry and Cruiser tanks expanded. With the losses of equipment and threat of invasion following the defeat of France, the General Staff required a large increase in tank production from industry. In November 1940, Prime Minister Churchill confirmed that greater output was important when he stated: 'At this stage in tank production numbers count above everything else. It is better to have any serviceable tank than none at all.'[1] While accepting that quantity output could be detrimental to the quality of the tanks under production, this gave industry the opportunity to improve the latest designs and assembly techniques before introducing them to the production lines.[2]

The success of the policy for quantity production is shown in Table 3.1 with the increase in output from 1,379 tanks in 1940 to a wartime peak of 8,622 in 1942, producing a total of 14,838 standard gun tanks for that period. Less than half of these were worthwhile Matilda and Valentine tanks. The others were Light tanks, problematic Cruiser tanks, and unsatisfactory Churchill tanks before production of these were successfully modified or reworked. The General Staff cut the British tank programme from 1943 to concentrate upon a smaller number of quality designs, convert other tanks to a supporting role and incorporate more tanks from the United States to achieve the total number required each year. As a result, British industry delivered 12,181 standard gun tanks from 1943 until April 1945. Two-thirds of these were front line ready Churchill, Heavy Churchill, Cromwell, Challenger and Comet tanks, and Valentine tanks for the Soviet Union. The remaining tanks were from the obsolete and diminishing programmes. By comparison, the mainstay of German tank production throughout the war was the Panzer Mark IV. The Mark III ceased production in 1943 and was superseded by heavier Panther, Tiger and King Tiger tanks. Production in the United States concentrated upon the Sherman Medium tank and the Stuart Light tank.[3]

Table 3.1 Tank output in Britain, Germany and the United States, 1940 to 1945

Year	Britain	Germany	United States
1940	1,379	1,139	331
1941	4,837	2,373	4,052
1942	8,622	2,159	24,997
1943	7,217	7,552	29,497
1944	4,000	7,903	17,565
1945	964	924	11,968
Total	27,019	22,050	88,410

Sources: The National Archives, AVIA 46/188, 'Monthly Deliveries of Infantry and Cruiser Tanks by Firms, 1939–1943', draft official history narrative by D. Hay, after 1950, pp. 269–71; CAB 120/355, 'A.F.V. Production', 1943; CAB 120/356, 'A.F.V. Production', 1944–5; H. C. Thomson and L. Mayo, *United States Army in World War II, The Technical Services, The Ordnance Department: Procurement and Supply* (Washington: Department of the Army, 1960), reprinted 1968, p. 263; L. Ness, *Jane's World War II Tanks and Fighting Vehicles: The Complete Guide* (London: Harper Collins, 2002), pp. 86–8 & 187.

To provide a greater understanding behind these headline figures, this chapter will begin by showing how the fluctuating terms of reference for each Tank Board meant that the tank programme alternated between meeting the demands of the Ministry of Supply and of the General Staff. New orders for existing and the latest Infantry and Cruiser tanks were placed between January 1939 and June 1940 at the time of the Dunkirk evacuations. The cost price of each tank will be compared, including how the American Sherman tank provided under Lend-Lease was unexpectedly similar to the British Cromwell tank. Industry produced tanks of greater quality and firepower during the second half of the war, while the General Staff relied upon large numbers of tanks from the United States to fulfil the balance of requirements. The General Staff decision to choose the Meteor tank engine instead of the Ford V8 from the United States gave British tanks greater operational mobility and increased assurance of delivery once production of the Meteor had transferred from the Ministry of Aircraft Production. The General Staff requirement for greater armour protection was impeded until the Meteor engine became available and until industry had transferred to welded turret and hull construction. Finally, industry planned for the anticipated return to peacetime civilian markets from late 1943, while the General Staff wanted part of the post-war production of the Centurion tank to be provided by the newly formed and state owned Royal Tank Arsenal.

The changing terms of reference of each Tank Board

The General Staff priorities for the tank programme during rearmament had to balance the need for Light and Cruiser tanks in case of war with Italy in the Middle East, and Infantry tanks for the expected return to trench warfare on the Continent against Germany.[4] From October 1938, the General Staff prioritized the Middle East by specifying that two-thirds of the tank programme provide Cruiser tanks. However with the outbreak of war, the General Staff reversed these requirements in December 1939 so that two-thirds of the programme now favoured the slower but better armoured Infantry tanks.[5] With the increased urgency for war production from 1940 until 1943, the ability of each Tank Board to meet General Staff requirements altered with the different terms of reference provided by each Minister of Supply.

The terms of reference given to the first Tank Board in June 1940 highlights government policy and General Staff requirements, when the army had experienced the military reverses and evacuations from France. An early draft suggested that the board was meant to 'consider the whole situation regarding the design and production of Tanks' and advise the Minister of Supply regarding future action. This general remit was jointly amended by the War Office and Ministry of Supply at the end of May 1940, which put production before design to reaffirm that the continued 'production' of existing tanks took precedence over the 'design' of new models.[6]

A key factor in the formation of General Staff requirements was the battlefield performance of the Matilda tank in France during 1940, when compared to the Light and Cruiser tanks. Essentially, the Light Mark VI tank was obsolete in terms of armour and armament, and while the two-pounder armed Cruiser tanks had the best gun available, the armour protection could not withstand enemy anti-tank guns of 50 mm calibre or heavier.[7] The Matilda tank had defeated every type of enemy tank during the French campaign with the best combination of armour protection and the two-pounder gun. However, the Matilda tank had reliability problems due to driving long distances before coming into action, which was an operation for which this Infantry tank had not been designed to perform. The need for greater operational range and tactical mobility was to be fulfilled by Cruiser tanks. As a result, the Director of Armoured Fighting Vehicles, Major-General Vyvyan Pope, stated at the opening meeting of the first Tank Board later in June, that the General Staff priorities for all tanks were heavier armour first, then powerful armament and finally absolute reliability.[8] Following the mobile warfare experienced in France and later in the Western Desert against the Italians, the General Staff changed the tank programme in December 1940. As such, requirements were distributed as 70 per cent Cruiser tanks, 21 per cent Infantry tanks and 9 per cent Light tanks, while still emphasizing greater armour protection, armament and reliability.[9]

A contradiction existed for the terms of reference for the second Tank Board when announced during the first meeting in January 1941. The board had the explicit requirement to consider the design, development and production of tanks and make decisions to meet the requirements of the General Staff as quickly as possible. However at this occasion the Minister of Supply, Sir Andrew Duncan, emphasized that Prime Minister Churchill had insisted upon the maximum production of current tank models during 1941, without interference caused by changes in design. Therefore, the second Tank Board could only meet General Staff requirements during 1941 when these did not conflict with the mass production of existing designs.[10] This conflict was illustrated when the General Staff requirement for heavier tank armament could not be introduced, because 100 six-pounder guns would have meant forfeiting the production of 600 two-pounder guns. This was unacceptable when increased output was required, although the decision to continue producing lesser armament delayed the arrival of British tanks with greater high explosive firepower until later in the war.[11]

The difference between the fluctuating General Staff requirements during the first and second Tank Boards and the actual production over the same period reveals the disparity between the pressures upon industry to respond to the short-term demands on the battlefield. With the requirement for Light tanks diminishing by June 1941, the proportion of Infantry tanks desired by the General Staff increased to 30 per cent, with Cruiser tanks remaining the preferred type at 69 per cent.[12] However, the existing production programme was still weighted in favour of Infantry tanks due to the difficulties and disruption to output that would result from a sudden change-over. Therefore, the General Staff had to accept more of these slower tanks during 1941 and into 1942 than they ideally required.[13]

To illustrate, 4,837 tanks were produced during 1941 divided between 3,351 Infantry tanks, 1,413 Cruiser tanks and 73 Light tanks. This meant that industry was still meeting the requirement of December 1939 with the Infantry tank programme representing over two-thirds of the total number delivered. The total number of tanks produced during 1942 had increased to 8,622 in accordance with the increased programme from 1940, although the number of Cruiser tanks continued to fall short of General Staff requirements at 3,329 or 39 per cent of the total. The balance was still dominated by 5,275 Infantry tanks and only 18 Light tanks as planned.[14] Therefore, the limitations of the first and second tank boards to meet General Staff requirements resulted from the inability to switch industry to the production of the desired Cruiser tanks quickly enough with the minimum of disruption.

The third Tank Board from August 1941 remained executive in function, with terms of reference that were similar to the second board, but with the exception of no longer meeting the requirements of the General Staff as soon as possible. In essence, while the General Staff requirement focused on Cruiser tanks mounting the six-pounder gun and a small number of similarly armed Infantry tanks, the board still had to maintain large-scale output. This meant a continued increase in the production of the two-pounder gun armed Matilda and Covenanter tanks during 1941 and 1942. The two-pounder armed Valentine, Churchill and Crusader tanks also remained in production during this time even when supplemented with six-pounder variants during 1942. To assist in the short-term production of battleworthy tanks, the Ministry instructed the board to accelerate the modifications on existing designs in addition to the expansion of tank output.[15] The Valentine tank continued in production to meet the requirements of the General Staff, until superseded by the demands of the Soviet Union for this particular tank into 1944, under the supply protocols to provide munitions, equipment and raw materials for their war effort.[16] By November 1941, Minister of Supply Lord Beaverbrook changed the terms of reference so that the third Tank Board could now take executive decisions on meeting General Staff requirements.[17]

The continuation of existing tank production was re-emphasized in September 1941, when the Tank Board chairman Geoffrey Burton confirmed that the Ministry of Supply programme could only change very slowly. This was noted by Beaverbrook in attendance, who stated that the 1942 production programme must therefore continue unchanged. As a result, the problematic Covenanter tank would remain in production until October 1942, and the Matilda tank was expected to finish as late as February

1943.[18] However, the Covenanter tank did not complete until January 1943 and Matilda output extended until August, delaying the introduction of the later Cruiser tanks designed to replace them.[19] As examined in greater detail in Chapter 5, these deferments kept the labour force together at the tank factories by avoiding inactivity during a premature change-over from one tank model to another. Furthermore, a hasty cancellation of the obsolete Matilda and Covenanter tank programmes was avoided during 1942 and 1943 because as discussed in Chapter 6, the United States was providing greater numbers of tanks under Lend-Lease to support the British war effort.

The diminishing General Staff requirement for Light tanks from 1941 can be attributed to design and development problems, in addition to the tactical necessity for the greater armour and firepower provided by Infantry and Cruiser tanks. Problems with cooling the engine on the Tetrarch tank meant that no production was possible during the first 3 months of 1941.[20] Despite delivering 6 tanks in April, the production problems caused by engine difficulties were exacerbated when the assembly works of Metropolitan-Cammell sustained severe bomb damage.[21] This resulted in irregular output as illustrated by 13 tanks in June, 7 in September and 11 in November.[22] The following 4 months delivered only another 16 tanks before the programme terminated in March 1942, having produced only 100 tanks in total.[23]

A similarly poor situation occurred with the later Harry Hopkins Light tank, which in November 1941 had a planned total output of 2,400. The General Staff only required 1,200 tanks at this time, so to meet the optimum rate of production the other 1,200 tanks were to be provided to the Soviet Union under the supply protocols.[24] This was consistent with Soviet requirements that included Light tanks as part of the aid programme.[25] The Harry Hopkins tank was due to start production in July 1942; however, problems with the suspension meant that the first tank was delayed until July 1943. In any event, none were shipped to the Soviet Union and only 102 tanks were produced.[26]

The terms for the fourth Tank Board from May 1942 under the non-executive chairmanship of Lord Weir, made no reference to General Staff requirements and was meant to resolve the issues of policy relating to tank development and production for the Ministry of Supply. Different from the three previous occasions, the fourth board was given the responsibility of considering specific qualitative factors of tank design, such as reliability, mobility, armour and armament.[27] The General Staff formalized these requirements during the final meeting of the fourth Tank Board in August 1942, by prioritizing the 'qualities' for tank performance as reliability first and foremost, followed by armament, speed and radius of action, and finally armour protection. This had effectively reversed the position of June 1940 which had prioritized armour, armament and then reliability.[28]

As demonstrated in the previous chapter, the executive fifth Tank Board was the most successful by operating continuously from September 1942 until April 1945, as a result of the greatly enhanced organizational structure. Aside from this prima facie evidence, the fifth Tank Board benefited from the political, strategic and industrial changes over the same period, which gave fewer occasions for the board or the terms of reference to change as before. As illustrated later, by the end of 1942 the relationship between the 'user' and 'supplier' became synchronized when the Secretary of State for War, P. J. Grigg, and the Minister of Supply, Sir Andrew Duncan, decided upon tank policy on a joint basis for the fifth Tank Board to implement. This resulted in the elimination of obsolete tanks as industry transferred to new designs from 1943, which met the operational requirements of sustained reliability and mobility to pursue an offensive strategy overseas. The Valentine tank continued at a reduced level to meet Soviet demand into 1944, while the balance of General Staff requirements were fulfilled by the growing dependency upon tanks from the United States under Lend-Lease, as examined in Chapter 6.

The cost of Infantry and Cruiser tanks

Between January 1939 and June 1940 a total of 5,773 Light, Infantry and Cruiser tanks were ordered to meet General Staff requirements, distributed among 16 manufacturers with half of them undertaking orders for at least two different tank designs.[29] The total number ordered reflected General Staff requirements from December 1939 with 60 per cent of the programme represented by 3,481 Infantry tanks, together with 1,858 Cruiser tanks and 434 Light tanks. The total number of tanks requested from industry also included a number of continuation orders, partly in response to the sudden loss of equipment on the Continent during the evacuations from France. For example, the Valentine order with Vickers-Armstrongs increased by a further 300 tanks on 29 May 1940, from the original order of 275 tanks placed on 6 May 1939.[30] Similarly, Birmingham Railway Carriage & Wagon Company received a new order for 300 tanks on 12 June 1940 to add to their original order of 225 tanks placed on 29 June 1939.[31]

The continuation orders for the Valentine tank were placed without the benefit of any operational experience, as the first deliveries did not commence until early June 1940 from Vickers and in August from both Birmingham Railway and Metropolitan-Cammell.[32] Instead, the first production Valentine tank from Vickers had performed satisfactorily enough during testing to give the General Staff the justifiable confidence to place additional orders. Furthermore, the Valentine tank met the requirements for the increase in production now being demanded from industry following the loss of equipment in Europe.[33] As discussed in Chapter 6, a similar approach was adopted in Canada with the order for 488 Valentine tanks with the Canadian Pacific Railway Company to equip a Canadian army tank brigade.[34]

The continuation orders for the Matilda tank were made in the knowledge of recent battlefield experience in France, which the Director of Mechanization, Major-General Alexander Davidson, brought to the attention of Vulcan Foundry in June 1940. Davidson was keen to emphasize that the proven fighting capabilities of the Matilda tank had meant that new orders were being placed with increased confidence.[35] While this commentary would have given encouragement to Vulcan Foundry for their efforts, this optimistic opinion was later tempered by the General Staff when Major-General Pope raised the problems of mechanical reliability during the opening meeting of the first Tank Board.[36]

The cost of the 5,339 Infantry and Cruiser tanks ordered from January 1939 to June 1940 amounted to over £78 million. While the Infantry tanks represented 60 per cent of the total order, in accordance with General Staff requirements at this time, they accounted for 69 per cent of the total cost due to the higher basic cost price for each tank. For example, the cost for each Cruiser tank ranged between £12,000 for the Covenanter and £13,700 for the Crusader. By comparison, each Valentine tank cost £14,900 and each Matilda tank £18,000. The contracts branch of the Ministry of Supply adopted a new pricing structure from March 1941, resulting in a general lowering of prices although there was no uniform percentage reduction. Essentially, the first four Cruiser tanks were limited to a flat £7,500 each as they were obsolete and production had ended or would complete shortly after March 1941. Where production expanded after March 1941 and continued into 1943, such as with the Covenanter, Crusader, Matilda and Valentine tanks, prices fell between 37 and 43 per cent. At this stage in 1941, the basic price of the new Centaur and Cromwell tanks currently under design were estimated at £10,000 each.[37]

As similarly experienced in the aircraft industry, these reductions in production cost during the war were in contrast to the overall increase in assembly weight and complexity, and with the rise in engineering wages overall. By 1941, the aircraft programme was incorporating the latest advances in the Merlin engine to improve the Spitfire, the production of the Manchester bomber was being prepared for the transfer to the Lancaster, and arrangements were being made to introduce the De Havilland Mosquito. To illustrate the declining cost of these aircraft, the Ford Merlin engine fell from £5,640 in June 1941 to £1,180 at the end of the war. The cost of the Lancaster bomber was cut from £22,000 for the first production model to £15,500 in 1944, and the Mosquito fell from £6,000 in 1941 to £4,200 by 1945.[38]

On the face of it, the estimated cost of the Cromwell during 1941 at £10,000 compares favourably with the calculated cost for the United States to provide Britain with Sherman tanks under Lend-Lease during 1944. To illustrate, a total of 8,961 Sherman tanks were expected during 1944 for a value of $485 million or approximately $54,123 per tank.[39] The Dollar–Sterling exchange rate during Lend-Lease has been valued by the British official history at $5.3 to £1. This meant that each Sherman tank delivered to Britain during 1944 cost £10,211 to produce, compared to the estimated £10,000 cost of the Cromwell tank at March 1941.[40] These similarities are out of proportion with the greater economies of scale available in American industry examined in Chapter 6, which should have resulted in a much lower cost price for the Sherman tank. In reality, the overall value of providing these tanks to Britain was actually greater when including the shipping costs, which have been estimated at over 10 per cent of the total Lend-Lease aid provided to Britain and the Commonwealth during 1944.[41]

The example of American industry illustrates how the estimated and average production costs for each tank varied by manufacturer. By the spring of 1943, the cost of each Sherman at the Chrysler Tank Arsenal was $42,400, compared to $70,000 at the Federal Machine and Welder Company. The main reasons for this disparity were that the arsenal was wholly owned by the government while the Federal Machine plant was privately owned, and that the prices related to different models of Sherman tank. Furthermore, the initial contract price for each Sherman tank at the new General

Motors Fisher Tank Arsenal was over $67,000, although this was reduced once the actual production costs had been calculated to become one of the lowest overall.[42] When considering the differences in total output from these three firms, the variations in contract price and the ability of Fisher to lower the cost with experience becomes apparent. While being unable to separate between particular models and types, Chrysler produced 22,234 tanks throughout the war, compared to Fisher with 13,137 tanks, while Federal Machine only assembled 540.[43]

Transformation of industry to quality production

The transformation of industry to produce tanks of greater quality was discussed among senior General Staff and Ministry of Supply officials, during the final meeting of the fourth Tank Board in August 1942. In this instance, the non-executive chairman Lord Weir stated that the tank programme must now meet the requirement for improved reliability and quality as expected from the new Cromwell tank.[44] To meet these requirements as soon as possible, in February 1943 the General Staff sought to reduce Crusader and Valentine production for this year.[45] However, as examined in Chapter 5, the speed at which the tank programme could change was affected by development problems, the existing contractual commitments and the avoidance of unused or interrupted labour resources during the change-over. As a result, the production forecast for 1943, as determined in November 1942, expected nearly 1,650 Crusader tanks, over 2,050 Valentine tanks, including those to be shipped to the Soviet Union, and 965 Cromwell tanks.[46] Despite the emphasis upon transforming the programme, the tank industry only produced 532 Cromwell tanks, while 1,684 Crusader and 1,798 Valentine tanks were delivered under the existing production arrangements.[47]

The General Staff insistence upon tanks with greater reliability was complemented by the requirement for increased tank armament with a range of firepower options. The eventual transfer from the two-pounder to the six-pounder gun during 1942 gave British tanks much greater armour-piercing capability, although they still lacked an effective and available high explosive ability. This issue was raised by the Soviet authorities upon receiving the first six-pounder armed Valentine tanks, with the additional tactical concern that these tanks lacked machine guns to engage infantry and lightly armoured targets.[48] A high explosive shell was under production for the six-pounder gun with 100,000 rounds already supplied to the British army in North Africa by February 1943.[49] The requirement for six-pounder high explosive shells was confirmed by the General Staff during March 1943.[50] During May 1943, the output of six-pounder high explosive shells was expected to reach 300,000 per month by October, but the front line troops would not receive these shells in meaningful quantities until late December.[51] Ultimately, this programme could not be completed because the experience of combat in North Africa meant that British tank policy now demanded the greater high explosive capability of the new 75 mm tank gun.

The requirement for greater high explosive rather than armour-piercing firepower on British tanks was jointly formalized by P. J. Grigg and Andrew Duncan in April

1943. This divided tank armament for the 1944 programme with 10 per cent of the vehicles mounting the 95 mm close-support howitzer, 60 per cent with the 75 mm gun, and the remaining 30 per cent with the six-pounder gun. The last requirement was to fulfil the armour-piercing role under the expectation that the six-pounder gun would be replaced with front line tanks mounting either the dual-purpose and high-velocity 77 mm or 17-pounder guns.[52] The former related to the Comet tank from February 1945 with the latter mounted onto the Challenger tank and Sherman Firefly conversion from the Normandy campaign, until the Centurion tank was introduced after the end of the war in Europe. Meanwhile, the existing six-pounder armed tanks made a significant battlefield contribution during the 1944 and 1945 campaigns in Italy and north-west Europe, especially when firing the new 'Sabot' ammunition.[53] This round gave between 45 and 50 per cent greater armour penetration at short to medium range and was more than half the weight of the best capped shot.[54]

The General Staff requirement for the production of Infantry and Cruiser tanks for the 1944 tank programme was estimated at the beginning of 1943 to be 7,600. By July 1943, Prime Minister Churchill approved a reduction in the current 1943 and expected 1944 programmes to accept an additional 3,000 tanks from the United States spread across both years. This will be examined in greater detail during Chapter 6 and was designed to redirect some British industrial capacity towards the production of railway locomotives, rather than importing these from the United States and taking up valuable shipping space. As a result, the number of tanks to be produced in Britain during 1944 was reduced to 6,900, with the Centaur programme sustaining the biggest reduction.[55] At the beginning of 1944, Grigg and Duncan jointly recommended a further reduction to 5,280 vehicles during 1944, with the expectation of at least 8,500 tanks from the United States.[56]

In addition to receiving greater numbers of Lend-Lease tanks, there were a number of operational reasons behind these successive reductions in the British tank programme. By July 1943, the Liberty powered Centaur tank was deemed unfit as a front line gun tank and was therefore relegated to a training role in addition to some anti-aircraft tanks and 95 mm armed close-support tanks for the Royal Marines Armoured Support Group. In an example of 'user' feedback, trials conducted with the standard Centaur tank by the 9th Armoured Division revealed that 23 out of 129 vehicles suffered from clutch failure, which could only be remedied by redesigning the entire clutch system.[57] This meant that the number of Centaur tanks deemed 'unfit for action' by this defect equated to 18 per cent, which was consistent with the findings from March 1943 examined in Chapter 5.

By 1944, the majority of front line tanks under production were the Meteor engine powered Cromwell, Challenger and Comet tanks, while the Churchill programme had now expanded to include the Heavy version.[58] The sustainable transition to the production of battleworthy tanks during 1944 consisted of 2,223 Meteor engine tanks, 1,062 Churchill tanks and 280 Valentine tanks to meet the residual Soviet requirements under the aid programme. The production of tanks not destined for front line action, such as the Harry Hopkins Light tank and the Cavalier and Centaur Cruiser tanks, were now limited to 435. The remaining programme for 1944 produced 4,102 tank adaptations, such as 17-pounder gun or Duplex-Drive tanks, with 3,266 conversions being carried out on Sherman tanks received from the United States. The output of standard Infantry and Cruiser tanks during 1944 was only now meeting the General Staff requirement of December 1940, with at least two-thirds of the programme providing the necessary mobility with reliable Cruiser tanks.[59] The 1944 aircraft programme underwent similar quality based reductions, which cut the unsatisfactory or fully developed Stirling and Wellington bombers and Hurricane fighters, to concentrate production upon the Lancaster, Halifax, Spitfire, Tempest and Mosquito.[60]

The same quality based rationale was applied to the 1945 British tank programme which was estimated during January 1944 at 5,500 together with 5,000 tanks from the United States. The British programme had now eliminated the Centaur completely and while maintaining a strong Heavy Churchill contingent, the Meteor powered Cruiser tanks now accounted for over 70 per cent of expectations.[61] With the recent successes in north-west Europe following the Normandy campaign, and notwithstanding the setback at Arnhem, the 1945 tank programme was reduced during October 1944 with the expectation of the war ending by 31 March 1945. This new programme amounted to 2,850 British tanks split almost equally between the Heavy Churchill on the one hand and the Cromwell, Comet and Centurion on the other, plus 2,730 tanks from the United States.[62] As examined later in Chapter 6, this reduction in the 1945 programme was premature, especially when there was a shortfall of Lend-Lease tanks from the United States during 1944.

Deciding upon the Meteor engine

A tangible transfer of industry to the production of quality tanks was demonstrated by the emergence of mechanically reliable vehicles. The principal reason why this became possible on the latest Cruiser tanks was the adaptation of the Merlin aero-engine into the 600 horsepower (hp) Meteor tank engine, replacing the older, problematic and insufficiently powered 300 to 395 hp Liberty engine. The necessity of designing the Meteor engine to be interchangeable with the Liberty was emphasized by William Robotham from Rolls-Royce and the Chief Engineer Tank Design on the third, fourth and fifth Tank Boards.[63] The Cromwell tank was the first production model to be designed and fitted with the Meteor engine with deliveries beginning in December 1942.[64] This could not have occurred sooner as there were insufficient supplies of Meteor engines to begin installing them until late 1942, resulting in Cavalier and Centaur tanks having to be supplied with Liberty engines instead.[65]

Much of the delay in obtaining enough Meteor engines was because the Ministry of Aircraft Production was understandably reluctant to redirect their Merlin engine capacity to the tank programme until mid-1942, with a commitment to produce 3,000 tank engines.[66] While the original plan had Rolls-Royce delivering 500 tank engines by December 1942, this quickly reduced to just 37 under the condition that the supply of aero-engines always took precedence.[67] This decision was in accordance with British strategy during 1942, which increased heavy bomber production for the area bombing campaign against Germany, alongside the growing contribution of American air power.[68] Therefore, with the delivery of Meteor engines outside the control of the

Ministry of Supply, a production order for 2,000 tank engines was placed with Morris Engines in October 1942.[69]

The British Tank Engine Mission to the United States at the end of 1942 identified that the developmental 500 hp Ford V8 engine could be an alternative to the Meteor for the latest Cruiser tanks under production or design. The mission 'emphatically' recommended that the Meteor order with Morris Engines be abandoned and replaced with immediate preparations for the production of the Ford V8, albeit once this engine had been adopted by the US Ordnance Department.[70] The manufacturing benefits for the British tank programme of accepting the Ford V8 were that fewer machine tools and man-hours were required for assembly, with the result that three Ford engines could be produced for every two Meteor engines.[71] The fifth Tank Board decided unanimously against cancelling the Meteor order in favour of the prospective Ford V8 because: the Meteor had been reliable under trial; the Ford was not interchangeable with existing British tanks carrying either the Liberty or Meteor; and that the Meteor provided an extra 100 hp.[72] Ultimately, the Ford V8 did become an engine of good quality albeit after many additional and prolonged tests. When mission chairman Sir Miles Thomas learnt of this development during January 1944, he confirmed the same to Lieutenant-General Ronald Weeks who was present at the Tank Board meetings.[73] Weeks replied that despite being a good engine, the risk of solely relying upon the Ford V8 would have been too great.[74] Weeks elaborated on this comment after the war, by highlighting that problems would have resulted from becoming dependent upon the Ford V8 and spares from 3,000 miles away.[75]

Following the rejection of the Ford V8 engine, Rover Company received an order for 3,000 Meteor engines in March 1943, thereby ensuring the future supply of reliable engines for the tank programme.[76] Further to the order for tank engines, Rover purchased the 'rights' of the Meteor engine from Rolls-Royce for £5,000 plus the transfer of 3 Rover Patents.[77] The production forecast for the different Meteor orders had Morris Engines starting deliveries in April 1944 and with Rover in May. The order organized by the Ministry of Aircraft Production with Rolls-Royce and Henry Meadows was due to complete in September 1944, thereby placing all Meteor engine production under the control of the Ministry of Supply.[78]

While engines for the tank programme were secured with sustained Meteor production, Thomas confirmed to tank parent firm Leyland Motors during July 1943 that Liberty engine production had to be maintained to retain the workforce during the transfer.[79] As a result, Morris Engines built the Liberty until May 1944 when the strength of Meteor output permitted the final 94 Liberty engines to be cancelled and the remaining material used as spare parts.[80] With Meteor powered tanks taking precedence during 1944, the remaining Liberty engines and spares went towards the production or conversion of 619 Cavalier and Centaur tanks.[81]

While tank losses during the Normandy campaign compelled an increase in Cromwell production as examined in Chapter 5, the General Staff considered that the Meteor orders with Morris Engines and Rover were sufficient to meet the tank requirements for 1945.[82] With the end of the war in Europe in May 1945, cancellation orders were sent to Morris Engines and Rover which cut each contract by 1,000 engines.[83] To offset this loss of work, Thomas stressed to the Ministry of Supply that Morris Engines now had sufficient capacity to receive more orders for wheeled vehicles.[84] With Meteor engines providing British Cruiser tanks with increased power and reliability, British tank design could now meet the General Staff requirement for operational mobility with greater armour protection.

Increasing armour protection

The senior civilian and military authorities discussed the problems of adding heavier armour to existing tanks or new designs during the first meeting of the 'Tank Parliament' in May 1941. This forum was introduced by Prime Minister Churchill to provide the Ministry of Supply, the War Office and the armoured divisional commanders with the freedom to express opinions in a parliamentary style discussion.[85] Peter Beale draws the incomplete conclusion that the four meetings were simply a waste of time and a forum for just 'platitudes and posturing'.[86] Ronald Lewin gives the 'Tank Parliament' the benefit of the doubt by describing how the opportunity for an open discussion was 'nullified' by Lieutenant-General Giffard Martel, commander of the Royal Armoured Corps. Martel assembled his divisional commanders beforehand to prepare fixed responses to likely areas of discussion, albeit without Major-General Percy Hobart who would not go along with Martel's scheming.[87] Essentially, Martel did not want the views from others to interfere with the organization or techniques of the Royal Armoured Corps.[88]

The four 'parliament' meetings were held from 5 May to 19 June 1941 and were well attended with Churchill, Lord Beaverbrook, senior members from the Ministry of Supply and the War Office, and the commanders of the 1st, 6th, 8th, 9th and 11th Armoured Divisions. While the Tank Parliament was short-lived, it brought the users into direct contact with senior members of the government to highlight particular or common concerns and made everyone aware of the potential remedies. The first meeting established that an increase in armour protection would require a tank engine of much greater power to maintain mobility, and that the added weight would cause difficulties for the tracks and suspension.[89]

The lack of a suitably powerful and reliable engine affected the Cruiser tank programme until the second half of the war when the Meteor engine was introduced. To illustrate, the main Cruiser tanks under production during 1941 and 1942 had maximum armour protection of 40 mm on the Covenanter with the 280 hp Meadows engine and up to 66 mm on the Crusader with the 340 hp Liberty engine. While the Cavalier and Centaur tanks from 1943 both had slightly enhanced Liberty engines, the armour thickness was limited to 76 mm and as such these tanks remained unsuitable. The introduction of the 600 hp Meteor engine permitted an increase in armour protection to 101 mm on the welded Cromwell and Comet tanks, and then later to 152 mm on the Centurion tank.[90]

The German tank programme went through a similar transition from the Panzer Mark III with the 296 hp Maybach engine and 50 mm of armour early in the war, to the later King Tiger powered by the 690 hp Maybach engine and 150 mm of better protected sloped armour. In contrast, the tank programme in the United States remained largely undeveloped when compared to Britain and Germany, due to continued mass production of the Sherman tank. For example, the difference between the Grant tank from 1941 and the Sherman tank during 1944 was a slight increase in armour protection from 51 mm to 76 mm and an equally minor improvement in engine power from the General Motors 375 hp engine on the Grant to the Chrysler 425 hp engine on this Sherman variant.[91]

The ability of German tank and anti-tank guns to penetrate Allied armour at considerable distances in North Africa, in 1942, provided the British General Staff with the requirements and limitations of increasing the levels of armour protection. A report from the Middle-East Headquarters, in December 1942, emphasized that German gun positions in open country should be engaged at over 2,000 yards whenever possible to reduce the likelihood of being hit. With regard to ranges of 1,000 yards or less, the report unequivocally stated that tank armour could not protect against heavy tank and anti-tank guns, especially when they are concealed.[92] This comment identified the tactical difficulties that the Western Allies confronted when the war moved away from the desert, and into the close environments of Italy and north-west Europe. In respect of tank policy, by February 1943 both the Ministry of Supply and General Staff abandoned the requirement for British tanks to withstand the German long 75 mm and 88 mm guns.[93]

The British authorities first identified the combat capabilities of the Tiger tank from the intelligence reports and initial experiences in Tunisia during late 1942.[94] Lieutenant-General Martel describes how a disabled Tiger tank was studied in the field during February 1943, resulting in the MI-10 Technical and MI-14 German branches of British Military Intelligence providing detailed specifications.[95] Another Tiger was later captured intact during April 1943 and while the transfer to Britain for examination was delayed until October, this was still eight months prior to the Normandy campaign.[96] While no longer developing standard tanks to protect against the heaviest German guns, the General Staff placed a requirement during April 1943 for a special assault vehicle with greater armour protection.[97] The pilot for this Tortoise tank weighed over 70 tons, mounted a limited traverse 32-pounder or 94 mm gun and 229 mm of frontal armour.[98] There are noticeable similarities between the Tortoise and German Jagdtiger deployed during the Normandy campaign, which was heavier in weight, had 250 mm of frontal armour and mounted a 128 mm gun.[99]

When considering the operational value of the Tortoise, in April 1944, General Montgomery doubted whether the exceptional weight would permit rail transportation and bridge crossing, and questioned the length of time needed to assemble the vehicles before an attack.[100] The Tortoise project did not expand beyond six pilot models; however, the Tortoise superstructure did withstand a direct hit from the latest German 88 mm gun during a firing trial in July 1945. In this case a new 88 mm gun achieved a penetration of 165 mm with a capped ballistic shot against the 229 mm of hardened cast frontal armour.[101] This result was consistent with the gun mounted on the King Tiger at a range of approximately 1,000 yards, which together with the British 17-pounder gun firing the Sabot round, could penetrate 208 mm at 500 yards.[102] Therefore, Britain could produce armour that defended against the best German tank and anti-tank guns, but the thickness required was so great that the vehicle became too heavy and operationally unworkable.

The production benefits of using cast armour were the avoidance of machining and riveting, thereby saving both time and labour resources with only the final assembly required. Furthermore, the use of cast armour eliminated the danger of rivets being forced into the tank interior to endanger the crew when the tank was hit.[103] The process was not without difficulties as casting involved complex designs and required highly skilled labour.[104] During January 1942, the third Tank Board reported that the technique for casting armour had improved, as demonstrated by the successful trials of firing six-pounder shot against the cast turret of the Churchill tank.[105] Despite this increase in quality, the use of cast turrets was still limited by the lack of available casting capacity, with the executive fifth Tank Board reporting in August 1944 that only half of the reworked Churchill tanks would get the better protected turret.[106] This problem continued into 1945 when deliveries of the new Centurion tank were unlikely to exceed 160 for that year due to the limitations of casting capacity.[107]

Another alternative to riveting was welded armour with the advantages for tank assembly of less time consuming machining, reduced weight and increased armour strength. While the benefits of welding were fully understood, such a significant and widespread adjustment to the production programme could not be made until 1943.[108] Until then the benefits of welding were applied on individual modifications to offset the extra weight of mounting the heavier six-pounder gun.[109] For example, during June 1941, the second Tank Board agreed to allocate the majority of tank welding capacity to produce the six-pounder gun turret on the Churchill tank to reduce the overall weight.[110]

In respect of the later tank designs, the Department of Tank Design asked Leyland Motors during June 1942 to produce a number of experimental welded tank hulls of the Centaur type. This was to assess the merits of a welded tank hull against riveted construction, in respect of the protection afforded, the saving in assembly man-hours, and the problems of maintenance in the field.[111] Similar improvements had occurred in the aircraft industry when the use of spot welding, together with a new system of factory control and assembly reorganization, had reduced the production time of the Halifax bomber at Handley Page by 20 per cent.[112] Despite making good progress by September 1942, the problems for Leyland Motors were the supply of armoured plate from outside sources and the availability of workers to prepare the plates prior to welding.[113] The Armoured Fighting Vehicle Liaison Committee agreed during November 1942 that the amount of welding in tank assembly should extend to the Centaur and Cromwell tanks as soon as possible.[114] During that month, Leyland Motors received an order from the Ministry of Supply for three welded hulls based upon the design prepared by the Leyland Motors' drawing office.[115]

In June 1943, the Ministry of Supply noted that the increased demands of welded hull construction meant that more armour plate would have to be ordered for the 1944 programme.[116] In the meantime, the fully welded front section of the Centaur tank provided by Leyland Motors in July 1943, demonstrated a much greater resistance to attack during firing trials.[117] Furthermore, when Leyland Motors transferred production to the Cromwell tank during November 1943, the first vehicles incorporated the fully welded front section from the Centaur design without modification.[118] In addition to the lack of skilled labour and welding experience, the shortage of welding equipment also prevented industry from completing the various production programmes. With particular regard to shipbuilding and tank production, shortages were overcome by matching the supply of equipment to the size of the demand.[119]

In the case of the Comet tank, specific welding equipment was designed by English Electric from November 1943 in preparation for the assembly demands of this all-welded vehicle. These 'manipulators' held and rotated the complete hull to the required position for each welding operation.[120] During January 1944, Leyland Motors received a similar welding manipulator from Davy United for the assembly of the Comet turret and immediately used this for welding the turret on the Cromwell tank.[121] When Comet production started in September 1944, Leyland Motors delivered 7 tanks by using 2 hull manipulators day and night with 6 welders employed per hull per shift.[122] During October, 4 manipulators were in use with an increased monthly output of 15 Comet tanks, and by December the number of welders engaged on Comet production had increased to 115 with a rise in output to 53 tanks.[123]

American tank design had not developed to the same extent as Britain and Germany in respect of armour thickness, with studies into plates of 127 mm and greater for standard gun tanks only commencing in 1945.[124] However, the practice of welding in the United States was employed much earlier than in Britain with techniques and equipment that produced a greater rate of output. For example, during a factory visit to American Car and Foundry by British Colonel H. G. Hoare in April 1941, the production of the Stuart tank revealed how the fitting and machining of individual armour plates on each tank was avoided. Instead, all the hull armour plate was produced to a standard size and then fitted directly onto the tank without carrying out the time consuming machining to ensure an exact fit in each case. The result was significantly quicker tank assembly. Gaps between the different armour plates were noted of less than 1 millimetre and while this appeared to be insignificant, bullet splash or hot metal fragments could still enter the fighting compartment when the tank came under fire.[125]

The change from a riveted to an all-welded turret on the Stuart tank was carried out by American Car and Foundry by applying a layer of welding to the edge of each plate before being placed into the assembly jig. This enabled any movement of the plate during assembly to be corrected by adjusting the layer of welding, rather than having to machine the plate separately to ensure a secure weld. These time-saving assembly techniques produced an impressive 8 tanks on the day of the visit under the expectation that output would increase to 15 per day or approximately 450 tanks per month.[126] The Tank Engine Mission to the United States, during the March 1942, discovered that this forecast was entirely feasible as American Car and Foundry was producing 420 tanks per month and working towards the maximum monthly capacity of 1,000.[127]

Changing to peacetime production

The ability of industry to meet General Staff requirements into the post-war period came under discussion by the government and individual firms late into 1943. A

War Cabinet meeting in October considered the general conversion of industry from war to peacetime production, with Prime Minister Churchill requesting that detailed plans be prepared as soon as possible. At this stage of the war, the service departments could not state precisely when each factory would be released from war production, especially given the prospect of a 'two-stage ending' against Germany and Japan.[128] However, the purpose of planning for the post-war period at this time was designed to avoid the mistakes made by the Lloyd George government during the First World War, which did not consider the matter of 'reconstruction' early enough and failed to provide the promised land 'fit for heroes'.[129] By December 1943, the Minister of Labour Ernest Bevin stated that the centralized controls on manpower with the Essential Work Orders should be maintained and demobilization should be withheld until after the victory against Japan.[130] As peacetime plans progressed during 1944, government ministers identified that the labour problem after the war would not be a shortage of work, but instead a shortage of workers to meet the expected demand.[131]

The investment in new buildings and equipment for war production discussed in Chapters 1 and 2 meant that British industry was well placed to take advantage of the expected demands of peacetime. For example, when comparing the post-war motor industry against the pre-war position, the productive capacity of commercial vehicles had increased by 60 per cent and motor cars by 20 per cent.[132] This preparedness went beyond mere physical capability, when commercial vehicle firm Leyland Motors and car firm Rover discussed during December 1943 the prospect of carrying out joint research and development after the war.[133] The benefits to both firms were that they could share the results of the investigations into engineering problems, while not being in direct competition in respect of sales.[134] This type of technological co-operation may have contributed towards the eventual acquisition of Rover by Leyland Motors during 1966. Peacetime production was considered again by Leyland Motors during June 1944, when a special Sales Conference was held to demonstrate to their salesmen that the post-war programme was under consideration.[135]

With the end of the war in Europe on 8 May 1945, Leyland Motors was advised by the Ministry of Supply that the Break Clause in the Comet contract would be enacted to reduce the overall number of tanks required. By this time, Leyland Motors had restructured factory operations so that the mass production of civilian vehicles could begin as soon as possible.[136] Later in May, the Ministry of Supply decided to terminate the Churchill rework programme by August, resulting in Vauxhall Motors transferring capacity to the Heavy Churchill, while Broom & Wade lost 150 workers.[137] During June, Gloucester Railway Carriage & Wagon Company received 3 months notice that the Break Clause had been applied to their Churchill contract, with cancellation taking effect in September or upon completion of the 185th welded tank if earlier.[138]

While the Break Clause had been invoked by the Ministry of Supply, in September 1945 John Fowler wanted to finish the contract of 150 Comet tanks to ensure an efficient transfer to peacetime production. As a result, the termination date was extended until 20 November or earlier if the firm had completed the remaining

27 Comet tanks.[139] With the reductions in the Comet and Churchill programmes, peacetime tank production was concentrated upon the principal General Staff requirement of the Centurion tank at an anticipated 40 vehicles per month.[140] With industry due to convert back to civilian production, the wartime government considered it necessary to place part of the post-war Centurion programme under direct state control by creating a Royal Tank Arsenal.

With the rejection by Leyland Motors to accept the parentage of the Centurion tank discussed in Chapter 2, the design and development remained under government control with 20 prototypes under production by Royal Ordnance Factories during 1944 rather than by private firms.[141] Prior to this involvement, the Royal Ordnance Factories had remained inactive on tank work since completing the small order for Light tanks in 1936, until 1943 when production capacity was used to convert Sherman tanks into the Firefly by mounting the 17-pounder gun.[142] The first six Centurion prototypes were sent to Germany in May 1945 after victory in Europe, for use in one regiment with crews from different units.[143] This selection ensured that the first Centurion tanks were operated by crews with extensive battle experience for the cross-country and firing trials north-east of Hamburg.[144]

In relation to the post-war programme, in February 1944 the Deputy Director-General of Ordnance Factories proposed that the Leeds Royal Ordnance Factory be converted to a Royal Tank Arsenal to establish a government owned factory for peacetime tank production.[145] During August, the chairman of the fifth Tank Board, Commander Micklem, agreed to the creation of a government tank arsenal producing 20 Centurion tanks per month.[146] By October, the General Staff supported this plan as they wanted to avoid the problems of being entirely dependent upon private sources of tank supply as experienced during the war.[147] The Leeds factory was chosen because it had good rail links and sidings for the transport of materials and finished tanks.[148] Furthermore, the factory required little structural alteration beyond the strengthening of gantries and provision for cranes to handle heavy tank weights, although the cost and installation of this machinery was valued at a substantial £625,000.[149]

The conversion of Leeds gave the post-war potential to increase output to 50 Centurion tanks per month if gun production was transferred to other ordnance factories. As many as 70 tanks per month could be achieved with the assistance of private contractors in the event that the General Staff required an even greater output.[150] This plan created the capacity that was comparable to peak Comet production at Leyland Motors of 68 tanks during March 1945, illustrating that the government was serious about securing control over some peacetime tank production.[151] The official history contends that the manufacture of tanks like the Centurion of 40 to 50 tons was not consistent with the post-war ambitions of heavy industry, and therefore lacked commercial viability.[152] While this was certainly accurate when considering those firms which became tank manufacturers as a result of war and then reverted to their prior industry in peace, it omits the background and strength of Vickers-Armstrongs. Between 1946 and 1957, Vickers produced 1,036 Centurion tanks of the Mark III variety or earlier.[153] As a result, the British tank programme came to a full circle with production that focused upon factories that were either owned by the government or Vickers-Armstrongs.

The expansion of state controlled munitions production to the tank programme could have been an extension of wartime policy and the Labour government post-war programme of nationalization. However, an example from either period can demonstrate that the nationalization of existing firms or industries was not always the preferred option. The wartime nationalization of airframe manufacturers Shorts Group was a last resort measure to improve the rate of production from this firm, through direct state control to meet the demanding bomber programme.[154] In respect of post-war motor manufacturing, the Labour government decided during 1948 to keep the industry under private ownership to maintain the strong export position, with central control relating to the allocation of raw materials.[155]

Conclusion

This chapter has examined how the demands upon increased output prevented the British tank industry from fully achieving General Staff requirements under the tank programme until 1944. While the General Staff responded to the changing nature of warfare by demanding that British tanks have greater firepower, reliability and increased armour protection, industry was either not able or not permitted to react to the same degree. As a result, many unsatisfactory and obsolete tanks were produced for much longer than desired. When the transfer to better assembly techniques for the quality designs was achieved during 1944, the British tank industry now provided vehicles that met the Allied requirement to carry out an offensive strategy overseas with greater operational mobility.

The introduction of the different tank boards from June 1940 to September 1942, discussed in Chapter 2, occurred with numerous changes to the terms of reference by each Minister of Supply. As a result, the priorities swung between meeting either the requirements of the General Staff with the concerns over the volume and condition of the tanks, or the Ministry of Supply which had to balance these demands against government munitions policy and changes to industrial capacity and labour. This changed from September 1942 with the introduction of the all-encompassing fifth Tank Board, which continually scrutinized the qualitative aspects of tank design and production. In addition, greater numbers of Lend-Lease tanks from the United States were accepted to fulfil the remaining General Staff requirements under the tank programme.

Up until the Battle of France, the General Staff sought a larger proportion of Infantry instead of Cruiser tanks based upon the expectation of trench warfare. This meant a greater overall expenditure due to the higher basic cost price of Infantry tanks when compared to Cruisers. The fighting in France justified the continuation orders for the Matilda tank, in keeping with the General Staff emphasis upon heavy armour and firepower, while the requirement for Light tanks diminished to insignificant levels. After the French campaign and with the experience of fighting the Italians in the Western Desert, the General Staff wanted greater operational mobility with the tank programme now required to provide a two-to-one majority in favour of Cruiser over Infantry tanks. However, the existing production arrangements could not reverse the pre-Battle of France priorities until 1944, resulting in more Infantry tanks than the General Staff desired.

General Staff requirements throughout the war maintained the emphasis upon improvements to British tank design in respect of armament, reliability and armour protection. In relation to firepower, the insistence upon uninterrupted production meant that Britain fell behind the United States in terms of high explosive tank armament and Germany for an effective dual-purpose tank gun. The British six-pounder gun became a successful anti-tank weapon, but the General Staff were seeking greater high explosive capability based upon the experience in North Africa. While high explosive six-pounder shells were under production, they were superseded by the increased capabilities of the new 75 mm gun, albeit at the expense of armour-piercing capability. As a result, the vast majority of British tanks performed either an armour-piercing or a high explosive role. Separate tank armament remained within British armoured units until the end of the war, although there was some improvement with the arrival of the dual-purpose 17-pounder armed Sherman Firefly and Challenger tanks from mid-1944, and the 77 mm gun armed Comet tanks from February 1945. All of these were superseded after the war with the introduction of the Centurion tank.

With the exception of the Valentine tank, the General Staff requirement for reliable tanks remained a problem for the British tank programme until 1943 when the Churchill tank had been satisfactorily reworked to become battleworthy. Chapter 5 will discuss how industry overcame the obstacles to reliability that included production problems, the existing contractual commitments and the avoidance of unused or interrupted labour during the change-over. An important transformation for the tank industry was the elimination of the problematic and underpowered Liberty tank engine on the Crusader, Cavalier and Centaur tanks, in favour of the preferred Meteor engine for the later Cromwell, Challenger, Comet and Centurion tanks. The Meteor gave these British tanks the prerequisite mechanical reliability, supported by the correct decisions to reject the Ford V8 engine from the United States and transfer production away from the Ministry of Aircraft Production to the Ministry of Supply.

In addition to increased reliability, the Meteor engine provided the tank programme with the ability to incorporate greater amounts of armour protection in the later Cruiser tanks. The quality of armour protection had improved by the latter half of the war because industry had gained the necessary experience and equipment or manipulators for the use of welding. By comparison, the armour thickness on American tanks did not substantially increase although welded tanks were mass produced much sooner than Britain because the machining of armour plate was reduced and an exact finish was not demanded every time. Both Britain and Germany produced armoured vehicles capable of withstanding the heaviest armour-piercing guns with the Tortoise or German Jagdtiger; however, these machines completely negated any attempt to maintain the initiative with operational mobility.

To take advantage of the large increase in productive capacity generated throughout the war, from late 1943 both the government and industry discussed and prepared for the return to peacetime civilian demand once the war contracts had been cancelled. The post-war tank programme concentrated upon the Centurion tank which met all three of the General Staff key requirements of having the best armament available with the 17-pounder gun, the greatest protection possible with 152 mm of sloped armour, and a reliable and powerful 600 hp Meteor engine to maintain operational mobility. The establishment of a Royal Tank Arsenal by the wartime government ensured that the peacetime production of the Centurion tank would not repeat the experience of being dependent upon civilian industry, beyond the well-known capabilities of Vickers-Armstrongs.

The Tank Workforce and Industrial Output

The experience of the factory workers towards achieving the increasing demands of the war effort requires examination for a further understanding of British industry during the period from rearmament until the end of the war. This will complement the analysis already undertaken during the previous chapters, concerning the transformation of British industry under greater centralized control, the expansion of productive capacity and the requirements of the General Staff. As a result, this chapter will examine the important issues relating to the role, skills and welfare of the factory workers, together with the consequences upon tank output by the actions of the employees, employers and the government alike.

To begin with, the impact of the war upon the home front will be highlighted by considering public and worker opinion towards both British industry and the overall war effort, including the response to Lord Beaverbrook's 'Tanks for Russia' week. The efforts to overcome the shortages in skilled labour included the expansion of dilution, the transfer of workers and the subcontracting of work, while trying to avoid provoking the Trade Unions. The call-up of workers to the armed forces was a continual drain on industrial manpower, although other reasons included health problems, dishonesty, dissatisfaction, domestic concerns and the relocation to work elsewhere. The effect of women entering the factories resulted in increased welfare provisions and the ability of firms to work seven-days-a-week. While women faced inequality in respect of wages, there were equal opportunities to gain new skills with the expansion of welding in tank assembly. Workers' holidays avoided exhaustion and reduced the number of industrial accidents. The effect that holidays had upon output was noticeable because these known periods of reduced activity were omitted from the production forecasts. Industrial action caused output to decline at individual firms, although the tank programme remained largely unaffected because these stoppages occurred at different times.

Public opinion towards industry and the war effort

During the war public opinion towards whether the stated demands of the government were being achieved by British industry was analysed by the social research organization, Mass Observation. In measuring public opinion towards industrial efficiency during August 1941, 35 per cent of the men and women interviewed considered that the British effort was inadequate compared to 27 per cent offering favourable responses. The problem with these results was that nearly half of the women and one-quarter of the men questioned stated that they lacked the information and level of understanding to form any opinion at all. Whether the opinion was based upon first-hand knowledge or hearsay, factory employers were blamed twice as frequently as the workers or the government for deficiencies in production, with claims of complacency and lack of momentum by employers since the crisis of 1940.[1]

One of the complaints made of workers was that they were motivated by higher wages, rather than supporting the war effort.[2] While wages did increase during the war as discussed later in relation to the inequality between men and women, the comments relating to worker motivation must also take into account the impact of inflation upon the overall cost of living. Significant price rises in basic foodstuffs, household goods and clothing were experienced during the first 18 months of war. The effect that inflation had upon rising earnings lessened with subsidies, greater rationing and price controls by 1942, although the value of other items continued to fluctuate, together with the cost of goods in the Black Market.[3] While wage rates did increase during the war, the working of longer hours and the availability of overtime to meet production targets had a much greater effect upon the rise in earnings.[4]

A small minority of those questioned during August 1941 blamed incompetent government officials for slowing output and encouraging profiteering. These complaints targeted the use and abuse of the 'cost-plus' system which allegedly slowed production and caused worker idleness.[5] The government had introduced the system of cost-plus for calculating the profit on contracts early in the war because sudden and unpredictable changes during production meant that a fixed price contract would be difficult to assess at the outset. Therefore, each contract was based upon the cost plus a fixed amount or the more lucrative fixed percentage which could be abused.[6] As illustrated by the Birmingham Railway Carriage & Wagon Company during November 1943, the firm now negotiated with the Ministry of Supply the rate of profit for all work completed during that year, rather than fixing the rate at the start of each contract as previously agreed under the cost-plus system.[7]

Similar complaints against the system of calculating profit were raised in the United States for the cost-plus-fixed-fee scheme, which reimbursed firms for the cost of approved expenses plus a fee based upon output. This scheme was sometimes considered to be excessive and encouraged firms to concentrate upon the sheer volume of output rather than industrial economy or efficiency. The difficulties in calculating the actual costs of production with the fixed fee or other fixed price contracts remained until the end of the war, when the final negotiations and adjustments took place.[8] In comparison to Britain and the United States, German industry generated increased profits from 1942 with the introduction of the fixed price system. This essentially eliminated the effect of taxes upon profits so that firms were encouraged to strive for greater output without a tax penalty. Another difference was the use of forced and slave labour which meant that German industry made greater profit with the lower wages paid to the workforce brought in from the occupied territories.[9]

In May 1943, the respondents to a Mass Observation questionnaire considered that the efficiency of British industry had increased over the previous year, although further improvements were still sought. The successful conclusion to the North African campaign contributed towards this positive outlook with the belief that British forces were now receiving adequate equipment in sufficient quantities.[10] Public opinion in this instance was matched by the information received from the front line. In late March 1943, General Montgomery wrote that on one occasion during the Battle of Mareth, the air assault consisted of 22 squadrons of fighters that included many Spitfires and Hurricane tank busters.[11] The quality of tanks being provided to North Africa was confirmed by a post-campaign technical report on the recent performance of all armoured fighting vehicles. Despite justifiable demands for greater firepower, the British army had received reliable Churchill tanks with excellent hill climbing ability, alongside battleworthy Sherman tanks under Lend-Lease to replace the problematic Crusader and obsolete Valentine tanks.[12]

The supply of equipment and materials from the United States under Lend-Lease also came under public scrutiny through the Mass Observation surveys, including comparisons to the perceived effectiveness of British industry. For example, the recent passing of the Lend-Lease Bill by Congress in March 1941 seemingly improved the morale of the respondents and helped to divert attention away from the effects of German bombing. However, the report raised the concern that the British response to receiving aid from the United States might cause a slackening of domestic war production.[13] By June 1941, Mass Observation noted that Lend-Lease had contributed towards an increase in confidence regarding the war and that favourable opinion towards the United States had risen from 27 per cent in October 1940 to 60 per cent by April 1941. While this was an improvement, the respondents were not overwhelmingly supportive of the United States, with examples of impatience and suspicion towards the actual timing of providing Lend-Lease aid. These misgivings did not extend to President Roosevelt who the respondents believed was doing his best to help Britain under difficult circumstances.[14] Mass Observation later reported that following the death of Roosevelt in April 1945, the British reaction was personal and genuinely sorry, and not just a series of standard tributes.[15]

As the war continued into 1943, almost two-thirds of Mass Observation replies considered that Lend-Lease was favourable or necessary for Britain, while most of the 14 per cent who were critical thought that the agreement gave the United States an advantage. A sizable 23 per cent could not provide an opinion either way, despite nearly two years of direct support from the United States. In respect of manufacturing, one-third of the respondents thought that the United States had a better industry than Britain, based upon the perception that production was quicker, more efficient and cheaper than British output. The 27 per cent who could not offer an opinion lacked the information or understanding to measure the efficiency of industry at home or abroad, similar to that expressed earlier in August 1941.[16] The claim that the United States was taking advantage of Lend-Lease was based upon the idea that the economic activity resulting from the agreement more than covered the cost of production. Under this argument, the access to British bases granted under the agreement was therefore surplus to the cost of Lend-Lease. While the increasing demands placed upon Lend-Lease expanded American industry during the war, this production was only achieved at the expense of and not in addition to the domestic civilian programmes.[17]

Government propaganda efforts with various 'War' week campaigns were used to stimulate public interest in supporting greater munitions output, as well as combating inflation by encouraging the public to take advantage of savings opportunities.[18] The tone of these propaganda efforts had to be judged correctly, otherwise the central message of the campaign could be misinterpreted or rejected. In one example, a Mass Observation report on public opinion in May 1941 following 'War Weapons' week in London, considered that a red bomb on a poster was inappropriate when considering the bombing of British cities to date.[19] For the public to react favourably to a propaganda campaign, the central message needed to resonate in public opinion and with those being specifically targeted.

Three months after Germany attacked the Soviet Union in June 1941, Minister of Supply Lord Beaverbrook encouraged industry to produce more tanks with the announcement of 'Tanks for Russia' week from 22 to 29 September. This campaign was designed to send more tanks to the Red Army and honour the first protocol with Moscow, which committed the Western Allies to supply the Soviet war effort with munitions, materials and equipment. A Mass Observation report at the end of the week noted how the campaign had energized the respondents with the belief that Britain was now providing something tangible to assist the Soviet Union. Those respondents who thought that even more was needed to support the Soviet war effort following 'Tanks for Russia' week would have taken some satisfaction upon hearing about the formal supply protocols later in October. The overriding opinion was one of necessity, with the realization that Soviet requirements took priority over British needs, otherwise Britain would lose an important ally and might become vulnerable to German attack again.[20]

This general feeling of public support for the efforts of the government and industry during tank week continued into the following week with the announcement that a record number of tanks were produced during the campaign. However, Mass Observation noted that the combination of 'Tanks for Russia' week and the reported continued resistance of the Red Army could transform this increase in overall opinion into complacency.[21] In the time from the invasion of the Soviet Union until the end of August 1941, Mass Observation carried out twice-weekly surveys in five London boroughs to measure the fluctuations in optimism and pessimism. While the accuracy of these figures were affected by the sampling errors typical of on-the-spot surveys, the results still demonstrated a basic understanding of events on the frequently changing Eastern Front.[22] This reaction to events continued during September when the fall of Kiev caused greater despondency among the respondents, but was soon replaced with greater optimism as tank week progressed.[23]

Skilled labour and production

The highly mechanized nature of the Second World War meant that manpower requirements had to be organized to provide the skilled workers to the factories to produce the equipment and skilled operatives to the services for ongoing maintenance and repair.[24] In Britain, the manpower situation came under greater centralized control from April 1939 with the introduction of peacetime conscription. While the General Staff did not consider compulsory military service to be an immediate priority, they recognized that it was inevitable in the long term.[25] Industrial conscription for men commenced after May 1940 when the new coalition government introduced the Emergency Powers Act to give Ernest Bevin, the new Minister of Labour, the power to direct any man to perform any service.[26] These powers extended to women at the beginning of 1942 when female conscription was required to replace the existing and inadequate system of female volunteerism.[27]

When compared to the United States, the mechanized nature of pre-war American society helped to provide the necessary skilled manpower and essential production facilities to comprehensively mechanize the armed forces.[28] The United States was unique among the Allies for not directing industrial labour or applying a compulsory service law universally.[29] Instead, the United States successfully mobilized resources by encouraging an extensive effort from all concerned.[30] In relation to German manpower, full employment had already been achieved in 1936 and wartime requirements were met by the continued and ruthless policy of using forced labour from the occupied territories and prisoners of war.[31] A great deal of German war production was carried out by using the traditional craftsmanship of skilled workers, whereas the United States used specialist techniques and equipment to employ greater numbers of semi-skilled workers. German industry was not completely devoid of mass production and any progress was hindered by initial shortages of the appropriate machine tools and by the later effects of dispersal to counter Allied bombing.[32]

The transformation of British industry during rearmament brought about changes and challenges to the skilled, semi-skilled and general labour force. Ironically, Britain's 'army of unemployed' could not transfer immediately to rearmament work because the Depression had reduced the number of apprenticeships to expand the overall skills base and because some skills were now superseded by industrial advances. Furthermore, the difficulties encountered with the Trade Unions during the First World War meant that industry could not increase the number of skilled workers by simply relying upon the 'dilution' of labour.[33] Dilution divided skilled work into tasks for completion by semi-skilled men, or by upgrading workers to a task that exceeded the level of skill that the union considered them permitted to undertake.[34] The chairman of Vickers-Armstrongs Sir Charles Craven, wrote to the Minister for the Co-ordination of Defence, Sir Thomas Inskip at the beginning of 1938, expressing concern that the lack of skilled labour had resulted in a great deal of deskilling. Deskilling was an extension to dilution that had semi-skilled workers operating machinery on work that would otherwise have needed a skilled engineer or craftsman. Craven emphasized that while the trades unions were completely opposed to any real dilution, they had not yet raised any serious obstacles.[35]

In common with other firms engaged on rearmament orders, Vickers subcontracted part of their work to firms which had skilled and semi-skilled men available to reduce the overall demand for more workers at Vickers.[36] Subcontracting was generally accepted by those unions opposed to dilution as it avoided the disruption caused by transferring labour from one firm to another, and maintained the employment of skilled workers at the contracted firms.[37] The effects of an acute shortage of skilled designers and workers upon the motor industry, during 1936, was that armament contracts prevented new vehicle research and restricted the development of existing models to tried and tested components.[38] Later in 1938, the motor firms engaged on the priority production of aircraft reduced the deficiencies in skilled labour with the use of subcontracting and the internal transfer of workers from the car factories affected by the recession to the 'shadow' factories for aircraft work.[39] With dilution and subcontracting being discussed within industry, the Chamberlain government avoided direct contact with the Trade Unions until 1938 for risk of encouraging demands for better pay and conditions. When the Air Ministry and War Office demanded increased munitions output in response to the German annexation of Austria or *Anschluss* in March 1938, the government decided that this would be achieved by seeking closer co-operation with the unions, rather than by reducing the production of civilian goods.[40]

The problems of labour supply continued during 1939 with AEC noting that the average number of employees per week during April 1939 was recorded as 120 fewer than April 1938.[41] To resolve this shortfall, AEC increased the number of 'boys' on production to 16 per cent, resulting in the number employed during May 1939 being greater than 12 months before.[42] Leyland Motors experienced similar problems in May 1939 when they had to transfer skilled workers from the night-shift to fill the vacancies in skilled labour in the day-shift. The number of workers on the night-shift had not increased over the same period, so this was presumably to the detriment of the work carried out during the later shift.[43] By the end of 1939, Leyland Motors warned that because the emphasis upon dilution had already upgraded the best semi-skilled workers, the quality of skilled work would deteriorate with each subsequent transfer. These later workers were expected to be less proficient with an increase in the level of scrap material and an anticipated reduction in piecework earnings.[44]

The effect that the outbreak of war had upon the workers was illustrated when the Nuffield Organisation reported that staff redundancies were necessary because wartime requirements had reduced the level of civilian demand. The firm compensated both men and women on equal terms for each completed year of service.[45] Similarly, the Rover Company noted that redundancies were unavoidable as a result of the reduction in working hours when the production of cars was cut from 250 to 100 per week. Rover managed to limit these redundancies by redirecting some employees to carry out work on air raid precautions.[46]

The completion of air raid precautions at Gloucester Railway Carriage & Wagon Company was supported by the out-of-hours weekend work of 74 employees, who volunteered to blackout windows and build shelters between 9 and 10 September.[47] A further example of volunteerism occurred during May 1940, when industrial workers responded in their thousands to join the new Local Defence Volunteers or Home

Guard, with some firms forming individual units such as the 10th Surrey (Vickers Armstrong) Battalion.[48] Similar Home Guard or Volkssturm battalions were forced upon German industry at the end of the war.[49] In some cases, local officials decided upon who should join, although the list of fit and available Germans of military age were still limited to factory workers or the officials themselves.[50]

From September 1941, industry received an increase in manpower following the temporary release of 8,000 skilled and semi-skilled Royal Air Force personnel from the Air Ministry. This decision was designed to overcome the shortage of similar workers in aircraft production after Prime Minister Churchill had asked for an increase in bomber output between July 1941 and July 1943.[51] The Ministry of Labour and National Service was surprised to receive this offer from the Air Ministry, as it was believed that the Royal Air Force currently had a shortage of skilled operatives.[52] While this was meant to support aircraft production, a small number of these Royal Air Force personnel were provided to the tank firms. Ruston-Bucyrus enthusiastically reported in January 1942, that despite being short of 300 workers for Crusader production, the 91 air force members quickly became very useful.[53] Leyland Motors received 3 men from the engineering section of the Royal Air Force and in February 1942 also reported that while the workers were not fully skilled, they were extremely versatile and became useful members of the machine shop.[54]

When the Royal Air Force personnel at Ruston-Bucyrus in Lincoln returned to the Air Ministry by December 1942, the firm stated that 50 to 60 semi-skilled workers were immediately required for the Crusader programme and that a further 200 to 300 would be needed by April 1943.[55] To minimize the loss in Crusader output at Ruston-Bucyrus, workers from nearby Ruston & Hornsby were loaned from their declining Matilda production, before returning early in 1943 to start work on the new Cavalier tank.[56] This temporary reallocation of workers to meet the changes within the tank programme is shown in Figure 4.1. This illustrates how Crusader output at Ruston-Bucyrus declined towards the end of 1942 with the loss of the air force personnel. This was followed by an increase in production with the transfer of workers from Ruston & Hornsby after the end of their Matilda programme. Crusader output decreased again when these workers returned to Ruston & Hornsby to begin work on the new Cavalier tank.

The number of skilled mechanical and engineering workers transferred from industry to the armed forces workshops ceased between November 1941 and August 1942. This decision followed the report from a committee headed by Sir William Beveridge, who was appointed by Ernest Bevin to investigate and ultimately corroborate the belief that the armed services, and in particular the army, were allocating skilled workers incorrectly. The War Office carried out a similar investigation and although they considered the number of inappropriate cases to be minimal, the system of allocating tradesmen was re-examined.[57] In Germany, the system of calling-up workers for the armed forces from the spring of 1941 was meant to protect vital industries by exempting tank firms completely, and providing other munitions firms with eight weeks notice to train replacement workers. However, this plan was based upon unrealistic expectations, especially when the situation on the Eastern Front deteriorated to have such an impact on manpower.[58]

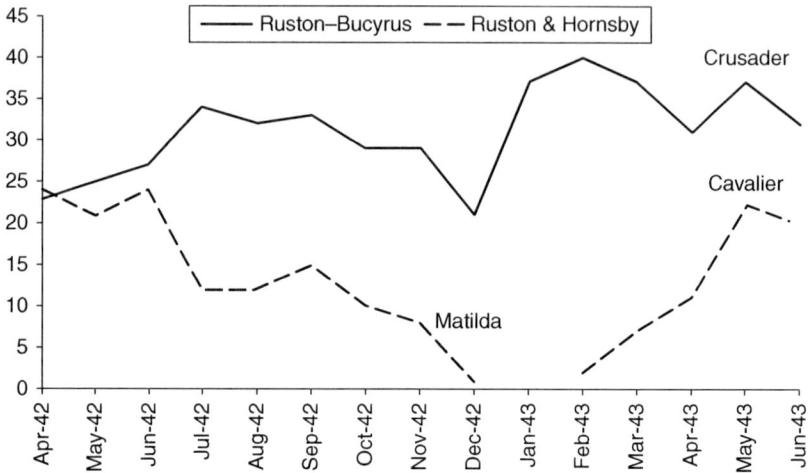

Figure 4.1 Tank output by Ruston-Bucyrus and Ruston & Hornsby, April 1942 to June 1943

Source: The National Archives, AVIA 46/188, 'Monthly Deliveries of Infantry and Cruiser Tanks by Firms, 1939–1943', draft official history narrative by D. Hay, after 1950, p. 271.

The difficulties in organizing the growing manpower requirements for British industry and the armed forces meant that full mobilization was not achieved until mid-1943, although an additional 1.6 million men and women had been added into the munitions industries. With all available manpower now engaged, the organization of requirements became a matter of balancing the distribution of men and women to meet the changing strategic situation. As the war continued during 1944 and into 1945, Britain maintained military strength by relying upon the increased mobilization and role of the United States to provide the additional men and equipment necessary for the final assault on occupied Europe.[59] In Britain, the reduction of weapons and equipment planned for the 1945 programme meant that the munitions industries transferred the available men and women to meet other manpower requirements.[60]

In addition to the demands of the services, there were many other reasons why individual firms continued to lose workers during the course of the war. Between January 1943 and May 1945, Leyland Motors had a total of 4,162 workers leave their factory in Leyland, the foundry at Farington and the factories at Chorley and Kingston-upon-Thames. Despite these departures, the total number of workers at these four locations over the same period grew by 835 from 8,960 to 9,795, with peak employment reaching 9,942 during September 1943. The overall rise in employment at Leyland Motors can be attributed to their continuing and increasing involvement in the tank programme, as the firm became the production parent of the consecutive Centaur, Cromwell and Comet tanks.[61] On the other hand, Vulcan Foundry ceased involvement in tank production following the completion of the Matilda contract in May 1943, and was transferred to the core business of producing locomotives as discussed in Chapter 6. As a result, the number of workers at Vulcan Foundry fell from 3,625 in January 1943 to 3,103 by May 1945.[62]

Table 4.1 Reasons for leaving Leyland Motors, January 1943 to May 1945

Reason	Male	Female	Total
Health	1,042	575	1,617
Armed forces	567	18	585
Domestic concerns	85	472	557
Dishonesty or conviction	199	24	223
Transferred by government	162	15	177
Pregnancy	–	168	168
Redundancy	100	68	168
Dissatisfied with job	121	41	162
Return home or other work	102	44	146
Deceased	118	12	130
Unsuitable or unsatisfactory	66	33	99
Left without permission	22	14	36
Transfer to coal mines	28	–	28
Other	59	7	66
Total	2,671	1,491	4,162

Sources: British Commercial Vehicle Museum, Leyland Motors, M632 143/5, General Manager's Meetings, 1941–3, 'Reasons for Leaving', January to December 1943; M631 143/5, General Manager's Meetings, 1944–6, 'Reasons for Leaving', January 1944 to May 1945.

The reasons why the 4,162 workers left Leyland Motors from January 1943 until May 1945 are shown in Table 4.1. The number of male employees at Leyland Motors during these final 29 months of war in Europe averaged 77 per cent of the total workforce, while the proportion of men who left due to health reasons was 64 per cent. This meant that the number of female workers with health problems was larger than their 23 per cent share of the total workforce and was not attributed to pregnancy which was recorded separately. The number of females who left without permission or because of unsatisfactory performance or redundancy was similarly greater than the share of total women employed.

The gap between male and female workers widens even further when 85 per cent of those who left due to domestic concerns were women. Many of the reasons for these departures were caused by the continuing anxieties of food shopping, providing meals, essential housework and arranging for child care.[63] The death of an employee occurring as a result of an accident at the workplace will be examined later when considering the necessity to provide workers with sufficient opportunities for relaxation with factory holidays. Those workers sent to the coal industry were probably 'Bevin Boys' who became eligible for National Service, but were sent to the mines through the unpopular ballot system introduced by the Ministry of Labour to increase the number of coal workers.[64]

Women and welding in the workplace

With large numbers of men joining the armed services, the Allied nations recognized the necessity of mobilizing women to work in the factories and serve in the armed forces in a non-combatant role. Germany declined to use their female population to the same extent as the Allies until much later in the war. Instead, the Nazi regime relied upon both male and female labour from the occupied territories to overcome the shortages in manpower, and avoided using German women for as long as possible.[65] When comparing all the combatant nations, Britain ultimately directed women further than any other government.[66]

The introduction of women into factories compelled industry to extend the improvements to working conditions already instigated by Ernest Bevin, with the requirement for shared factory canteens and separate lavatories. Only about 1,500 factories had canteens in the workplace before the war. From November 1940, every workplace employing over 250 people and engaged on government contracts were required to provide canteens. By January 1941, construction and dock sites had to provide worker canteens, while other employers volunteered to install canteens under pressure from the inspectors, and before the regulations extended to these smaller firms. As a result, by April 1942 the number of workplaces with canteens in operation or under construction had increased to 8,300. Many factories operated more than one facility so the total number of canteens was even greater.[67]

To illustrate the effect on individual firms, in December 1940 Gloucester Railway met the recent legal requirements by opening the existing canteen facilities to all employees once the firm began employing women workers. Further measures included offering the widow of the former works manager the salaried position of welfare supervisor to assist the new female employees.[68] By August 1941, Metropolitan-Cammell had spent £15,000 on the construction and equipping of canteens at their Saltley, Midland and Old Park Works, plus £500 for the female lavatory and restroom at the Old Park site which had lacked these facilities to date.[69] While the workers welcomed these improvements to the workplace, the canteen operation was still subject to criticism for the quantity and quality of food, the standard of service, the cost of meals and whether management was making a profit.[70]

During the opening stages of providing aid to the Soviet Union during November 1941, more women were encouraged to enrol into the munitions industries as part of the 'Women in War Work' week in Coventry. Part of the campaign included an exhibition to emphasize the brutality of the German invasion of the Soviet Union and a street parade with women dressed in overalls, riding on tanks and working on aeroplane parts as they travelled. Home-made banners were also employed with messages of 'Tanks for women, good for slimming', 'Combine beauty with duty' and 'Russia doesn't ask for Thanks. What she wants is Britain's Tanks.' Despite these efforts to entice more women to enlist, the number of new recruits fell well short of the target.[71] This disappointing result was due to the restriction of only offering full-time work, when part-time opportunities could have relieved some of the concerns by men and women alike, regarding food shopping, providing meals and essential housework.[72] This failure should not detract from the success of the campaign to continue advertising the necessity of providing still greater amounts of aid to the Soviet Union, and of the importance of the British tank industry and the workers to achieve this.

The impact of female conscription from the beginning of 1942 upon the organization of labour at the workplace was illustrated at Leyland Motors. The introduction of women into the Leyland works in June 1940 enabled more semi-skilled male workers to be transferred to skilled work under the dilution scheme.[73] From July 1940 and as a result of the growth in women workers, Leyland Motors changed from a two-shift system of 90 hours per week, to a three-shift system of 135 hours.[74] The increase in female workers following conscription permitted essential areas of Leyland plant to work continuously seven-days-a-week from April 1942.[75] The decision to widen conscription to women workers was generally well received by those interviewed by Mass Observation at the end of 1941, with nearly two-thirds providing favourable responses. Many of the respondents considered that this should have been introduced sooner and that women would be better placed in the munitions industry rather than entering the armed forces.[76] However, the Vice-Chairman of the Nuffield Organisation, Sir Miles Thomas, stated that the compulsory removal of female office staff to the production line or the forces would adversely affect the efficient operation of the parent system. The concern was that parent firm Mechanization & Aero had the responsibilities of buying, material control, spares allocation and the dissemination of information on behalf of the entire Crusader production group, and thus required the greater administrative support provided by female staff.[77]

The inequality in earnings between the comparative skills of male and female employees was released by a published Mass Observation report during 1942. This revealed that a Ministry of Labour census for July 1941 of 56,600 firms across war and other production recorded that on average men received £4.97 each week, which was more than twice the £2.22 earned by women. At the upper end of these figures, 12 per cent of male workers engaged on war production received more than £6 per week, compared to just 5 per cent for those workers on other production.[78] These figures can be illustrated further by reviewing the weekly earnings for employees at Gloucester Railway reported at the monthly board meetings, as shown in Table 4.2. A key reason why male earnings in July 1941 were less than the Mass Observation findings was because the firm had only delivered the first Churchill tank during this month. Gloucester Railway likely spent the nine months since the original order in October 1940 to retool and prepare the factory.[79] Female employees were either not working or recorded during this period. Once full production was underway, male weekly earnings had risen by May 1942 to exceed the level reported by Mass Observation. The inequality between male and female wages at Gloucester Railway

Table 4.2 Average weekly earnings at Gloucester Railway Carriage & Wagon Company, July 1941 and May 1942 (in £)

	July 1941 Men	May 1942 Men	May 1942 Women
Skilled	5.90	6.82	–
Semi-skilled	4.38	5.30	3.14
Unskilled	3.38	4.39	2.10
Average	4.55	5.50	2.62

Sources: Gloucestershire Archives, Gloucester Railway Carriage & Wagon Company, D4791/8/3, Board meeting reports and papers, 1939–42, 'Statistical Report' wages for July 1941 reported on 18 September 1941 and for May 1942 reported on 12 June 1942.

was consistent with the Mass Observation findings, as demonstrated when semi-skilled men earned more than semi-skilled women.

Without being able to distinguish between industrial and non-industrial workers, the number of workers interviewed by Mass Observation who were satisfied with their job role increased from 66 per cent in January 1942 to 72 per cent by May 1943. The number of female workers providing positive responses accounted for almost as many as male workers, although many women gave the appearance of not wanting to complain.[80] The increase in overall job satisfaction would have been strengthened by the marked improvement in opinion from those workers who approved the length of the working day. Crucially, the number of respondents who worked between 7 and 9 hours each day increased to 59 per cent by May 1943, compared to 47 per cent in January 1942.[81]

Female factory workers would have had greater job satisfaction as they became more proficient in the new skills of machining, riveting, lathe work and wiring, and welding on aircraft and tank assembly.[82] However, many of these tasks were deemed 'women's work' due to the process involved, resulting in these women getting paid less than those women employed on 'men's work'. This created a subdivision of inequality for the female workforce beyond the general differences in pay between men and women already discussed. Furthermore, women on part-time work because of domestic responsibilities did not receive the benefits provided to full-time workers, such as bonus and overtime rates, and the availability of unemployment and accident insurance.[83] The range of welding opportunities for women also occurred in American industry, together with similar classifications of work to justify the differences in wages.[84] An example of gender equality was experienced at Leyland Motors with the formation of a 'welding school' in April 1943 to meet the increased volume of welding on the Centaur tank. The school trained male and female workers to produce welded 'test pieces' for the Chief Metallurgist to examine, and if approved the candidate commenced work on tank production.[85]

The increase of welding in factories was not without worker side-effects. Despite the use of goggles and face masks during 1942, workers received contact burns and 'arc-eye' or 'welder's flash' due to the intensity of the welding flame.[86] By September 1944, 20 per cent of the trainee welders at Leyland Motors had requested alternative employment for health reasons due to the extreme heat. Another health concern reported by welders related to the presence of smoke fumes during welding which could not be easily extracted, especially in enclosed spaces such as the interior of the tank hull.[87] The Chief Inspector of Factories recorded in 1939 that the blackout increased the problems of poor factory ventilation because insufficient attention had been given to how this wartime necessity affected the working environment.[88] The chief inspector reported for 1945 that these problems continued throughout the war, and even the design of new factories built as part of the expansion of industrial capacity had not given enough consideration for improved ventilation.[89] A partial solution to the problems of ventilation in tank welding was carried out at Leyland Motors in December 1944. This was the installation of an air chute to direct fumes towards the ventilators, and a curtain by the open outside door to allow fresh air to circulate without significantly lowering the temperature or causing a draught.[90] Despite these efforts, the level of absenteeism in welding peaked at 33 per cent in January 1945, resulting in additional work on one Saturday and later for a whole weekend to maintain the required rate of output.[91]

Worker holidays, accidents and output

The availability of paid annual worker holidays in Britain during the 1920s was limited to approximately 1.5 million workers. By 1937, the combination of collective agreements and the reaction by some employers before the introduction of the Holidays with Pay Act during 1938 had provided around 3 million workers with paid annual holidays. The legislation had the effect of increasing the total number of eligible employees to 11 million by 1939, with an estimated 15 million workers by 1943.[92] Unpaid breaks were taken before 1939, when the motor industry made redundancies to deal with seasonal demand and by enforcing a three-month 'holiday' in the summer prior to the start of the Motor Show.[93]

Following the evacuations from Dunkirk and with the continuing fighting in France during the remainder of June 1940, the government cancelled all holidays in both war and other industries. The main reasons for this decision were to avoid interrupting munitions output and to ensure that transport facilities supported the needs of the services and domestic evacuation, and not those travelling to and from their holiday destination.[94] By the end of July, Ernest Bevin stated that employee exhaustion would affect production levels, unless a short factory stoppage was permitted, if rotation was not appropriate.[95] Towards the end of 1940, Bevin reached an agreement with the employers' and workers' associations that firms engaged on essential production should have a one-day holiday on Christmas Day, with Scotland taking New Year instead.[96]

A serious side-effect of working longer hours and the reduction in holidays during 1940 was a 40 per cent increase in recorded accidents, with a disproportionate amount experienced by new workers.[97] By the final years of war, the return of holidays had improved the accident rate with fewer hours being worked and more time available for new workers to become accustomed to the dangers of factory work.[98] The figures reported by the Chief Inspector of Factories show that the number of 'fatal accidents' across industry fell from a peak of 1,646 during 1941 to 851 by 1945, which was fewer than the 944 recorded for 1938. 'Non-Fatal Accidents' peaked in 1942 at 313,267 and likewise fell each subsequent year to 239,802 during 1945, although this was still 60,643 accidents higher than 1938.[99]

In respect of the circumstances of the different accidents, the report book of Birmingham Railway from November 1944 to July 1945 provides a small number of examples to compare against the chief inspector's findings to highlight the overall frequency. In general terms, the proportion of accidents caused by the use of powered machinery fell from 17 per cent in 1942 to 15 per cent by 1945, due to greater preventative measures that were backed-up by legal enforcement. All the other causes were 'non-machinery' related, in which manual handling accidents became slightly more common over the same period from 26 to over 27 per cent. This occurred at Birmingham Railway when two tank fitters strained themselves while lifting a steel plate, while another tank fitter required hospital treatment after sustaining a hernia when lifting a tank door. The chief inspector reported that these types of injuries were preventable through increased mechanization and greater use of lifting machines. The recording of employees falling within the workplace remained between 13 and 14 per cent of all accidents from 1942 to 1945. At Birmingham Railway, two tank fitters fell into the 'tank pit' on different occasions when they lost their footing nearby, while a female tank electrician fell down elsewhere due to poor lighting. Other types of accidents recorded by the chief inspector related to the use of hand tools, being hit by a falling item and 'stepping on or striking' against an object.[100]

The annual factory holiday for one week during the summer returned in 1941, so that the workers received the necessary rest and recuperation and the factory plant could be overhauled and repaired where necessary. The affect that these holidays had upon industrial output can be illustrated by a number of examples from 1941 to 1944. At Vulcan Foundry, the summer break from 20 July 1941 caused a reduction in the number of employees from over 2,800 in the week before to just over 400 during the holiday week.[101] This resulted in Matilda tank output at Vulcan Foundry falling by 23 per cent during July compared to the average output of the previous three months. A similar decline in output of 21 per cent occurred during July at English Electric for the Covenanter tank, with Metropolitan-Cammell sustaining a 17 per cent reduction in Valentine tank output, indicating when holiday periods were taken at these firms as well.[102]

The published Mass Observation report for 1942 noted that those munitions firms which only provided a one-day holiday during Christmas 1941 to limit the effect on output, actually recorded a high rate of absenteeism for a few days afterwards. As a result, the affected firms increased the hours of work in the weeks prior to a holiday period to recover the expected lost time and output caused by the unofficial days taken after the holiday. This policy was applied factory wide, despite some workers preferring just the one-day holiday rather than having to work the extra time beforehand to balance the expected days off later. The report concluded that most workers just required a period of relaxation rather than pleasure during the holiday, with the opportunity to get away from the continuous demands of war work.[103]

For 1942, the government advised industry that the annual one-week holiday should be staggered between April and September to ensure the efficient continuation of production and to avoid pressure on the transport system. Additional worker holidays included the Bank Holidays on Easter Monday, Whitsun and August, plus two days over Christmas or New Year.[104] The fluctuations in tank output caused by holidays would be immediately detected by the Ministry of Supply because production figures were reported on a weekly basis for individual tank models. The importance of maintaining this practice was re-emphasized by Prime Minister Churchill in

December 1942, meaning that individual manufacturers and tank programmes were constantly scrutinized to identify the reasons for any fall in output.[105] The weekly schedule of tank output was maintained until January 1944 when Churchill agreed that this could now be provided on a monthly basis.[106]

The effect that factory holidays had upon weekly tank output can be illustrated by the late Whitsun holiday in June 1943 and the summer holiday period during July. The tank programmes under examination excluded the Matilda tank which finished production in August 1943 and the Crusader tank which ended in September. Therefore, the attention was focused upon the production of the well-established Valentine and Churchill tanks, together with new Cavalier, Centaur and Cromwell tanks. In all five of these programmes, output fell in unison as a result of the 13 June Whitsun Bank Holiday, while the individual summer holidays caused a drop in output between 10 and 31 July.[107] In measuring these production figures against expectations, the supply Defence Committee received a joint report on tank policy during April 1943 from the Minister of Production, the Secretary of State for War and the Minister of Supply. This stated that the combined forecast for the production of Valentine, Churchill, Cavalier, Centaur and Cromwell tanks from April to September 1943 was 3,055.[108] By contrast, the tank programme actually delivered 2,730 leaving a shortfall of 325 tanks over this period.[109]

The effect of holiday downtime was not the only cause for this deficit as the production of the Cromwell tank had expanded more slowly than expected. However, given the proximity of the April forecast to the various holidays that followed, Prime Minister Churchill rightly criticized Minister of Production Oliver Lyttelton for not taking holidays into account.[110] The basis of this displeasure started when Churchill received the figures for the week ending 31 July which he described as: 'Dreadful. A shocking performance'. This was particularly relevant when Valentine production was excluded from British requirements as these were part of the aid programme to the Soviet Union.[111] Upon being 'shocked at the appallingly low output', Churchill asked Lyttelton to provide a full report and doubted that an explanation of summer holidays was sufficient.[112] In response, Lyttelton stated that forecasts did not allow for holidays as they occurred at different times for each workplace.[113] Churchill remained unconvinced and bluntly stated that the forecasts should have allowed for the certainty of annual factory holidays occurring over the summer period.[114]

To put this into context, by 1943 the British tank industry was delivering good quality Churchill tanks and had commenced production of the Cromwell tank, supplemented by increasing numbers of useful tanks from the United States as discussed in Chapter 6. Despite this positive outlook, the tone of Churchill's remarks emphasizes that sustained British tank output was just as important during 1943 as it was after the defeat of France, when equipment shortages were particularly severe. The inability to properly account for the effect of factory holidays upon industrial output was repeated again during July 1944, when the output of 125 Cromwell tanks fell well short of the planned 235 tanks for the month.[115] To illustrate how Churchill's 1943 warnings for calculating official forecasts were not followed, Leyland Motors reported that the decline in output for July 1944 was partly attributable to the annual worker holiday.[116]

Affect of strike action upon output

The possibility of industrial action causing a loss of output in Britain was a constant problem that grew between 1940 and 1944, despite the government making such strikes illegal. To illustrate, in the metal, engineering and shipbuilding industries there were 229 strikes in 1940, involving 40,000 workers for the loss of 163,000 working days. By 1944 there were 610 strikes, engaging 194,000 workers with over 1 million working days lost. The largest proportion of industrial action occurred in coalmining, which accounted for about half of the total working days lost in 1943 and two-thirds in 1944.[117] Industrial action was similarly banned by mutual agreement in the United States and enforced by legal penalties. However, strikes continued with nearly 3,000 taking place in 1942 for the loss of 4.1 million days and almost 5,000 strikes and 8.7 million days lost in 1944. When considering the different sizes of the workforce in Britain and the United States, these strike figures are actually not that dissimilar. Ultimately, the removal of the right to industrial action in response to the emergency of war had little effect upon the workers ability to express their grievances, whether they were unionized or not.[118]

By comparison, the German war effort was mostly disrupted by the effects of industrial action in the occupied territories, resulting in a variety of suppressive local measures, in addition to the arrests, detention, executions and deportations to concentration camps.[119] Against the risk of severe punishment, infrequent strikes were caused by the foreign labour transferred to German factories, with further disruption caused by those workers who fled the area due to the lack of food and Allied bombing during the second half of the war.[120] As for the German working class, industry never experienced significant action during the war, even when the Nazi regime came under extreme pressure in the final months before the defeat in 1945.[121] There were however examples of German workers using absenteeism as a form of surreptitious strike action. Separately, workers in a tank factory in Dortmund carried out a successful 1-hour strike against longer working hours by using a legal technicality relating to the notice provided. Apart from receiving nominal fines, the strikers were not punished.[122]

The rise in industrial action in Britain during the war occurred despite Communist Party influence within the factories from June 1941, which opposed such strikes and supported greater efforts to increase production following the German invasion of the Soviet Union.[123] The war on the Eastern Front brought strong industrial relations between the government, the employers, the trade union leadership and the workers themselves when Lord Beaverbrook announced the start of 'Tanks for Russia' week. In sponsoring this week, Beaverbrook placed the responsibility of producing 'more tanks than ever before in the history of our country' upon the shoulders of the workers concerned. For their part, the Trades Union Congress welcomed the prospect of achieving record levels of munitions output to assist 'their Russian comrades'.[124] This open support for the campaign was also expressed by tank factory workers, with those in the Midlands pledging 'to break all records from now on in aid of our comrades in Russia'.[125]

As part of tank week, the exploits of the tank industry were directly promoted by newspapers and the *Pathé* newsreel with well-publicized factory visits by the Soviet Ambassador Ivan Maisky, who appealed for 'tanks, please; more tanks; and yet more tanks'.[126] These visits portrayed a powerful image of solidarity for British relations towards the Soviet Union and of the consensus within British industrial relations to the response. Harold Macmillan MP noted this when he wrote to those firms producing the Valentine tank and attributed the success of the day to the enthusiasm shown by everyone involved and the publicity that followed.[127] An embarrassing situation involving the Soviet Ambassador was avoided during the planning of these factory visits because not all the tanks under production in Britain were actually sent to the Eastern Front. As a result, the factory visits to English Electric producing the Covenanter tank and Mechanization & Aero for the Crusader tank had to be cancelled.[128] The Soviet authorities did not want these two comparatively lightly armoured Cruiser tanks and instead requested that Britain provide Infantry tanks throughout the war.[129] High profile factory visits continued after tank week for those firms supplying the Soviet war effort, as shown when King George VI and Queen Elizabeth visited Vulcan Foundry during October 1941 to view the Matilda tank.[130]

Despite the Communist Party opposing industrial action, some shop stewards still applied the threat of industrial action for reasons linked to earnings and a suggestion of 'male chauvinism'. For example, in July 1942 a demand was made for the removal of all women from the Tank Erecting Shop at North British Locomotive because the women were deemed unsuitable and would lower the bonus.[131] In September, when the bonus was due to be shared among a team of men and women at North British Locomotive, the male tank workers argued that they had lost earnings by providing the women with extra assistance and threatened to walk out. The women eventually received a percentage.[132] To put this into context, disputes over wages accounted for 62 per cent of all strikes in the metal, engineering and shipbuilding industries from 1941 to 1944, plus a further 18 per cent directed towards the employment of particular workers. The remaining 20 per cent related to hours of work, working arrangements, rules and disciplinary measures and sympathetic action.[133]

The effect that industrial action had upon output was demonstrated during another strike at North British Locomotive, when Matilda production ceased in the three weeks until 19 December 1942.[134] As a consequence, the number of Matilda tanks delivered from this firm fell from 22 in November, and following an average of 25 for the previous 6 months, to just 9 during December. Following resolution of the strike the number of tanks delivered during January 1943 increased to 20, which was consistent with the planned reduction in the Matilda contract with production finishing in June.[135]

Later in 1943, Birmingham Railway encountered a period of industrial action for one week at the end of October that impacted upon the production of the Cromwell tank. While parent firm Leyland Motors had a Group Production Co-ordinator, they could not influence the industrial relations of the firms within the group. The managing director of Birmingham Railway, Harry Moyses, explained that the strike was due to a grievance relating to an increased rate of pay and resulted in the loss of over 76,000 production man-hours.[136] To estimate the effect that this strike had upon output, Leyland Motors recorded in November 1943 that approximately 5,640 man-hours were required to produce each Cromwell tank meaning that Birmingham Railway lost the production of approximately 13 tanks.[137]

The industrial action at Birmingham Railway meant that the Cromwell programme produced only 5 tanks during the strike week against 11 tanks delivered during the previous week.[138] However, this week-long stoppage had no discernible effect upon the upward trend of overall Cromwell production for the month. To illustrate, 24 Cromwell tanks were produced during September 1943, 46 tanks were delivered during October when the strike at Birmingham Railway occurred, and 108 tanks during November.[139] This continuing increase was due to the recent introduction of Leyland Motors to the assembly line with 32 tanks produced during November alone.[140] Therefore, while the strike at Birmingham Railway was individually significant, it should not be overestimated when compared to the expansion of the Cromwell programme over the same period.

During the final 12 months of war, the overall effect of strike action upon British industry diminished with the reduction in the number of working days lost from over 1 million in 1944 to nearly 528,000 in 1945.[141] This reduction was due to a number of factors including the effect of Defence Regulation 1AA that strengthened the Trade Unions' ability to deal with 'irresponsible elements'. In engineering, the majority of significant disputes were carried out by women and apprentices, many of whom were not unionized and therefore could not be controlled. Finally, engineering workers were concerned about the eventual return to peacetime conditions and did not want to lose work as a result of taking industrial action.[142]

Conclusion

British industry required large numbers of workers from rearmament until the end of the war to meet the expansion of capacity and achieve the different and changing government priorities and General Staff requirements for both quantity and quality output. The British workforce widened in size and participation with the conscription of men and women. The productive capabilities of workers became more efficient with the development of new skills and equipment. There was a general increase in the level of earnings and an improvement of welfare facilities within the factories. On the other hand, the experience of war production increased the likelihood of health problems and accidents occurring at the workplace and the threat or use of strike action to resolve disputes.

The opinion on the home front towards British industry, the war effort as a whole and the comparable situation in the United States was recorded by Mass Observation throughout the war. Rightful concern was raised regarding the efficiency of industry and whether the employers were profiteering from the emergency situation. Similar concerns were raised in the United States that firms were concentrating upon output at the expense of economy and efficiency. Public opinion towards industrial efficiency improved later in the war to reflect the greater quality of tanks under production and the benefits of Lend-Lease upon the British war effort. The impact and efficiency of American industry was noted by the British public with some concern that the United States was taking advantage of Britain in providing such quantities of aid. 'Tanks for Russia' week illustrated how the employers, the workforce, the unions and the general public could be encouraged to fully support a propaganda campaign because a successful outcome was desired by all concerned.

Various types of dilution were necessary to transfer skilled work to semi-skilled employees, while avoiding antagonizing the Trade Unions as experienced during the First World War. The method of subcontracting part of the work helped firms to overcome labour shortages, and also gained union support as subcontractors were able to retain their labour. Some firms were able to compensate for the lack of labour by transferring more 'boys' to the production line, and transferring skilled workers from the night-shift to make up the shortfall during the day-shift. The process of dilution continued, albeit against the concerns regarding the drop in efficiency following each transfer, as the best semi-skilled workers were upgraded first. An increase in output was achieved by the temporary transfer of skilled labour from either the Air Ministry or from another tank firm. While the call-up of workers for the armed forces drained manpower and disrupted factory operations, the combination of ill-health, poor worker performance and dealing with domestic issues could have a greater impact on the loss of employees.

The introduction and expansion of women into industry meant that additional lavatories and shared canteens had to be provided as part of an overall programme for greater welfare. The emergence of women also made it possible for some factories to extend shift work to 24 hours for seven-days-a-week, although female conscription could affect the administrative efficiency of a parent firm. While the expansion of welding in the workplace was important for increasing the skills of male and female workers alike, the process caused injuries and the toxic fumes and poor factory ventilation meant an increase in absenteeism.

The cancellation of summer holidays during 1940 was understandable in response to the heightened emphasis upon greater war production following the defeat of France. However, this could not be sustained for reasons of worker exhaustion and more importantly to reduce the number of industrial accidents. When factory holidays were taken in July 1941, tank output for that month fell by an average of 20 per cent. During July 1943, the effect upon tank output was even more striking when the forecast had not taken this foreseeable event into account. This lack of foresight was unacceptable to Prime Minister Churchill and despite reiterating the importance of the tank programme, the forecast for 1944 still ignored the impact that the summer holiday would have upon output.

The production forecasts could not account for the timing and length of industrial action nor the impact upon output. In one example, tank production was affected by a three-week strike at North British Locomotive at the end of 1942. However, this stoppage affected the declining and obsolete Matilda production so the effect upon the tank programme was minimal, as new tanks were coming into production during 1943. The loss of approximately 13 Cromwell tanks during the one-week strike at

Birmingham Railway during October 1943 was absorbed by the much greater output of the Cromwell programme as a whole.

Finally, a common issue discussed throughout this chapter related to worker's wages. To summarize, some public opinion thought that the workers were motivated more by the increase in wages than by supporting the war effort. However, wages were eroded by the increasing cost of living and the rise in earnings was more the consequence of working longer hours and overtime to meet production targets. While the dilution of semi-skilled workers was important, concern was raised regarding the effects that these supposedly less capable workers would have upon piecework earnings. In addition to the differences in pay between men and women generally, there was further financial inequality within the type of work carried out by women. Disputes over earnings remained the principal reason for taking industrial action, although 'male chauvinism' was sometimes used to justify the threat of strike action because of the perceived impact that women had upon lowering earnings.

5

Overcoming Production Problems and Delays

This chapter will discuss the difficulties that prevented British industry from achieving the required standard of production and examine how these problems were overcome to maintain high productivity. These factors will be illustrated by the experiences of British tank firms to meet the changes brought about by the General Staff discussed in Chapter 3, while comparing this situation to the aircraft industry and tank production overseas. Allied output improved in quality throughout the war by reducing the effects of material shortages, poor workmanship, inadequate factory inspection and the lack of spare parts. By contrast, the rigorous standards of German workmanship displayed earlier in the war deteriorated as their industry continued to be affected by these problems.[1] Industry in the United States achieved high levels of productivity by focusing their manufacturing upon the 'three charmed "S"s' of standardization, specialization and simplification.[2] British industry eventually developed these techniques as part of an overall increase in effectiveness and productivity.

To begin with, this chapter will show how the assembly line was affected by shortages of materials and components necessary to maintain a steady rate of production and complete the contract on time. The problems of reliability and mechanical breakdown involving many British tanks were due to both original design and poor workmanship. The standard of factory inspection for tank production was inadequate when compared to aircraft production that examined the work in progress. The front line vehicles were affected by the insufficient priority given to the supply of spare parts, until this programme was placed on an equal basis with the deliveries of completed tanks. Industry was given continuation orders for unwanted tanks because the replacement designs were not ready and a premature change-over would have caused inactive production and disrupted labour resources. The standardization of the British tank programme was completed by the eventual transfer of production to fewer designs that were reliable and required less servicing. The specialization of the tank programme was possible by concentrating production among fewer tank firms to deliver the standardized designs at a faster rate of output. The final element of greater productivity was achieved by the simplification of tank assembly that involved fewer man-hours to deliver the standardized tanks by the specialist firms.

Shortages of materials

Once a production order had been placed for munitions and the industrial capacity had expanded for the assembly firm to start production, there were a number of internal and external pressures which prevented each firm from maintaining the required level of output. Britain and Germany were both susceptible to the external pressure of enemy bombing, as discussed in Chapter 2. The internal pressures affected all the combatant nations, to include changes to the availability of labour reviewed in Chapter 4, and the unpredictable supply of raw materials and components. The British war effort was supported with food, fuels and materials from overseas allies, with the Soviet Union receiving similar assistance from the United States, Canada and Britain under the supply protocols. Germany was dependent upon imported metals and other resources from the occupied territories and trading partners like Sweden.[3] To cope with the shortages of assembly components and changes to the design with modifications, tank and aircraft firms had to remain flexible to ensure that output continued as uninterrupted as possible.[4]

The extent to which shortages in the supply of components delayed the completion of the contract can be demonstrated by the example of Leyland Motors for their total order of 654 Churchill tanks from June 1941 to September 1943. During the 28 months of production, the firm recorded delays in the receipt of bogie suspension units and final drives on 10 separate occasions. The effect that these shortages had upon tank output in each month was a 23 per cent fall in December 1941 and again during March and April 1942. A much greater decline of nearly 33 per cent was experienced during July 1942, again between November 1942 and January 1943, and finally from May to July 1943.[5] These shortages in production material delayed the completion of the Churchill contract by two months until September 1943, instead of July when Leyland Motors had expected the final tank to be delivered.[6]

One way of demonstrating the flexibility of industry to limit the disruption caused by material shortages was to produce the components in-house rather than relying upon subcontractors. In aircraft assembly, Gloster became 'self-contained' in the production of the Typhoon to avoid the difficulties experienced with the assembly of the Hurricane, which had been vulnerable to the shortages of components from other firms.[7] When the materials were produced by specialist firms, such as with armour plate, another way of keeping delays to a minimum was to take the matter outside the parent system. During May 1942, Crusader tank assembly firms Milners Safe and West's Gas both reported that the lack of armour plate was the main bottleneck in preventing them from meeting production targets.[8] In response, Sir Miles Thomas for parent firm Mechanization & Aero arranged for dependent firms to satisfy their armour plate requirements by making direct contact with the Ministry of Supply.[9]

While there were differences in the size of industrial capacity between Britain and the United States and Canada, North American production programmes was affected by the same supply pressures and shortages of material. During April 1941, British Colonel H. G. Hoare visited the Montreal Locomotive Works, which was a subsidiary of the American Locomotive Company, to inspect the general production of the M3 Medium tank. The visit revealed that the first hull and turret was expected from the General Steel Castings Corporation during May together with the first delivery of engines from another unnamed firm. However, shortages in the supply of transmissions caused a bottleneck to delay the likely delivery of the first production vehicle from June until the end of August 1941.[10] By comparison, Chrysler Corporation released their first M3 Medium tank during April 1941, because they produced their own transmissions in addition to supplying other firms.[11] During January 1942, President Roosevelt instructed industry to produce 45,000 tanks during the year. Despite increasing monthly output from 950 in January to over 4,850 tanks in December 1942, the annual total was still 20,000 vehicles below the target. While 45,000 tanks were greater than could be realistically expected, this shortfall was partly due to shortages of material, the irregular deliveries of material and an increased demand for spare parts.[12]

Poor workmanship

With the delivery of tanks to the front line delayed by shortages of materials and components, the armoured units experienced reliability problems with many of these vehicles because of inadequate workmanship and inspection in the factories. The pressure for increased output following the defeat of France in 1940 meant that these shortcomings continued on many British tanks during the North African campaign until 1943. The reliability problems faced by British tank units were alleviated with the receipt of tanks from the United States, however many of these vehicles also displayed initial problems of poor workmanship and inspection.

When considering the different Allied tank models used in North Africa, the superior armour and anti-tank firepower of the Matilda proved very effective against the Italians during Operation Compass and in the early battles against the Afrika Corps. However, the effectiveness of the Matilda tank was reduced by mechanical unreliability and limited operational range, and later by the increased armour and firepower on the Panzer tanks and by the forward deployment of German anti-tank guns.[13] The production of the Valentine tank was praised for being a dependable vehicle and mechanically superior to both the American Grant and Sherman. However, the fighting ability of the Valentine had become outdated due to the slower speed, inadequate firepower and insufficient armour.[14]

The majority of tank problems for British forces in North Africa related to Crusader production, with tank crews complaining how poor workmanship had caused unnecessary losses during combat.[15] Not all of the problems originating during production resulted in weakening operational capabilities. During January 1942, the Chief Mechanical Engineer for 13 Corps, Colonel Norman Berry, noted that while faulty casting had caused the suspension arms to break on a batch of new Crusader tanks, the workshops had repaired and returned the vehicles without affecting ongoing operations.[16] Furthermore, while mechanical breakdown had caused the majority of tank losses among a selection of Crusader tanks following Operation Crusader, the tank crews were more concerned about the danger of the German 88 mm anti-tank gun.[17]

With the Crusader tank facing criticism during February 1942, Sir Miles Thomas suggested to Lieutenant-General Giffard Martel at the Royal Armoured Corps that the firm's chief test driver be sent to North Africa to distinguish between necessary servicing and 'unnecessary tinkering'.[18] While Martel agreed to this action, he was convinced that the mechanical problems related to the fan drive and water pump after 200 miles and to oil leaks resulting from inadequate inspection during assembly.[19] Thomas was not prepared to attribute the problems to oil leaks because tests carried out on the Liberty engine at the experimental establishment in Farnborough, revealed that damage was caused when the engine was removed or overhauled in the field.[20] This argument was supported by a Ministry of Supply visit to North Africa around the same time, which noted the difficulty in changing the Crusader engine, compared to the speed at which the Grant tank engine could be replaced. However, this report criticized the design of the Crusader tank for the lack of attention given to the accessibility for maintenance.[21]

During June 1942, the Commander-in-Chief Middle East, General Claude Auchinleck, noted that Crusader faults had originated from 'careless assembly' in new Crusader tanks, including the inadequate tightening of nuts for oil joints. Auchinleck emphasized that these problems delayed operational requirements, when each tank had to be driven 150 miles before the faults became apparent and then required 200 workshop man-hours to make each tank fit for combat.[22] The Department of Tank Design recorded similar results during July 1942, when British tanks were tested over 1,000 miles to record when problems with the engine and transmission occurred under British environmental conditions. As expected the Valentine tank had the least problems with nearly 950 miles completed before a defect in the engine and no stoppages occurred in respect of the transmission. The Matilda tank produced a respectable average of 800 miles before both components failed, with the Covenanter tank travelling an average of 600 miles before mechanical failure. The rework scheme for the Churchill tank had doubled the mileage before an engine or transmission defect compared to the first production model, although the average mileage was still just short of 500 miles. The Crusader tank produced the worst test results with an average of 400 miles before a stoppage occurred. While this was greater than the distance reported by Auchinleck under desert conditions, the poor performance compared to the other tanks demonstrated that problems existed with the design and production of the Crusader tank.[23]

The concerns regarding the firepower, armour and especially reliability of British tanks in North Africa were given high profile attention, when they were discussed in parliament during the vote of no confidence debate on Churchill's premiership at the beginning of July 1942.[24] This was unwelcome publicity for the Crusader production firms, with Thomas arguing that many complaints were inaccurate and could not be corrected in public because of security reasons. In writing to the Crusader production group, Thomas stated that some Liberty engines were damaged at the dockside in Britain when the tanks were driven without water in the radiators. Thomas stated that while other causes contributed to mechanical failure, investigations in Britain revealed that the faults experienced in North Africa were reproduced when running the engine on a test bed without water for 10 minutes.[25]

Another cause of the problems with the Crusader tank was discovered upon arrival in North Africa when the vehicles had been inadequately prepared for the sea voyage, resulting in corrosion due to exposure and damage through vehicle collisions on deck.[26] The new Grant and Sherman tanks received in North Africa from the United States were also damaged by corrosion and collision sustained en route.[27] When Grant tanks were received in India with rusted components during 1942, the cause was attributed to the sea voyage together with the age and prior use of the vehicles.[28] These shipping problems occurred despite careful preparations in the United States beforehand that included coating the engines with oil, spraying the tank with a rust-preventative, and sealing both the engine and crew compartments with waterproof tape.[29]

The delivery of American tanks to British units in North Africa provided greater firepower, increased armour protection and overall reliability. These qualities had the benefit of improving the fighting spirit of the troops when compared to the problems in using some British tanks.[30] However, this front line experience does not take into account the workshop repair that was needed before these tanks were sent forward to be used by tank crews for the first time. The Grant tank has been described by the US official history as 'hurriedly designed' following German success in Europe during 1940, and was produced without adequate tests.[31] During February 1943, the Deputy Director-General of Fighting Vehicles at the Ministry of Supply, Colonel William Blagden, reported on the problems identified with 38 new Grant and Sherman tanks received in North Africa. These faults were a combination of excessive haste in production and inadequate inspection at the factory, together with the corrosion and damage caused during shipping.[32]

The 38 tanks examined revealed a combined total of 146 defects relating to manufacturing faults during factory assembly, with the majority occurring in the electrical system, the engine and the fighting compartment. The problems incurred during the sea voyage caused an additional 35 defects with moisture affecting the engine, the final drive and transmission, the electrical system and the fighting compartment. Finally, there were a further 15 defects from the internal and external damage caused by the collisions on deck.[33] A General Motors technician stationed in Cairo came to similar conclusions regarding the workmanship on other American tanks, when he recorded the misalignment of bolt holes and that some bolts had not been properly tightened. The technician concluded that rigid inspection was necessary at the assembly works especially when he had noted 84 separate defects on one tank.[34] These defects delayed the supply of Grant and Sherman tanks to British armoured units by three weeks while corrections were carried out at the base workshops.[35]

The additional work required on the American Stuart tank before being provided to front line units revealed problems of ergonomic design rather than poor workmanship or inspection. Colonel Blagden reported that the fighting compartment was cramped with insufficient head, leg or elbow room for the commander and gunner and the prospect of rapid evacuation was hampered by the shape and size of the turret escape hatches. The short distance from the tank floor to the turret roof meant that the commander was exposed from the waist upwards and there was no communication between the driver and commander. Blagden expressed the reluctance to remedy these problems because it involved cutting into new production tanks, however workshop action was necessary to provide the front line with suitable equipment.[36]

Inadequate inspection

The task of inspecting war production was particularly daunting given the overall pressure for increased output and the competing demands of the different services. While the mechanical and electrical components used in tank production shared similar functions with motorized vehicles, it was not possible to ensure that the thousands of assembly parts had been fitted correctly. The system of tank factory inspection was deemed inadequate by Martel during February 1942 when discussing with Thomas the problems with the Crusader programme. These comments were later repeated in July, when the Deputy Chief of the Imperial General Staff, Lieutenant-General Ronald Weeks stated to Thomas that tank firms were responsible for perfecting the system.[37] In an attempt to improve the production and the reputation of the Crusader group, Thomas emphasized to each firm that every tank leaving the factory must be mechanically capable of achieving the operational requirements of the army.[38]

There were also shortcomings in the method of official inspection in the factories when the Ministry of Supply only carried out a final inspection of each vehicle, leaving faults on the production line unnoticed.[39] This system continued until at least 1944, when Thomas rightfully argued that this method was in direct contrast to aircraft production that identified faults by examining the work in progress.[40] This technique was used on the production of the Lancaster and Halifax bombers where the main components were constructed and tested as separate units to be passed by the inspection staff. The individually completed sections were then transported from the component factories to the assembly works for the final stage of production.[41]

The limitation in the standard of Ministry of Supply inspection in factories was partly due to shortages in the number of available inspectors. During a meeting of the fourth Tank Board in July 1942, the Director-General of Tank Supply, Sir George Usher, highlighted the difficulties in retaining inspection staff when many good inspectors had been transferred to the Merchant Service as marine engineers.[42] To improve the level of inspection, the chairman of the Supply Council, Sir William Rootes, confirmed at the August Tank Board meeting that the Treasury had authorized the appointment of 300 additional inspectors, and the upgrading of 80 vehicle drivers.[43] The inspection situation improved with the formation of the new Armoured Fighting Vehicle Division under the chairmanship of Commander Micklem from September 1942 discussed in Chapter 2. This created a Director of Fighting Vehicle Inspection, with responsibilities to ensure that both the official and factory inspection of finished tanks were satisfactory.[44]

In December 1940 there were almost 900 inspection staff employed at the Tank Department, compared to 160 designers and 140 central administration staff. By June 1943, the number of inspectors had increased to 1,650, whereas the design section had greatly expanded to 745 and administration to 450 staff. As a result, the proportion of inspection staff fell from 75 per cent of the total number employed at the Tank Department in December 1940 to 58 per cent in June 1943. The increased emphasis upon the design section had doubled the size from just 13 to 26 per cent over the same period.[45]

Comparing the different rates of growth in the inspection and the design sections against the expansion in tank output from December 1940 to June 1943 can partly explain why faulty tanks were released to armoured units. Figure 5.1 illustrates how the gap between the numbers of tanks produced every six months and the number of official inspectors available to check for problems at the factories, widened considerably relative to the position in December 1940. The growth of the design staff was much stronger over the whole period and concluded with an extraordinary increase after December 1942. This improvement in official tank design resources provided the fifth Tank Board in November 1943 with details of the successful Centurion tank for the post-war programme.[46]

Despite the combined efforts of industry and the Ministry of Supply, improvements to the standard of production and inspection took time to achieve. By February 1943, Crusader tanks were still arriving in North Africa with faults that indicated carelessness in production and inspection. Of the 41 Crusader tanks examined from a number of firms, 30 tanks needed between 200 and 300 workshop man-hours

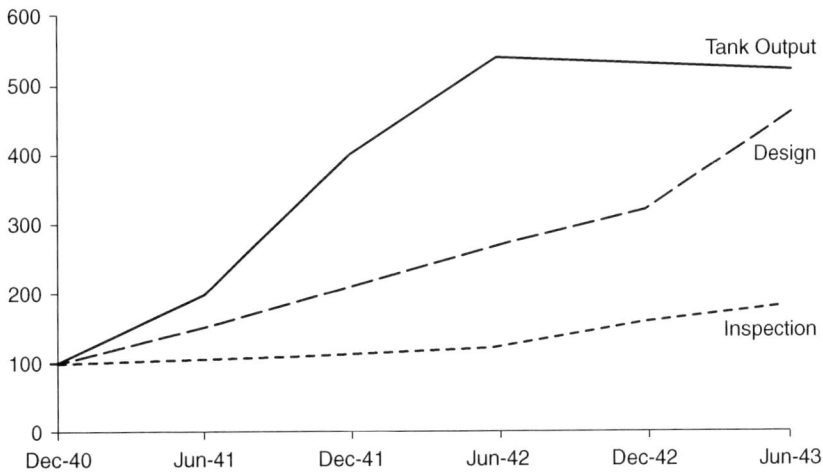

Figure 5.1 Index of the number of Tank Department design and inspection employees compared to the expansion of tank output from December 1940 to June 1943

Sources: The National Archives, AVIA 46/188, 'Numerical Strength of Tank Department', draft official history narrative by D. Hay, after 1950, p. 114; 'Monthly Deliveries of Infantry and Cruiser Tanks by Firms, 1939–1943', pp. 269–71.

each to correct production faults, with the remaining 11 tanks between 300 and 500 man-hours.[47] To put this into context, Mechanization & Aero reported that 6,050 machining and assembly man-hours were needed to produce each Crusader tank during 1943.[48] While there were variations in man-hours between the different firms, Mechanization & Aero would have incurred 248,050 hours to produce 41 Crusader tanks. By taking an average of the time necessary to repair the faults on all 41 tanks, a total of 11,425 workshop hours would have been required, which was less than 5 per cent of the total man-hours used in production at Mechanization & Aero.

By November 1942, the Minister of Supply Sir Andrew Duncan was expecting Crusader production to fall short of the 2,465 target for that year by 125 tanks. This shortfall was due to a number of separate factors including the importance of improved workmanship and inspection. The other factors accounting for this reduced output were the lack of armour plate, the shortage of supplies from the United States and that spare parts were taken from the production line to supply the tanks in North Africa.[49]

Insufficient priority for spare parts

The priority and distribution of spare parts should not be overlooked within the overall industrial programme and for the importance of keeping front line equipment in continuous working order. As Director-General of Army Equipment from 1941 and as Deputy Chief of the Imperial General Staff from 1942, Lieutenant-General Weeks highlights how the discussions over spare parts became very contentious when he recalls: 'I think I listened to more angry words about spare parts than almost any other subject.' Weeks used his General Staff experience to provide a generally realistic assessment of the 'life history of a spare part'. This included being regarded as a nuisance in the factory, the purpose being superseded by the demands on the production line, possibly being lost during transit or poor record keeping, never being used for its intended purpose, or simply forgotten about.[50]

The operational difficulties encountered by German motorized and mechanized units during the war demonstrated the consequences of not receiving enough or the right type of spare parts. The mobility of German units was hampered by the failing of industry to adequately support the mechanical requirements of the front line. The supply of spare parts was impeded by the logistical priority to provide fuel and ammunition and by distribution errors that shipped the wrong parts to the various units. This last problem was partly due to the many different vehicles being deployed, including the necessity to integrate captured French and Soviet equipment into German units.[51]

A discussion on policy relating to spare parts for North Africa was held in May 1941 during the second meeting of the short-lived Tank Parliament reviewed in Chapter 3. The Minister of Supply Duncan confirmed that the demand for greater output had directed spare parts to the production line, rather than issuing this equipment as spares to the tank units. A recent increase in the issuing of spares had not improved matters on the front line because the experience in North Africa had shown that more spare parts were necessary than previously estimated.[52] At a meeting of the second Tank Board during July 1941, the Director of Armoured Fighting Vehicles, Major-General Vyvyan Pope, argued that the fighting in North Africa fully justified the production of Crusader tank spares at the expense of new tank output.[53] However, as discussed in Chapter 3, this was contrary to the policy of greater tank output and industry would take time to react to any increase in spares production.

The British campaign in North Africa was also affected by the shortage of spare parts from the United States for the Grant tanks used during the Battle of Gazala in May 1942. In a post-action report in July, Averill Harriman from the US Embassy in London confirmed to the Under Secretary of War that the field workshops had cannibalized 65 new Grant tanks to distribute the components as spare parts. This was required before the start of battle to keep the remaining vehicles operational, and again during June when 15 tank engines were removed and sent forward to repair those tanks disabled on the front. In relation to tank maintenance, Harriman stated that the Grant tool kits were lacking track adjusting tools and special wrenches, and that they only had 3 handbooks for each regiment of 36 tanks.[54]

A long-term solution to improve the supply of British spare parts was highlighted by George Usher at the third Tank Board in January 1942, as the Cruiser tank programme would eventually become more standardized with the Cromwell tank.[55] However, Cromwell production did not start until the end of 1942 and mass production was not reached until a year later. As a result, in October 1942 the spares programme for current tank models was adjusted to ensure that firms would ultimately supply spares simultaneously with new tanks.[56] The transformation of the tank programme to meet the greater priority for spares was shown at Mechanization & Aero from 1939 to 1944. The total sale of spare parts on the Ministry of Supply trading account was just 4 per cent in 1939 with tanks, engines and gear boxes making up the remainder. From 1940 to 1942, the proportion of spare parts grew from 12 to 22 per cent of total sales. Spares accounted for 37 per cent in 1943 and then 45 per cent in 1944, bringing the supply of spares almost level with tanks, engines and gear boxes.[57]

The supply of aircraft spares also fluctuated over the course of the war to meet the demands placed upon the programme. During the Battle of Britain, the production of spare parts was reduced so that industry could deliver more aircraft to front line squadrons. This was similar to the policy of providing spare parts to tank production to supply more vehicles for the North African campaign. From 1942, it was more economical to allocate some of the resources used for spares production to aircraft repair instead of aircraft production because more aircraft were provided to the air force. Some firms, such as Vickers-Armstrongs, allocated more resources to producing spare parts than to the production of new aircraft.[58]

The shortage of spare parts for armoured units based in Britain came under top level scrutiny in July 1941, when the supply Defence Committee noted that 26 per cent of tanks in static workshops or with units were recorded as 'unfit for action'.[59] When this number deteriorated to 27 per cent in the following week, Prime Minister Churchill understandably wanted this reduced and judged that the number of tanks deemed unfit should not exceed 10 per cent. Churchill instructed the Secretary of State for War, David Margesson, to put forward proposals to remedy the situation.[60] Margesson was considered a 'Chamberlainite' and one of the 'Guilty Men' blamed for the policy of appeasement and the inadequate preparation for the military campaigns in 1940. Later he was deemed to have been an ineffective Secretary of State particularly in relation to the defence of Singapore.[61]

While these opinions are not disputed, Margesson identified the departments or units responsible for reducing the high proportion of unfit tanks with a series of common sense recommendations. First, the Ministry of Supply should achieve the balance between the production of tanks and ancillary equipment, which industry was working towards from late 1942. Secondly, the War Office should contact the manufacturers direct for tanks awaiting spare parts for more than 14 days. Thirdly, the unit workshops would increase the speed at which they affected repairs with the proper allocation of technicians, including taking skilled labour from industry as highlighted in the last chapter. Fourthly, improvements in maintenance would be achieved once the crews had become better skilled in operating their tanks, as discussed below. Finally, Margesson suggested that a complete overhaul in static workshops should occur after a certain mileage and that ongoing repairs be carried out in unit workshops when the spares and skilled personnel position had improved.[62]

Margesson's suggestions took time before becoming effective as unfit tanks increased by one point to 28 per cent in September 1941, although the tanks awaiting spares after 14 days had reduced from 10 per cent in June to just 3 per cent.[63] By September 1942, the situation improved when the number of unfit tanks accounted for 21 per cent with a further reduction to 18 per cent by November.[64] This remained unchanged by March 1943 and was still greater than the 10 per cent sought by Churchill.[65] This highlights the conflict between demanding the mass production of tanks on the one hand without an adequate spares policy and still maintaining a sufficient quantity of battleworthy tanks within armoured units on the other.

Continuation orders and cancellations

At some point during the manufacturing process the authorities had to decide whether to place a continuation order for the equipment under assembly or interrupt the production run by cancelling the contract for a new design. Even the decision to maintain production of an existing model could cause disruption when design modifications were incorporated based upon operational experience. In essence, the decision had to balance the loss in output by interrupting the existing production run, against the anticipated increase in quality through changes to the design or introduction of a new model.[66] For the manufacturers, continuity in production permitted the firm to devise production strategies that included ordering the right amount of material supplies and organizing the appropriate machine tools and labour.[67]

Historians have argued that the decisions to maintain rather than cancelling the production of obsolete British tanks during the first half of the war affected the fighting capabilities of front line units during 1941 and 1942 and even as late as 1944 in Normandy.[68] While this is credible, this does not fully appreciate the decision making at the time, which had to measure the effect upon tank output, labour resources and the supply of materials when an obsolete tank programme was cancelled. In the case of the Valentine tank, continuation orders were necessary because of the political decision to provide these tanks to the Soviet war effort with production finishing in May 1944.[69]

Between December 1940 and April 1941, English Electric and Leyland Motors both received two continuation orders for the Covenanter tank.[70] This was not a misguided expression of confidence in an unreliable vehicle, as the second Tank Board stated that continuation orders would ensure that the firms incurred 'no gap in production' before transferring capacity to the new designs expected during 1943.[71] An important reason for avoiding inactive production was the retention of labour, rather than having workers mandatorily sent to another firm that required the same manpower. Sir Miles Thomas on behalf of the Crusader production group stated these concerns to the Ministry of Labour and National Service during August 1942, when discussing the upcoming transfer of production to the Cavalier or Centaur tank. Thomas raised objections to losing any skilled labour because these workers were essential to complete the change-over to the new tools and jigs required for the machining and assembly of the later tank designs.[72] The risk of inactive production prevented the Covenanter programme from being cancelled outright, although the third Tank Board emphasized in August 1941 that this tank was unsatisfactory and contracts should be completed as quickly as possible.[73] As a result, Leyland Motors was immediately requested to raise their deliveries to 40 per month, although the highest individual output achieved was 35 tanks during August 1942.[74]

This continuation policy was also applied to the Churchill programme during 1942, when George Usher argued in January that following completion of the original 3,000 vehicles a further 1,000 tanks were necessary to ensure that a break in production was avoided.[75] Major-General Weeks wrote to the Tank Board chairman Geoffrey Burton to express his concerns regarding this proposal for a variety of justifiable reasons. These included the following: the high percentage of unfit Churchill tanks, the incapability of the maintenance department to repair many vehicles at the same time and the large number of the mechanical problems due to defects in design.[76] This last complaint necessitated the 'rework' programme, the benefits of which will be discussed later. Burton conveyed the same concerns to the managing director of Vauxhall Motors, C. J. Bartlett, as the parent firm for the Churchill production group.[77] When a break in production was discussed again during the next Tank Board meeting in February 1942, Major-General Macready stated that the General Staff could not use more than 3,000 Churchill tanks in any event. As a result, the Tank Board agreed that no additional Churchill tanks be ordered and that Vauxhall Motors should attend a special meeting to discuss the situation.[78] A compromise was reached at the meeting in February for an order of 500 additional Churchill tanks, instead of the 1,000 requested, to avoid a break in production and to prepare for the expected transfer of Churchill capacity to a later tank design.[79]

The completion of 3,500 Churchill tanks was expected during May 1943, at which point industrial capacity would change-over to start production on the

Cromwell tank.[80] While the Churchill continuation order was meant to prevent a loss in output, by August 1942 the Secretary of State for War P. J. Grigg and Minister of Supply Duncan anticipated that the change-over would still sacrifice the equivalent of 400 production tanks.[81] This was accepted by the operations Defence Committee, who authorized the detrimental impact of the change-over upon overall tank output.[82] General Staff policy towards limiting the Churchill programme remained for the rest of 1942, with Weeks advising the Armoured Fighting Vehicle Liaison Committee in December that production should cease at 3,500.[83] The technical problems with the Cromwell prototype delayed the start of production with the result that the Churchill continuation orders became the less favoured but only viable option.

In weighing up the delay of the Cromwell programme, Grigg and Duncan estimated during January 1943 that Vauxhall Motors would not start Cromwell production until early 1944, which was four to five months after completing the Churchill contract. Similar to the earlier concerns raised by Thomas, this break would cause a reduction of the labour force in those firms waiting to change-over to the Cromwell tank. To minimize this risk and limit any gap in production, a further order for 500 Churchill tanks with the latest modifications in design was jointly recommended by Grigg and Duncan.[84] The War Cabinet approved this decision therefore retaining Vauxhall Motors on the Churchill programme until the end of the war and increasing the total order to 4,000 tanks.[85] This was discussed at the next meeting of the fifth Tank Board later in January, with the General Staff stipulating that these 500 extra vehicles be fitted with the new 75 mm medium velocity gun currently undergoing trials.[86]

In addition to the risk of lost output and inactive or reduced labour resources, cancelling a tank order in preparation for a later tank design could also affect how component suppliers provided the material to finish the original contract. In February 1942, it was agreed that London, Midland and Scottish would cancel their remaining Covenanter order at Crewe and redistribute the material requirements between Leyland Motors and English Electric.[87] The final material for Covenanter assembly should have arrived at Leyland Motors by November 1942 when production was due to change-over to the new Centaur tank. However, this material did not arrive until January 1943 because of an understandable shift in focus by the suppliers to provide materials for the Centaur tank, at the expense of residual Covenanter requirements. Therefore, the expansion of Centaur production was impeded for two months until January 1943, while Leyland Motors had incomplete Covenanters taking up valuable floor space.[88] English Electric likely had the same problem when the mass production of the Centaur tank only began when the Covenanter order had completed in January 1943.[89]

Standardization with fewer tank designs

The transfer to quality tank production from 1943 discussed in Chapter 3, resulted from the emphasis upon standardization as one of the 'charmed "S"s' of greater productivity. The decision to standardize production among the latest Churchill,

Cromwell and Comet tanks was because they were intrinsically reliable, had reduced servicing requirements in the field and could be produced in large numbers. British aircraft production had already standardized and simplified the mass production of the bomber programme by December 1941 without sacrificing quality.[90] By comparison, the German war programmes were the least coherent with naval production fluctuating between capital ships and submarines, aircraft production emphasizing anti-aircraft guns at the expense of fighters, and an army programme that lacked standardization and was too sophisticated.[91] On the other hand, the United States and the Soviet Union demonstrated how the standardization of war production could be successfully applied on a much larger scale with the output of vast numbers of Medium tanks.[92]

The poor reputation of reliability for British tanks produced during the first half of the war was overturned from 1943, when tank firms received operational feedback which confirmed that quality production for the latest tanks had been achieved. In March 1943, a technical report on the North African campaign stated that the reworked Churchill tanks of the 25th Army Tank Brigade had completed 400 to 500 miles, without the mechanical problems experienced with the earlier models.[93] By May 1943, the Churchill tanks within this brigade had completed an average of over 500 miles across mountainous terrain and over 700 miles over the Tunisian countryside.[94] During June 1943, Lieutenant-General Weeks wrote to Vauxhall Motors to emphasize how the Churchill tank had contributed towards victory in North Africa. Weeks praised the ability of the Churchill to climb very steep slopes and that the tank had demonstrated the prerequisite reliability necessary to give the infantry the support when they needed it the most. In contrast to the criticism received earlier in the war, Weeks gave special tribute to those involved in production for the quality of the workmanship.[95]

During the Italian campaign, Eighth Army Commander Lieutenant-General Oliver Leese confirmed to the War Office that the Churchill tank had performed well under sustained anti-tank fire during the attack and breaching of the Adolf Hitler Line in May 1944. Leese reported how the combination of this armour protection, the ability to cross rough terrain and the effectiveness of the six-pounder gun, gave the Churchill tank crews a great deal of confidence.[96] When mechanical or production defects required the attention of the manufacturers, the tank was sent back to Britain for examination and correction. During the Normandy campaign, the welding joints of the glacis plate of a Heavy Churchill tank failed when hit by a 150 mm high explosive shell. This forced the plate into the fighting compartment injuring the driver and gunner. The tank was returned to Britain for inspection by the Department of Tank Design and Vauxhall Motors. Meanwhile, the field workshops modified the remaining Heavy Churchill tanks by welding a piece of armour plate to both sides of the glacis as a support.[97] By December 1944, permanent modifications were introduced to new production tanks by increasing the quantity of the weld metal on the internal and external joints of the glacis plate. Tank crews identified these changes as the modified tanks were marked with the letter 'K' instead of 'H'.[98]

The combat performance of British tanks was questioned once again during the Normandy battles forcing Field Marshal Montgomery to prohibit the circulation of 'alarmist reports' issued outside the regular distribution channels, in order to avoid undermining morale.[99] This fear originated from the combat differences of the Cromwell and Sherman tanks compared to the better armed and armoured German tanks. Montgomery's concern was that troops were 'developing a "Tiger" and "Panther" complex – when every tank becomes one of these types: compared to the old days when every gun was an 88mm', highlighted during North African campaign.[100] To put this 'complex' into perspective, only about 30 per cent of German tanks during the Normandy campaign could be considered superior to standard Allied tanks, with the Tiger tank accounting for only 5 per cent.[101] Given this numerical disparity, Montgomery was right to take action against 'alarmist reports' as he believed that better tactics were the key to defeating German armour through outflanking manoeuvres and wherever possible using the 17-pounder gun.[102] Improved tactics were even more important when the close proximity of the enemy in Normandy meant that the armour protection of any tank was inadequate against a heavily armed opponent. However, Allied tanks in north-west Europe had greater operational capabilities than German armour. This meant that the Allies had superiority in the quantity and quality of tanks to achieve an offensive strategy, while German tanks were mostly limited to a defensive role.

The operational capabilities of the Cromwell tank was shown in July 1944 when Leyland Motors received information that the tank had performed very satisfactorily in Normandy and notices were posted throughout the factories to inform the workers.[103] Following the breakout from Normandy, Major-General Gerald Verney commanding the 7th Armoured Division, extended this praise for the ability of the Cromwell to travel long distances without serious maintenance or breakdown. In a letter to the Director, Royal Armoured Corps, Major-General Raymond Briggs, which was later forwarded to Birmingham Railway Carriage & Wagon Company, Verney stated that despite being in continuous action for three weeks with little chance for maintenance, the rate of mechanical failure was extremely low. Verney wanted the workers involved in the production of the Cromwell to be informed of the progress achieved during recent combat.[104] The general reliability of the Cromwell tank without lengthy maintenance during prolonged operations did not reduce the need for spare parts, as shown when Birmingham Railway received new orders in April and August 1944, and January 1945.[105]

In November 1944, the Department of Tank Design stated that the overall increase in reliability and efficiency of British tanks over the past three years was partly due to the improvements in the requirement and standard of crew maintenance.[106] This was consistent with the expectations of Margesson during July 1941, when he reported on the different methods to reduce the number of unfit tanks. The changing requirements for maintenance on British tanks during the war is shown by the different instruction books of the earlier Valentine and Churchill tanks compared to the later Cromwell tank. Both the Valentine and Churchill tanks required the gear box oil to be checked on a weekly basis and changed after 2,000 miles. This was arguably too high even allowing for the greater reliability of the Valentine tank. After checking the engine oil each day, the difference in quality between the two tank engines was shown by the requirement for a complete oil change every 500 miles for the Churchill Bedford engine, whereas the Valentine General Motors engine was every 1,000 miles.[107] The periodic checks were retained for the later Cromwell tank for 1945, although the gear box required an oil change at the more reasonable 1,000 miles. The change in engine oil increased to every 1,500 miles, thus reflecting the greater reliability of the Meteor engine.[108]

In order to give British tank production some greater context, it should be noted that pre- and post-war motor cars in Britain had similar or even greater servicing requirements. In 1939, the Austin Ten could have required a complete change of engine oil after 1,000 miles, as part of the after sales care recommended by the manufacturer.[109] After the war, the engine and gear box on the Riley 100 H.P. required an initial oil change after the first 500 miles, following which the engine oil was replaced every 1,500 miles and the gear box oil every 5,000 miles.[110] With the mechanical components used in British tank and motor manufacturing having basic similarities, the standard of tank design, production and maintenance was quite remarkable when considering the vast differences in size, weight and operational usage. The problems of the Crusader tank and the Liberty engine earlier in the war were avoided because the greater reliability of the later tanks reduced the need for extensive field repair and maintenance which could contaminate the tank components.[111]

The effectiveness of British tanks during the campaign in north-west Europe was summarized by Montgomery during February 1945. This commentary unfavourably compared the performance of German tanks during the Ardennes offensive in December 1944 to the earlier capabilities of British and American armour during September as highlighted by Verney. Montgomery claimed that the German offensive would have reached the Meuse in 36 hours had they been equipped with British tanks, while 21st Army Group would not have cut off the Pas de Calais region in 8 days after the Normandy campaign had they been equipped with German armour.[112] In response, tank veteran Peter Beale criticizes both Montgomery and the quality of British tanks, by stating that the statement was 'not only farcical in the eyes of the tank crews in the north-west Europe campaign, but criminal'.[113] This comment has merit when considering the direct combat comparisons between the German heavy tanks and the British Cruiser or American Medium tanks. However, Beale misses the central point of Montgomery's statement which considers the different operational requirements of the two campaigns, together with the numerical and mechanical superiority of Allied armour. Lieutenant-General Martel argues that German heavy tanks were best suited for defence and lacked 'the necessary mobility' for the operational requirements of the Ardennes offensive.[114] Furthermore, British armour averaged a greater mileage per day in the pursuit of German forces from the Seine to Brussels, than the German Panzer units of 1940 achieved from the Meuse to the English Channel.[115] As for American tanks, General George Patton criticized the slow speed and poor range of the Tiger and Panther, and claimed that the Third Army would have sustained 100 per cent road losses had it used the Tiger on the route to the Moselle River during September 1944.[116]

Specialization with fewer tank firms

The second method that contributed towards British industry achieving greater productivity, and another one of the 'charmed "S"s', was the specialization of tank assembly from 1943. Rather than introducing any new firms to tank assembly, the production experience and techniques were concentrated among fewer tank firms to specialize in carrying out the final assembly. These changes improved the quality of workmanship in the British tank industry to complement the standardization of production among the battleworthy Churchill, Cromwell and Comet tanks. This was a reversal of the problems earlier in the war, which was dominated by the production of too many unreliable and unsatisfactory tanks in response to the demand for increased output.

Between 1943 and 1945 the number of firms working on tank assembly fell from 27 to 19 following the cancellation of the Matilda and Crusader contracts. When the Valentine programme was reduced to just Vickers-Armstrongs and following the cancellation of the Covenanter, Cavalier and Centaur programmes, a further contraction was achieved to just 11 firms for the production of the remaining Churchill, Cromwell and Comet tanks. For those firms now specializing in tank production, the Churchill programme continued with 6 firms, namely Broom & Wade, Charles Roberts, Dennis, Gloucester Railway Carriage & Wagon Company, Newton Chambers and the parent firm Vauxhall Motors. The Cromwell programme consisted of Birmingham Railway, English Electric, John Fowler, Leyland Motors and Metropolitan-Cammell. Of these firms, Birmingham Railway produced the short-lived Challenger tank, whereas the other 4 firms transferred to the later Comet programme.[117] The aircraft industry went through a similar process of concentration in which the main design firms dealt with ongoing modifications, while the mass production of the well-established designs was given to the better resourced state owned factories.[118]

The focus upon fewer tank models permitted the surplus industrial capacity to specialize on tank conversions or other non-tank work in support of the war effort. For example, Beyer Peacock, London, Midland and Scottish, North British Locomotive and Vulcan Foundry all returned to their core industry of locomotive production, as discussed in the next chapter, while Fodens and Morris Commercial Cars returned to wheeled vehicles. Mechanization & Aero, Morris Industries Exports and West's Gas converted completed Crusader or Centaur tanks to an anti-aircraft role. Ruston-Bucyrus transferred to engineering stores, and Harland & Wolff concentrated upon Admiralty work again. In addition to the production of Cromwell and Comet tanks, Metropolitan-Cammell also worked on the Valentine and Sherman Duplex-Drive conversions, while Birmingham Railway produced engineering stores together with the Cromwell and Challenger tanks.[119]

One of the problems for assembly firms following a substantial and sudden reduction of production orders, such as the Centaur programme, was the storing of materials and completed tanks that were now surplus to requirements. In response to this concern, Mechanization & Aero stated that unless the excess material already received for the diminishing Centaur programme was taken away, they would refuse to accept any future deliveries. To avoid a blockage at the works, the Ministry of Supply located an appropriate site with suitable rail and road facilities in Burton-on-Trent, which was not already connected to the tank programme to hold the unwanted material. A similar scheme had been arranged for storing completed Crusader tanks awaiting conversion at locations as diverse as Dudley Zoo, the Caledonian Meat Market, Tate & Lyle and the British Reinforced Concrete Company.[120]

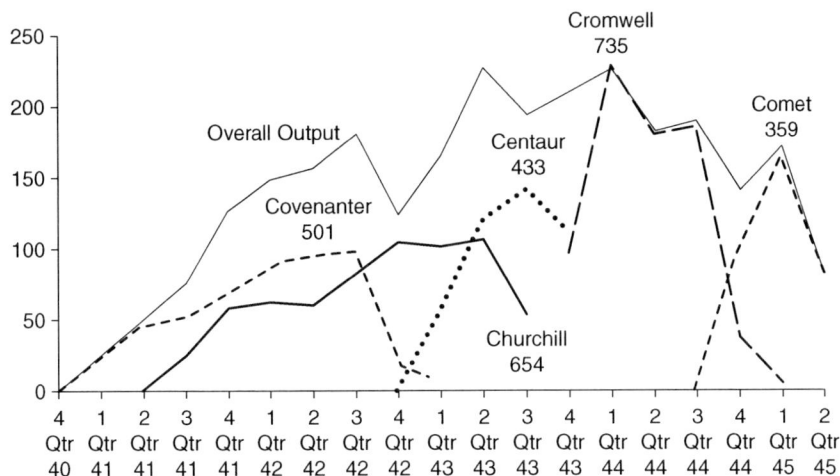

Figure 5.2 Tank output by Leyland Motors, December 1940 to May 1945

Sources: TNA, AVIA 46/188, 'Monthly Deliveries of Infantry and Cruiser Tanks', pp. 269–71; British Commercial Vehicle Museum, Leyland Motors, M632 143/5, General Manager's Meetings, 1941–3; M631 143/5, General Manager's Meetings, 1944–5.

The level of increased productivity through the improvement in techniques and experience is shown in Figure 5.2 for the quarterly output of Leyland Motors for five tank programmes from December 1940 until May 1945. The graph demonstrates that production of the later Cromwell and Comet tanks expanded faster and in greater numbers over a shorter period than the earlier tank programmes, while still affected by material shortages.[121] In respect of the total output for each quarter, Leyland Motors delivered almost as many Cromwell tanks during the first quarter of 1944 than the combined output of Churchill and Centaur tanks during the second quarter of 1943. Similarly, Comet output during the first quarter of 1945 nearly reached the combined deliveries of the Covenanter and Churchill during the third quarter of 1942. The significance of these examples was that only front line tanks were produced during 1944 and 1945, whereas the earlier years included the output of unbattleworthy Covenanter and Centaur tanks.

The immediate transfer from the Centaur to the Cromwell tank during the fourth quarter of 1943 was due to the design similarities between the two models, which avoided a costly change-over period and resulted in a sustainably high output of Cromwell tanks. The Comet tank had a number of design and production differences including a welded hull construction, which required specific jigs or 'manipulators' as discussed in Chapter 3. While this change in assembly organization resulted in an initial loss of output, Leyland Motors reported that labour resources had not been affected by the change-over and as seen in Figure 5.2 a high rate of production was quickly established.[122] The end to the war in Europe accounts for the decline in Comet deliveries during the second quarter of 1945.

Simplification with fewer man-hours

The final method in which British industry achieved greater productivity, and in keeping with the last of the 'charmed "S"s', was through the simplification of the manufacturing process with each of the later tank designs requiring fewer man-hours to complete. There are difficulties when using man-hours to measure industrial effort, especially when considering the differences in the size of the order, the available capacity and the experience of the firms producing the equipment. This was demonstrated in aircraft production during 1941 and 1942, when the assembly of the Spitfire Mark Vc at the Supermarine works incurred 13,000 man-hours, compared to 10,400 hours at the larger and more experienced Castle Bromwich factory.[123] Furthermore, improvements in production organization resulted in reducing the 'direct man-hours' necessary to assemble the Lancaster airframe from 51,000 man-hours in 1941 to 20,000 by 1945.[124]

In tank production, the overall machining and assembly for each Centaur tank at Leyland Motors required approximately 5,600 man-hours compared to 6,900 hours for the Covenanter, and 6,050 hours for the Crusader at Mechanization & Aero. The reductions in man-hours to assemble the 28 ton Centaur is in contrast to the increase in weight when compared to the 18 ton Covenanter and 20 ton Crusader.[125] This was similarly experienced in aircraft production with the heavier aircraft requiring less manpower per pound of weight than to assemble the lighter models.[126] Leyland Motors reported during November 1943 that the 28 ton Cromwell tank required an extra 40 hours assembly time compared to the Centaur, due to the additional work to prepare and install the Meteor engine.[127] Despite the additional work on the Cromwell, the total requirement of 5,640 man-hours was still less than the Covenanter and Crusader, and as shown in Figure 5.2, Leyland Motors delivered more Cromwell tanks over a shorter period.

When comparing these results to the production of Panzer tanks, German industry was particularly inefficient until the tank programme had converted to 'flow production' in 1943. This meant a reduction in the number of man-hours necessary to assemble the Panzer Mark III from 4,000 to 2,000.[128] Despite this improvement in productivity, by 1943 the Panzer III was no longer an effective front line tank, especially when compared to the Cromwell, Sherman or Soviet equivalents. Overall, the ability of British industry to produce operationally effective Cromwell tanks in large numbers improved the prospect of increasing output in response to the demands of the front line, such as following the invasion of north-west Europe in June 1944.

When considering the attritional nature of the Normandy campaign, the loss of over 400 tanks during Operation Goodwood did not cause equipment shortages for front line units, although morale and confidence did suffer.[129] Many of the British and American tanks lost by the 7th, 11th and Guards Armoured Divisions during the operation were recovered and repaired in the field for future operations.[130] Those tanks which could not be repaired immediately were shipped back to Britain in the hope that they could be rebuilt, as shown when a number of Cromwell tanks were sent to Leyland Motors during July and August. However, the close proximity of the Normandy battles meant that Leyland Motors considered the majority of these tanks to be beyond repair, as the damage was too severe.[131] A similar return to industry was ordered by Hitler during November 1943, to bring damaged tanks from the Eastern Front closer to the spare parts which were in short supply on the front line. The attempt to expedite the repair of tanks was unsuccessful because of the delays incurred in transportation and that the scheme strained the already limited industrial resources.[132]

During July 1944, Leyland Motors noted that the losses of Cromwell tanks during the Normandy campaign could only be replaced by the delivery of new tanks direct from the production line.[133] As shown in Figure 5.3 for the Cruiser programme as a whole, the necessity for greater Cromwell output delayed the start of Comet production, but more importantly slowed the rate at which these more advanced tanks came off the assembly line to begin equipping front line units. As illustrated, the Cromwell programme was meant to reduce the monthly output of tanks after July so that production would cease altogether by the end of 1944. The Comet programme was supposed to start in August, under the expectation of large-scale deliveries being possible due to the similarities between the two tanks as demonstrated at Leyland Motors. However, due to the demands of the Normandy campaign, Cromwell output was increased during August with the result of deferring Comet production until September. The rate of output for the new Comet tank was much smaller and slower than expected because Cromwell production was maintained until April 1945 with deliveries that exceeded Comet output until January 1945. Despite delaying the introduction of Comet tanks to armoured units, the ability to suddenly increase production of the Cromwell demonstrated that the British tank industry had transformed to produce good quality tanks at a high rate of output.

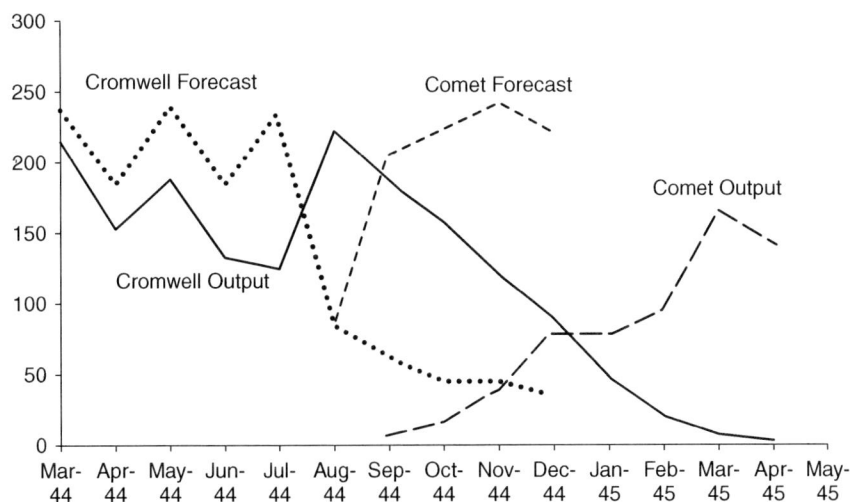

Figure 5.3 Cromwell and Comet tank forecasts and output, March 1944 to April 1945

Sources: TNA, AVIA 22/454, 'Centaur/Cromwell Planning', 9 November 1943; CAB 120/356, 'A.F.V. Production', March 1944 to April 1945.

Conclusion

The productivity of the British tank industry increased during the war to provide British units with better quality equipment resulting in improved performance in combat. This was achieved by the eventual standardization of the tank programme, the specialization of the tank firms and simplification of tank assembly. This was made possible by overcoming the shortages in materials and components, inadequate workmanship and inspection, the insufficient priority given to spare parts and the need to continue producing unwanted tanks. These production problems were not unique to the British tank programme as they also affected the aircraft industry in Britain and tank production in the United States and Germany.

The standardization of the tank programme could only be achieved once reliable tank designs had been developed and put into full production. This meant that continuation orders for unwanted tanks were necessary to keep the labour resources in situ and minimize inactive assembly lines, until reworked Churchill tanks and the new Cromwell and Comet tanks became available. Unlike many of the earlier British tank designs, these later tank models were very reliable, were less prone to mechanical breakdown and had fewer servicing requirements. This was similar to the adoption of the Sherman tank by the United States and contrary to the heavy tanks used by Germany. By focusing upon a smaller range of British tank models the variety of different materials and components necessary for assembly was reduced. This avoided many of the delays experienced earlier in the war, when frequent and unpredictable material shortages could reduce monthly output by up to one-third and delay the completion of a tank contract by a few months.

The specialization of the tank industry was achieved when production of the standardized designs was concentrated among fewer firms, permitting other firms to work on tank conversions or transfer capacity to their core industries or non-tank work. The positive effect on productivity was shown by the almost seamless transfer from Centaur to Cromwell production and the later change-over from the Cromwell to the Comet tank. The ability to specialize in the production of battleworthy tanks was achieved by overcoming the earlier problems of inadequate workmanship and inspection. Many production faults could have been identified had official inspection taken place before the tank was fully assembled and had there been enough inspectors to match the large increase in output. The increased numbers of official inspectors after June 1942 complemented the transfer to standardized tank designs and simplified assembly techniques. A number of other faults were caused by corrosion and collision due to the inadequate preparations before shipping the tanks overseas.

The simplification of tank assembly was demonstrated by the fewer man-hours required to assemble the later tank designs, making it possible to increase production of the Cromwell tank to replace the heavy combat losses during the Normandy campaign. Delays caused by shortages of materials and components were eased when firms produced the requirements in-house and when bypassing the parent system to obtain the items direct from the Ministry of Supply. The simplified nature of tank assembly was coupled with the greater priority given to the production of spare parts, so that they could be delivered on an equal basis with new tanks. This ensured that armoured units did not repeat the experience of the first half of the war, when the number of unfit tanks was over one-quarter of the total tank strength.

Finally, the British tank industry compares favourably with the examples from the other domestic and foreign tank programmes, especially when aircraft production had priority and North American industry had greater capacity as examined in the next chapter. The mass production of British aircraft became standardized and simplified with the reduction in man-hours needed for assembly, and when spare parts were used to repair damaged aircraft instead the same resources being used on new aircraft production. The aircraft programme had a stronger inspection regime throughout the war that examined the work in progress before reaching the final assembly stage. Tank production in the United States was similarly affected by the shortages of materials and spare parts and by inadequate workmanship and inspection, before improvement and high productivity was attained. By contrast, Germany found these problems increasingly more prevalent and more difficult to overcome as the war progressed.

6

Influence of North America upon the British Tank Industry

The present examination of the British tank programme has considered the military, political, strategic and industrial pressures upon achieving the demands of the British war effort from rearmament until the end of the war. This chapter will broaden this assessment by examining how North American industry influenced British policy and the tank programme from 1940 until 1945. Ultimately, Britain benefited from the ability in North America to concentrate production within large factories that were strategically immune to the threat of enemy attack. To illustrate, the United States produced a total of 88,410 Light, Medium and Heavy tanks between 1940 and 1945 from the combined facilities of 17 manufacturers, with just five of these firms accounting for 69,385 tanks.[1] The Canadian programme was less extensive and produced 5,794 tanks and other armoured fighting vehicles from 1941 until 1945, the vast majority of which were produced by the facilities of just two firms.[2]

To consider the influence of North American production upon the British tank industry, this chapter will begin by reviewing the production of Valentine tanks in Canada which were supplied on behalf of British requirements to the Soviet Union. The British tank programme in the United States was limited to providing tank components following the failure to secure contracts for British tanks by American industry. As a result, Britain purchased American tanks while competing against the War Department for the same vehicles, and many of these orders were later sold back to the United States at a cost that was discounted or *gratis*. The exchange of tank related information and equipment between Britain, Canada and the United States illustrated the extent of collaboration throughout the war. Britain accepted a greater number of tanks from the United States to eliminate the production of unsatisfactory British tanks. The reductions in the British tank programme during 1943 and 1944 meant that some tank firms returned to producing locomotives in Britain, rather than importing these bulky items via Lend-Lease and consuming valuable shipping space. The consequences of becoming overdependent on tanks from the United States was demonstrated when the deliveries of Lend-Lease tanks to Britain were cancelled late in 1944.

The British tank programme in Canada

The British government took advantage of the manufacturing potential of North America before the outbreak of war by setting up the British Supply Board in Ottawa, together with an office in New York under Arthur Purvis. When war was declared in September 1939, the Ministry of Supply formed the British Purchasing Commission in Ottawa, while the arms embargo in the United States prevented war production from this source. When this legal obstacle was removed in November 1939, Purvis was sent to Washington DC to establish contact with the US Government and became chairman of the British Purchasing Commission, now relocated more prominently to the business centre of New York.[3] The method of purchasing arms from the United States was restricted to a 'Cash and Carry' basis that meant each nation was limited to their ability to pay and transport the munitions in non-American shipping. This arrangement favoured Britain over Germany given the differences in dollar reserves, and that German shipping across the Atlantic was extremely difficult and infrequent.[4]

Britain placed a range of overseas orders before the increased pressures on obtaining war material in response to the German offensive in the West during May 1940, which revealed the level of British buying power and priorities at this time. For example, between October 1939 and April 1940 the Ministry of Supply used £96 million of American, Canadian and other European and worldwide currencies to order a variety of raw materials for the British war programme. A further £5 million was spent on machine tools and another £1 million on industrial equipment and stores. The combined orders for explosives over this period was the single largest munitions expenditure at £12 million, with a further £14 million spent on other munitions. During this early stage in the war, tanks and transport only accounted for £2 million of the total £130 million spent. The importance of North America was demonstrated when the United States accounted for 31 per cent and Canada for 52 per cent of the total purchases.[5] Following the defeat of France in June 1940, the selective nature of British purchases changed to a policy of 'arms at any price' to meet the increased demand for munitions.[6]

With the presence of British purchasing officials in Ottawa shortly after the outbreak of war, the Ministry of Supply sought to enlarge the British tank programme by contracting Canadian production facilities. As a result, during October 1939 the Ministry of Supply via the British Purchasing Commission in Ottawa, ordered 100 hulls for the Valentine tank from the Canadian Purchasing Board. These hulls would presumably be transported to Britain for the fitting of components and equipment for the finished tank to be allocated to an armoured unit.[7] By December, the Ministry extended this programme for the assembly of 200 complete Valentine tanks. A similar output was organized to equip the Canadian army tank battalions being offered to Britain, which could not be supplied by British industry.[8] At the beginning of 1940, the Ministry of Supply offered to supply the drawings for the jigs and fixtures necessary to support the emerging Valentine tank programme in Canada.[9]

The production of Valentine tanks in Canada was temporarily halted during March 1940, when the Director of Mechanization Brigadier John Crawford and the

Canadian Purchasing Board agreed to consider producing the prospective Churchill tank instead. This was confirmed with the offer of drawings and that the purchasing board should inspect the mock-up tank at Woolwich. In addition, engineers from Canada were invited to view the prototype under production at Harland & Wolff in Belfast.[10] These site visits may not have taken place, however the drawings were provided and the Canadian Purchasing Board confirmed during April that the tank components could be produced in Canada.[11] Many of the features on the Harland & Wolff prototype were retained by the draughtsmen of Vauxhall Motors and the Mechanization Board for the design of the later Churchill tank.[12] Given these similarities, the discussions relating to the Harland & Wolff prototype could also relate to the later Churchill tank had a production order been placed with Canadian industry.

On 22 May, Crawford stated that Canadian firms could assemble complete Churchill tanks in Canada before shipment to Britain. Another option was for Canadian firms to produce the engines, gear boxes, suspensions, tracks and gun mountings for the assembly of tanks in Britain, therefore reducing the amount of shipping space required for complete vehicles.[13] With the deteriorating military situation in France during May and June 1940, the Ministry of Supply suspended the programme to produce Churchill tanks and components and instead placed an order for 300 Valentine tanks with the Canadian Pacific Railway Company in Montreal. This decision was made because the first production Valentine tank by Vickers-Armstrongs had performed satisfactorily and production could start immediately.[14]

Following the events in Europe, the demand for greater production was repeated by the Canadian government with the Minister for National Defence authorizing the production of 488 Valentine tanks to equip a Canadian army tank brigade.[15] For Britain, the prospect of receiving this tank brigade equipped with Valentine tanks produced in Canada would have taken the pressure off British industry to provide the same equipment. This was emphasized in January 1941, when the Secretary of State for War David Margesson stated that Britain was 'entirely agreeable' to Valentine production in Canada under the expectation that the tank brigade would arrive in Britain in the summer of 1941.[16] While this plan lapsed with the German invasion of the Soviet Union in June, Britain benefited from Canadian Valentine production as these tanks were sent to the Red Army to supplement British obligations under the supply protocols to provide raw materials, munitions and equipment.

Once the order for 300 Valentine tanks was received at Canadian Pacific in June 1940, the firm instructed their representatives in London to acquire the specifications and drawings.[17] A visit was organized for a few Canadian Pacific employees to the works of Vickers-Armstrongs in Newcastle-upon-Tyne on 20 June, to gain a better understanding of the production processes.[18] Later in August, the Canadian Minister of Munitions and Supply, Clarence Howe, considered that the Valentine tank would be exceptionally difficult to assemble and questioned whether mass production could be achieved in Canada.[19] British industry during the war delivered an average of 120 Valentine tanks per month during the first 2 years of production from just 3 firms. In comparison to the first 2 years of the Churchill programme, the 11 firms involved delivered 130 tanks per month on average, whereas the 9 firms under the

Crusader programme produced 110 tanks per month.[20] Even though the Churchill programme used a number of smaller firms such as Beyer Peacock and Dennis, and the Crusader programme used Lysaght and Milners Safe, the difference in comparative output between these programmes illustrates that the Valentine tank could be mass produced.

During September 1940, the British War Office informed the Canadian government that the combat experience in France had emphasized the need for greater numbers of Cruiser tanks with increased speed and mobility.[21] At the same time, the Canadian General Staff decided to produce American Medium tanks, although the Valentine programme continued with production expected to start in February 1941 at 3 tanks per day. As a result, the British order for 300 tanks would finish in August 1941, with the Canadian order for 488 tanks completing by February 1942.[22] If the Canadian authorities then wanted to replace the proposed tank brigade with an armoured brigade equipped with the preferred Medium tanks, then the 488 complete Valentine tanks would be offered to Britain.[23]

With the first production Valentine tank expected in February 1941, Canadian Pacific reported in January that the absence of component drawings had caused delays and the firm were producing their own based upon the sample tanks provided by Britain.[24] The armour plate from Dominion Foundries to assemble the hull of the first Valentine tank was not delivered to Canadian Pacific until February, with other components such as the electric traverse gear for the turret still outstanding.[25] The components for the assembly of 12 tanks were received at Canadian Pacific by the beginning of May, although there was a lack of skilled labour for fitting and machining the armour plate.[26] Despite these delays and shortages, the first Valentine tank was completed later in May, which was 11 months since receiving the order in June 1940. This was 2 months sooner than the 13 months that Vickers-Armstrongs took to deliver the first ever Valentine tank.[27] However, Canadian Pacific were producing an existing design that had been proven by Vickers beforehand, rather than generating a new tank from the beginning.

Even with production underway, the Valentine programme at Canadian Pacific continued to be delayed by a series of unsatisfactory and time consuming production techniques. An army officer carrying out a factory visit in October 1941 noted how mass production was being impeded by a lack of appropriate equipment or machinery. These included the use of paint brushes instead of spray guns, the use of hand rather than hydraulic jacks and the general use of hand tools overall. The combination of material delays and obstructive assembly practices meant that the original forecast for the production of 105 Valentine tanks from May to September 1941 had to be lowered to just 30 tanks.[28]

In response to the Allied requirements from October 1941 to supply the Soviet Union with materials and equipment, Britain increased the Valentine programme in Canada to 1,420 tanks. By May 1943, all but 32 of these Canadian Valentine tanks had been shipped direct to the Eastern Front.[29] Canadian Pacific achieved this by overcoming the earlier unsatisfactory production methods to complete 420 tanks by April 1942 and deliver an expected 75 tanks per month thereafter.[30] Therefore, Canadian Pacific produced an average of 57 Valentine tanks per month across the

2-year programme. This was greater than the individual production of Vickers-Armstrongs that achieved an average of 47 tanks per month during the first 2 years of their programme.[31] Ultimately, Valentine production by Canadian Pacific reflected the majority of Canadian industrial effort during the war, with 66 per cent of production activity allocated to Britain, the United States and other Commonwealth and Allied nations. The remaining 34 per cent of Canadian war production was provided to the Canadian armed forces.[32]

The British tank programme in the United States

To assist the production of tanks in Britain, the British Purchasing Commission placed orders with North American firms for the supply of components, such as the $2.5 million contract in May 1940 to support the final assembly of 250 Valentine tanks. The individual contracts included gun mountings from York Safe and Lock, transmissions from Buckeye Traction Ditcher and suspension units from American Car and Foundry.[33] The suspension order was inspected during April 1941 when British Colonel H. G. Hoare visited the American Car and Foundry works. At this time the contract was nearing completion, although the firm was reluctant to undertake another order as they considered the Valentine suspension unit to be too difficult and too expensive to make.[34] In respect of engines from General Motors for the Valentine tank, the second Tank Board noted during May 1941 that increased Valentine output was now more likely as these engines were being received from the United States.[35] During the 6 months to the end of April 1941 the Valentine programme delivered an average of 100 tanks per month. With the receipt of engines from the United States, average output increased to 140 tanks per month over the 6 months from May 1941, despite the reduction sustained in July as a result of the annual week-long factory holiday discussed in Chapter 4.[36]

The purchasing of tank components from North America continued after 1940 with at least 18 firms by the middle of 1942 supporting the tank programme in Britain, and the Valentine tank in Canada. The Valentine programme was supplied by 13 firms across the full range of components that included engines, transmissions, suspensions, tracks, armour plate and other castings. Seven firms assisted the ongoing Crusader programme with transmissions, tracks, armour plate and castings, while only one firm provided tracks to Matilda production reflecting the decision to finish this programme during 1943. The new Centaur programme had three firms providing transmissions and castings demonstrating that Britain took advantage of North American industry to support the latest tank programmes at home, while receiving increasing numbers of Lend-Lease tanks, as examined later.[37]

With the purchase of components for British tanks underway during 1940, the next logical step was to place orders for the complete assembly of Matilda and Crusader tanks in the United States, with the Valentine tank already under order in Canada. During the deteriorating military situation in France during June 1940, a French mission to the United States discussed the possible assembly of 12,000 French B1-Bis tanks under a production group headed by Baldwin Locomotive. While there was a lack of capacity for moulded armour plate, an impressive 10 tanks per day could be achieved by the end of 1940, if the American authorities gave priority for the necessary machine tools. These discussions were taken seriously as it was proposed that a few specialists and a complete B1-Bis tank be shipped from France to the United States for examination. British interest in this project was expressed with the hope that production tanks would be delivered on an equal basis between Britain and France.[38]

While the defeat of France ended the French mission, British tank units would have benefited from receiving the proven B1-Bis tank in large numbers from the United States for the campaigns during 1941 and 1942. This supply would have achieved both the overriding requirement for increased output to replace the losses following the evacuations from France, and provided British forces in North Africa with greater firepower when comparing the B1-Bis to British and German equivalents. The French tank had slightly less armour protection than the British Matilda, although both were matched in terms of speed for the designed infantry support role. The B1-Bis had a larger and single 270 hp engine, together with greater firepower than current British tanks by incorporating a turret mounted 47 mm anti-tank gun and hull mounted 75 mm high explosive gun.[39] In relation to German armour during 1940, the B1-Bis tank was superior to the Panzer Mark IV in respect of armour and overall firepower, although the German tank had greater speed and range of action. However, the B1-Bis was at a disadvantage tactically with the crew taking on multiple responsibilities and that the main 75 mm gun was hull and not turret mounted, thereby limiting the effectiveness of the gun to wherever the tank was facing.[40]

The question of how the B1-Bis would have performed under desert conditions from an operational standpoint will have to remain unanswered given the lack of opportunity. However, given the limitations of British armour during 1941 and 1942 in terms of numbers, reliability and high explosive firepower discussed in the previous chapters, the potential of receiving numerous B1-Bis and spares from the United States would have been useful before the large-scale deliveries of Grant and Sherman tanks. This possibility ended later in June 1940, when the General Staff advised the first Tank Board that they would not be taking over the French arrangements for the B1-Bis because they favoured the production of British tanks in the United States instead.[41] However, this was made on the assumption that the United States was still prepared to produce foreign tanks that did not meet the demands of the US Army, bearing in mind the recent defeat of France and the current risks to Britain.

The possibility of placing orders for Matilda and Crusader tanks with American industry was explored by a British mission to the United States after the defeat of France, under Major-General Ridley Pakenham-Walsh. During August 1940, the discussions revealed that modifications were needed to the Crusader power system, transmission and tracks, to harmonize the vehicle with the equipment under production for American tanks.[42] The United States was understandably reluctant to produce British tanks as this nation could 'go under' at any day. This would have resulted in American factories producing British equipment which was unsuitable for the US Army. The British mission quickly recognized that production of the Matilda or Crusader tank in the United States was not going to be possible, so ordering the new American M3 Medium tank was considered as an alternative.[43]

The inability to secure production of the Crusader tank in the United States contributed to the expansion programme in Britain after November 1940, discussed in Chapter 2, with the introduction of a further six tank firms to the existing three Crusader assembly firms. The failure of a British tank programme in the United States was not the rule, as there were notable examples of American industry producing British equipment in large quantities. These included the Lee-Enfield Rifle, the Rolls-Royce Merlin aero-engine, the Mark XIV bombsight, the No. 19 wireless set, the Universal carrier and the 6-pounder or 57 mm anti-tank gun. Some of this equipment was also used by the United States for their war effort.[44]

Purchasing American tanks for the British war effort

The US War Department responded to the fighting in Europe during 1940 by instigating a programme to produce thousands of new tanks.[45] This greater emphasis had followed a general expansion in material for the US Army with $75 million spent during 1938 and 1939, and $150 million approved for 1940 including the Chrysler Tank Arsenal in Detroit.[46] A serious obstacle for any country wanting to purchase tanks designed in the United States was that official policy prohibited the release of technical information until a sizeable order had being placed. Britain could not reasonably be expected to place a large cash order without first understanding the characteristics of the vehicles on offer. To overcome this problem, President Roosevelt's representative Henry Morgenthau agreed during May 1940 that this information could be obtained by a British army officer, via an examination of the tank during production and testing.[47] This gave Britain the opportunity to scrutinize the equipment before making an outlay in dollars or gold.

During June, the M2A1 Medium tank was inspected by a Lieutenant-Colonel from the Royal Tank Regiment, who was concerned about the vulnerable 32 mm of armour and that mass production would take time to achieve.[48] This delay was illustrated when the order for 1,000 M2A1 tanks with Chrysler in August 1940 was not expected to start production until September 1941 at 100 tanks per month and finish in August 1942. However, this contract was later cancelled in August 1940 and replaced by the new M3 Medium tank. Chrysler released the pilot of this new tank after just 7 months and the first production tank after 11 months.[49] With Britain unable to secure the production of the Matilda or Crusader tank in the United States, the General Staff confirmed to mission leader Pakenham-Walsh during August 1940 that an order for 1,500 M3 Medium tanks was acceptable.[50] When the new M3 design was discussed by the Dewar Tank Mission later in 1940, it was noted this tank had greater firepower than the Crusader, but concern was raised regarding the height of the vehicle, especially when including the turret cupola. The position of the wireless set in the main hull instead of the turret as per the British standard was also questioned.[51] As a result of these the comments, the M3 Medium became the Grant tank by incorporating a 'British turret' that removed the cupola and moved the radio equipment.[52]

The first cash contracts for 1,686 Grant tanks were placed during the final quarter of 1940 involving Pullman-Standard Car, Pressed Steel Car and Baldwin Locomotive, together with an order for 400 of the prospective Sherman tanks with the Lima Locomotive Works. These contracts were coupled with additional orders for armour plate, engines, guns and mounts with a further six firms. The total amount of these contracts was over $132 million, plus a further $16.5 million to expand the existing industrial capacity.[53] Each contract was presumably the maximum that could be placed with each firm having increased the capacity and the minimum number to make the production cost effective. British equipment such as sand shields, smoke generators and smoke bomb throwers were installed separately at one of the Tank Depots in the United States, therefore avoiding any interruption to the production line at the tank firms.[54]

By the end of 1940, a total of $3.2 billion worth of munitions orders had been placed with American firms by the British Purchasing Commission. While these orders created new capacity and exposed American industry to the processes of ordnance production, they conflicted with the similar attempts by the United States to equip their own armed forces.[55] By 1942, the arrangements under Lend-Lease had superseded British contracts as the means of supplying the British war effort from the United States. To illustrate, of the 951 tanks shipped to British forces by the end of 1941, only 165 were sent under British contracts.[56] With Lend-Lease deliveries providing the greatest impact on the British war effort, the War Department purchased large quantities of the munitions generated by the British contracts. This transferred 653 Grant and all but one of the 400 Sherman tanks to the War Department for the cost of $66 million or approximately half of the original order.[57] This purchase did not include the additional plant paid for under British contracts to expand the industrial capacity, and was instead leased to the War Department for the nominal rent of $1 per year. During the course of the war some of the equipment and building expansions were sold for about 30 per cent of the original value, while $6.8 million worth was deemed irrecoverable. This capacity ultimately supported the American war effort, including the equipment that Britain was receiving under Lend-Lease.[58]

In addition to the purchase of Grant tanks, early in October 1940 the British authorities in the United States also considered ordering Light tanks from American Car and Foundry, with deliveries expected early in 1941.[59] Rather than financing this order in cash, the British authorities considered paying for these Light tanks by giving up 300 aero-engines under production in the United States, possibly the extremely important Merlin.[60] The British War Cabinet was unlikely to agree to this exchange when they had refused to raise British tank production at the expense of aircraft and air defence under the Priority of Production Directive, examined in Chapter 2. The cash purchase of 200 Light tanks direct from American Car and Foundry was agreed later in October.[61] By late January 1941, the inability to finance tank orders meant that Britain became wholly dependent upon the anticipated introduction of Lend-Lease to continue benefiting from the large production capabilities of the United States.[62]

Despite this lack of buying power, British officials still inspected the production progress of the remaining cash orders, such as the factory visit to the Baldwin Locomotive Works by Colonel Hoare during April 1941. This revealed that despite rushing the final assembly of the first M3 Medium tank for the US Army, the reliability of American tank design and the competence of American industry was indicated when the tank performed well on the testing track.[63] The completion of the original British cash contracts were obstructed by the need to provide the same equipment for the simultaneous expansion of the armed forces in the United States. The scheduled output for M3 Medium tanks from July 1941 expected to deliver 570 tanks to Britain by December 1941, compared to 505 tanks for the US Army. From January 1942, the US Army would receive an increasing number each month, while British deliveries were capped at 180 per month until the contract finished.[64] Ultimately, the necessity for British cash contracts to supply the front line with tanks from the United States was less important when the weight of Lend-Lease became available, and the remaining order been sold to the War Department.

Allied co-operation and exchange of information

The benefits of North American industry for the British war effort were supported by the mutual exchange of information and equipment between the Western Allies. An early example of co-operation in relation to tank production was seen during September 1940, when representatives of the British mission to the United States attended a meeting of the Canadian Joint Committee on Tank Development discussed in Chapter 2. This meeting reviewed the current Valentine programme in Canada, together with the possibility of using Canadian industry to produce the M3 Medium tank, the British six-pounder gun and various armoured cars.[65] During February 1941, the Canadian Chief of the General Staff, Major-General Harry Crerar, suggested an informal meeting in Montreal for British, Canadian and American officers to exchange information relating to tank design. While this was an ad-hoc arrangement and was not formally recognized by any government, it provided the means for the different military authorities to examine the latest tank developments.[66] The range of issues considered during the meeting included cast armour, tank armament and power traverse, the differences between steel and rubber tracks, and tank radio equipment.[67]

By August 1941, the Canadian Military Headquarters in London contacted the Ministry of Supply to propose the formation of an Armoured Fighting Vehicle User Committee in Britain. The committee would initiate the testing of vehicles and components shipped to Britain from Canadian production.[68] In response, the tank design department in Britain agreed for the Canadian vehicles to be included into the very full programme of trials to be carried out at the experimental establishment at Farnborough. In a further example of co-operation between Britain and Canada, the secretary of the Canadian user committee was attached to Farnborough to witness the trials taking place, while a British Royal Engineers officer became a permanent member on the committee for the Ministry of Supply.[69] The committee meetings occurred over a period of 26 months until December 1943 and discussed the trials of tank guns, engineer tank adaptations, tank transporters, the arrangement of the tank fighting compartment and tank crew clothing.[70]

The increased co-ordination on tank policy between the British and American authorities began before the United States entered the war in December 1941. US

Army Colonel G. A. Green was added to the third Tank Board from August 1941 as a part-time member. Green had the dual task of advising the board on design and production issues and act as a liaison officer for the United States.[71] The attendance by Colonel Green extended to the fourth and fifth Tank Boards until his involvement ended on 22 November 1943.[72] This type of collaboration was not isolated, as demonstrated when the US Chief of Ordnance, General Charles Wesson, visited London during September 1941 to obtain British opinion on tank and artillery design based upon their combat experience over the previous two years.[73]

Following the attack on Pearl Harbor, the military relationship between Britain and the United States strengthened again when Field Marshal Sir John Dill was appointed to Washington to keep distrust and misunderstandings to a minimum.[74] Specific collaboration was formalized in March 1942, when the British Tank Mission to Washington secured a joint agreement with the US Tank Committee for the mutual exchange of information and the co-ordination of plans.[75] A similar agreement was signed in September 1942 between Britain and the Soviet Union, but this became a one-sided arrangement with Britain providing technical detail and equipment with little reciprocation from Moscow.[76] Likewise, the majority of Soviet equipment obtained by the United States came from captured German sources, who had originally taken it from the Red Army.[77]

The manner in which British tank conversions were incorporated into American armoured formations demonstrated how the Anglo-American agreement worked in practice. For example, between June 1942 and December 1943, the Research and Development Service in the United States received regular reports from Britain relating to the Duplex-Drive system on the Sherman tank.[78] In another example, Britain supplied details of the Canal Defence Light adaptation to the Grant turret which assisted night river crossings with a powerful and dazzling searchlight. This information permitted the US Ordnance Department to build 500 turrets over 18 months, therefore saving 2 years of preliminary work. While this device was not extensively used during the war, the benefits and importance of the collaboration were obvious.[79]

Allied ordnance officers were never denied access to British research and development information while attached to the various experimental stations or proving grounds in Britain.[80] One area of limitation was identified during September 1943 when the Department of Tank Design chose not to supply the Canadian Military Headquarters in London with the latest information relating to British tanks. This inflexible approach was not due to security restrictions, but because the number and frequency of adjustments resulted in a great deal of work to compile and distribute the new books. Therefore, the restriction was meant to keep the recipients to just those groups who were actively involved, so that they received the updated information in a timely fashion.[81] As for the co-operation from the United States, British military personnel and industrialists visited many factories during the war to consider whether American techniques could be incorporated into British industry for greater productivity.[82] From mid-1943 onwards, US Ordnance provided Britain with thousands of technical and industrial reports each month, detailing important and mutually beneficial information on production processes.[83]

Lend-Lease supply of American Tanks

The benefits of Lend-Lease for the British war effort were the supply of much needed raw materials, equipment and munitions, which Britain could not produce or otherwise purchase from their own resources. On the other hand, Lend-Lease was primarily designed to keep the war away from mainland United States and the industrial equipment provided to Britain could not be used for exports in competition with the United States.[84] The effect of Lend-Lease upon the British tank programme was the expectation of large numbers of battleworthy tanks, so that British industry concentrated upon producing tanks of greater quality and transferred some firms to other essential war production.

The impact of Lend-Lease upon the Canadian government was to offer a similar type of credit system; otherwise Britain would divert orders from Canada to the United States. As a result, the War Committee in Ottawa agreed during March 1941 to finance the entire British deficit in Canada. In return, Britain maintained their existing production orders and obtained all their Canadian dollar requirements from Canada. Later in January 1942, Canada used the funds generated from the sterling to dollar exchanges in London to provide Britain with an interest-free loan valued at C\$700 million for the duration of the war. Furthermore, Canada provided the gift of war supplies and food to the value of C\$1 billion. This was later superseded in 1943 by 'Mutual Aid' where Canada helped to finance British and Allied purchases in the Dominion.[85]

The ability of the United States to supply the various requirements of the different allied nations via Lend-Lease, demonstrated the extent of American industrial strength. Much of this production capacity was generated after September 1940 by the combination of British cash contracts and War Department orders and facilities like the Chrysler Tank Arsenal. This expansion was important as the US Chief of War Plans, Major-General George Strong, revealed to British mission leader Pakenham-Walsh during August 1940 that the American army programme was currently 60 per cent of the British army programme.[86] This estimate proved realistic when the United States produced 4,383 tanks during 1940 and 1941, which was 71 per cent of total British tank output of 6,216 over the same period.[87]

Following the German invasion of the Soviet Union during June 1941, President Roosevelt demanded an increase in tank production to 2,800 tanks per month, although American industry produced no more than 900 vehicles during December. To remedy this shortfall, efforts to increase tank output had taken place in 1941 to take effect during 1942. One important step was raising the priority status for tank production, similar to that carried out in Britain with the revised Priority of Production Directive in November 1941. Another development was the decision to construct the General Motors Fisher Tank Arsenal with the potential capacity to assemble 1,000 Sherman tanks per month.[88] By spring 1943, the tank industry in the United States was producing nearly 4,000 vehicles each month from 16 factories at an overall cost for tools, equipment and buildings of \$250 million.[89]

The effect of changing production from the Grant to the Sherman tank from mid-1942 meant that nearly 5,000 Grant tanks remained in American service and surplus to requirements by 1943. Some of these were adapted with the Canal Defence Light device or deployed as recovery or training vehicles, while the remainder were dismantled for spare parts or scrapped.[90] In respect of British requirements, the North African and European theatre armies received the latest Sherman tanks, while the British army in Burma under Lieutenant-General William Slim continued to fight with older Stuart and Grant tanks. Despite being obsolete, the Grant was capable of combating Japanese Medium tanks and was very useful in overcoming Japanese bunkers.[91]

Grant, Lee and Stuart tanks were also provided to Australia under Lend-Lease from 1942 as part of the general strengthening of defences, so that the United States could use Australia as a base of operations following Japanese attacks in the Pacific.[92] Together with Matilda tanks from Britain, these vehicles provided a supply of armour which the Australian tank programme could not match, with their first Sentinel pilot delivered in January 1942.[93] These Allied vehicles relieved some of the fears of quantitative deficiency in Australia that had similarly existed in Britain from mid-1940. However, the Australian authorities noted that the Allied tanks were becoming increasingly obsolete. During April 1942, the Grant and Lee tanks had serious problems, while the Stuart tanks required extensive modification to make them battleworthy. In common with existing opinion, the Australian authorities noted that the Matilda tanks were too slow and could not operate over long distances.[94] By February 1943, 255 Lee tanks had required numerous modifications and were restricted to training purposes rather than combat deployment.[95] Until May 1943, the Australian army had received 1,624 tanks from overseas sources, including 487 Stuart and 757 Grant and Lee tanks and 380 Matilda tanks.[96]

During May 1943, Lend-Lease liaison officer Averell Harriman wrote to Prime Minister Churchill to recommend that Britain reduce domestic tank production and become more dependent upon the United States by accepting a further 3,000 Sherman tanks. To support this proposal, Harriman stated that a significant overproduction of Sherman tanks was expected, despite the American tank programme being reduced during late 1942 to meet the demands for more shipbuilding and escort vessels. Politically, Harriman argued that President Roosevelt could not justify the loss of thousands of tank workers if output was cut further, especially since tank production had been promoted as a great success of the government and industry. Finally, the Soviet Union had decided not to request American tanks under the supply protocols, meaning that the production surplus would expand unless Britain accepted more tanks. In exchange for reductions in the British tank programme, Harriman suggested that British industry increase locomotive production as examined later.[97]

The availability of large numbers of Sherman tanks from the United States during 1943 similarly affected the Canadian programme currently producing the Grizzly tank. This was essentially a Sherman tank that incorporated a smoke mortar and British wireless equipment. With Canadian Pacific Railway producing the Valentine tank during 1942, the capacity of the Montreal Locomotive Works was being prepared for an order of 1,200 Grizzly tanks. The similarities with the Sherman design meant few production problems were encountered and the first vehicle deliveries were delayed by only one month to August 1943. However, the availability of many Sherman tanks from the United States during 1943 resulted in the cancellation of the Grizzly programme with the final 188th tank delivered in January 1944. The decision to cancel the Grizzly tank after just five months in production was supported by the British General Staff, because Montreal Locomotive could transfer capacity to the much desired 25-pounder armed Sexton self-propelled vehicle used by British forces.[98]

In response to Harriman's request, in July 1943 Churchill approved the decision to accept a further 3,000 Lend-Lease tanks from the United States at the expense of the Centaur tank, with the adjustment taking effect against British tank requirements for 1944. The British authorities stipulated that as many tanks as possible should be the latest production models mounting the new high-velocity 76 mm gun. Harriman later confirmed that 4,000 Sherman tanks would mount the larger gun during 1944 or 3,500 if Britain wanted 1,000 self-propelled tanks among the Lend-Lease deliveries.[99] The American 76 mm tank gun was meant to provide the Sherman tank with greater armour-piercing capability as the existing 75 mm gun could not penetrate the latest German tanks. While the new gun had an increased muzzle velocity, firing trials in the United States revealed that the latest shot could only penetrate the equivalent frontal armour on the German Tiger tank at no more than 300 yards.[100]

During 1943, the British authorities also considered the 76 mm gun from the United States for the design of the new Comet tank, instead of mounting a comparable British tank gun that would have consumed industrial resources. The ammunition and spares for the 76 mm would have been supplied by American industry and the requirements for the Allied armies using this tank gun on the battlefield would have been standardized. Despite these benefits, the General Staff decided upon the British high-velocity 77 mm gun, which had greater armour-piercing performance and avoided the complete redesign of the Comet turret and stowage had the American 76 mm been adopted.[101]

The demand for American production tanks mounting greater firepower was expressed within the United States, similar to the criticism raised in Britain regarding the lack of enough heavily armed British tanks, as reviewed in the earlier chapters. The American authorities emphasized that the tank programme could not be immediately transformed and therefore the existing production arrangements had to be maintained.[102] This response was plausible given the difficulties of changing the production programme from one design to another as already discussed in relation to British industry. Although the United States relied upon greater numbers of lesser-armed Sherman tanks on the battlefield, rather than a smaller number of better armed and armoured heavier tanks. This was again similar to the British decision to mass produce the Cromwell tank, which met the requirement for greater operational mobility.

An alternative to mounting the 76 mm gun on the Sherman tank was to mount the high-velocity and available British 17-pounder gun, as successfully demonstrated on the Firefly tank. Brigadier Macleod Ross, who was the British chief technical liaison officer at the Detroit Tank Automotive Center from 1942 to 1945, criticizes the US Ordnance Department for not adopting the British gun simply because it was 'Not Invented Here'.[103] This decision was taken despite the 17-pounder gun completing firing trials that were superior to the larger American 90 mm gun used on the later Pershing tank. Furthermore, to assist in the assembly of 17-pounder armed Sherman tanks in the United States, Britain had offered to supply 200 guns and recoil mechanisms per month, together with drawings to show how the gun would be mounted.[104]

The condemnation of US Ordnance was repeated by General Bradley when recounting how General Eisenhower had reacted angrily to the combat limitations of the new 76 mm armed Sherman tanks during the Normandy campaign. These results were despite Eisenhower receiving earlier assurances from US Ordnance that this gun would be sufficient to engage all German armour. To increase the firepower in American armoured units, Bradley asked whether British industry could convert US Army Sherman tanks to carry the 17-pounder gun as demonstrated on the Firefly. However, this was not possible as Royal Ordnance Factory capacity was already overloaded with existing work to meet the requirements of the British General Staff.[105]

Overall, the expansion of industrial capacity in the United States produced over 72,000 Light, Medium and Heavy tanks between 1942 and 1944. The vast majority of these tanks were produced by the Chrysler Corporation, American Car and Foundry, General Motors, the Cadillac Motor Company and the Pressed Steel Company.[106] Total American output was over three-and-a-half times greater than the 19,839 standard Light, Infantry and Cruiser tanks produced by British industry during the same period.[107] To demonstrate British dependency upon Lend-Lease to support an offensive strategy across the different theatres, the United States supplied nearly 20,000 Grant and Sherman tanks to British and Commonwealth forces during these three years.[108] The difference between the numbers of British and Lend-Lease tanks was even greater when unbattleworthy British tanks were not sent to the front line. As a result, after deducting the output of the Light, Covenanter, Cavalier and Centaur tanks from 1942 to 1944, Britain produced 16,712 front line tanks compared to the 20,000 tanks received from the United States.[109] In addition to providing a greater number of battleworthy tanks, Lend-Lease permitted British industry to concentrate upon quality tank output and redirect other capacity to tank conversions or other essential war work such as locomotive production.

Effect of Lend-Lease upon British industry

A large increase in Lend-Lease Sherman tanks was provided during 1943, giving British industry the time and opportunity to develop the Cromwell tank to a high standard. This meant that the Cromwell tank did not enter mass production prematurely and avoided the problems experienced by the earlier Crusader and Churchill programmes.[110] As examined in the previous chapter, this provided British tank crews with Cromwell tanks that were extremely reliable and required less maintenance to meet the operational requirements of the Allied advance in north west Europe during 1944 and 1945. The decision to accept more Lend-Lease tanks resulted in reduced production of the unsatisfactory Centaur tank and supported the build up of American forces in Britain under operation 'Bolero'. Together with the initial D-Day preparations under operation 'Roundup', the Minister of Production Oliver Lyttelton emphasized to Prime Minister Churchill in August 1942 that these operations required large numbers of locomotives. At this stage, British industry was directed towards war production so locomotives from the United States would be supplied fully constructed, thereby consuming valuable Lend-Lease shipping space.[111]

Lieutenant-General Brehon Somervell from the US War Department offered a solution to this problem earlier in June 1942, by recommending that locomotives be built in Britain from materials supplied by the United States. The Ministry of Supply had reviewed and rejected this possibility because locomotive production would interfere with tank output, as both programmes required the same heavy machinery. However, with the United States expected to significantly increase tank deliveries during 1943, the Centaur programme was reduced by 918 tanks to transfer the industrial capacity to locomotives.[112] In quantifying these changes, Lyttelton confirmed to Churchill that 454 locomotives would be constructed from the capacity released from tank production. With regard to shipping space, Lyttelton estimated that 70,000 measurement tons would be saved below deck or the full carrying capacity of 8 to 10 cargo ships. This saving in shipping space was even more important as complete locomotives were exceptionally difficult to handle, especially against the comparative ease of shipping extra tanks instead.[113] Churchill raised concerns over the reduction in British tank production for 1943, but nonetheless acquiesced having recognized the considerable benefits for Lend-Lease shipping.[114] Steel production in Britain was similarly reduced in 1944 as a means to increase shipping space by accepting finished steel from the United States, rather than importing the bulky iron ore.[115]

Four British tank firms transferred to locomotive production after the completion of their existing tank contracts. The final Covenanter tank from the Crewe location of London, Midland and Scottish was delivered during August 1942 when the factory began work on locomotives. The last Churchill tank from Beyer Peacock was delivered during March 1943 permitting the change to the production of locomotives the same month. In respect of the Matilda tank, Vulcan Foundry and North British Locomotive finished their tank contracts in May and June 1943 respectively, with the transfer to locomotives occurring in June and July. When the London, Midland and Scottish works at Horwich completed their Matilda contract in February 1943, the factory assembled the Centaur tank until November when the firm then began producing locomotives similar to the Crewe location 15 months earlier.[116] Locomotive production was important because the estimated number of locomotives required for civilian and military use during 1943 was 6,000, while Britain and the United States were only expected to provide 4,700 for the year.[117] By comparison, German industry produced over 5,300 locomotives during 1943 having benefited from a sizeable redirection of labour that also increased the tank workforce by over 60 per cent.[118]

The order book for Vulcan Foundry from 1938 to 1945 shows the impact that this redirection of industrial capacity had upon the firms concerned, as illustrated in Figure 6.1. To begin with, the orders for 130 Matilda tanks for £1,170,000 placed during 1938 dominated the order book into 1939. The continuation orders for the Matilda during 1940 following the fighting in France carried the strength of this war work into 1941. With the order book declining during 1942 and with the completion

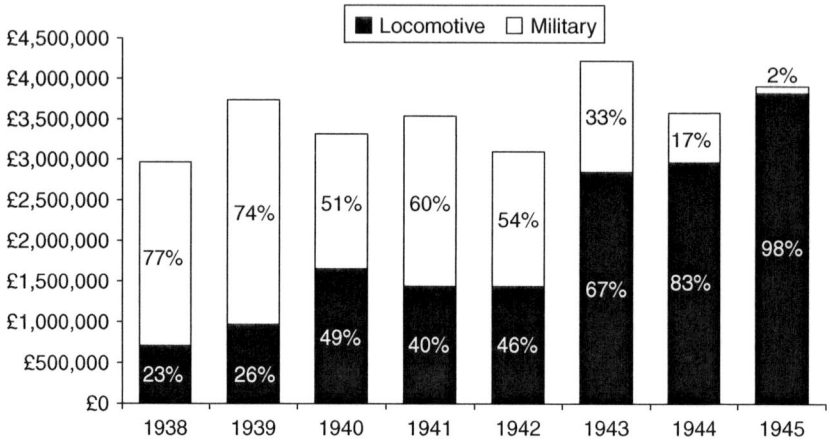

Figure 6.1 Average value of the Vulcan Foundry order book, 1938 to 1945

Source: Yearly averages taken from monthly figures reported in Bodleian Library Oxford, Vulcan Foundry, MS. Marconi 2739, Board Minutes 1934–40 and MS. Marconi 2740, Board Minutes 1940–5.

of the Matilda contract during 1943, Vulcan Foundry needed either another tank order or the transfer of capacity to non-tank work. Vulcan received the latter during 1943 with a considerable order of £1.8 million for 160 'Austerity' locomotive engines in May and again in July for a further 94 engines for £896,000.[119] The production of military equipment declined during the last years of war with limited orders for Matilda spare parts during January and June 1943, and the completion of other Ministry of Supply and Admiralty contracts during 1944 and 1945.[120] With the growing expectation of an end to the war during 1945, Vulcan Foundry received an order of £1.2 million for 100 'Liberation' locomotives in February.[121]

The Australian War Cabinet took similar advantage of overproduction in the United States during 1943 by seeking 310 Sherman tanks under Lend-Lease at the expense of cancelling their unsatisfactory Sentinel tank programme in July. General Douglas MacArthur supported this decision because it promoted the standardization of equipment between the Allied forces and redirected the skilled Australian workforce to urgent ship repair and the construction of small craft and railway wagons.[122] The final authority to obtain these Sherman tanks remained unfulfilled by June 1944, with little prospect of receiving them with the demand on American armour during and following the Normandy campaign.[123] By the end of January 1945, the Australian authorities had abandoned the Sherman tanks in favour of 310 British Churchill tanks. Despite an attempt to secure 150 of these heavily armoured tanks for the post-war army, the Australian authorities cancelled the order in January 1946.[124]

With the expectation of the war ending by 31 March 1945, the British tank programme was reduced in October 1944, with the four firms involved in Comet production being notified in November that their contracts were being curtailed. The effect on each firm varied, with parent firm Leyland Motors only requiring a 6 per cent reduction in the total contract, compared to 25 per cent at John Fowler, and nearly 30 per cent at English Electric. Metropolitan-Cammell received the largest reduction of 60 per cent with all four contracts due to complete between July and December 1945.[125] These reductions were made on the understanding that Britain would receive 8,961 Sherman tanks under Lend-Lease during 1944. However, by October there was already an accumulative shortfall of nearly 3,500 Sherman tanks under this arrangement.[126] This deficit was later exacerbated by the cancellation of Lend-Lease Sherman tanks during November and December 1944. The War Department admitted to British officials in Washington that this was partly because they had underestimated the total tank requirements for 1944.[127]

This miscalculation by the United States was a consequence of halving the American tank programme during the final years of war. From the final quarter of 1943, overall capacity was reduced from 8,000 to 6,600 tanks per month with the elimination of Lima Locomotive, Pullman-Standard, Ford and Pacific Car and Foundry. Another 4 firms ceased tank activity during 1944 resulting in a further reduction of monthly capacity to 4,000 tanks, with the departure of American Car and Foundry, Baldwin, Marmon-Herrington and the Fisher Tank Arsenal. One of the issues with the American tank programme was that monthly tank output was half of the total capacity available, even when resources were concentrated later among fewer tank firms.[128]

From the British point of view, the Secretary of State for War P. J. Grigg stated that the American shortage during 1944 was also because the United States had underestimated the minimum requirements for both wastage and reserves. Essentially, both Britain and the United States were at fault for cutting back their respective tank programmes prematurely, with the expectation of an earlier victory against Germany. The first concern for the British authorities caused by the cessation of Lend-Lease deliveries was an estimated depletion of reserves of 500 Sherman tanks per month. This would result in a complete exhaustion in Italy by mid-April 1945 and in north-west Europe by mid-June. The second and more immediate concern was a shortage of Sherman tanks suitable for conversion to the 17-pounder armed Firefly.[129] The combination of diminishing reserves and fewer Firefly tanks than anticipated brought about the same kind of anxiety about shortages in equipment that occurred following the defeat of France. Ironically, earlier in August 1944, the War Cabinet had highlighted to the Select Committee on National Expenditure that the receipt of large numbers of Sherman tanks during 1943 had in part removed this 'fear of a quantitative deficiency'.[130]

The re-emergence of this concern is illustrated in Figure 6.2, which shows the monthly deliveries of 5,492 Sherman tanks during 1944, compared to the 3,142 Churchill, Heavy Churchill, Cromwell and Challenger tanks delivered by British industry. This meant that the United States provided 2,350 more tanks than British front line output. However, with the exception of April and July, the United States did not provide enough tanks each month to achieve the required 8,961 Sherman tanks expected under Lend-Lease for the year, meaning that Britain had an accumulative shortfall of 3,469 tanks. The reduction in Lend-Lease deliveries from August until October was because more Sherman tanks were given to American armoured units instead of to Britain. These were used as direct replacements for the heavy losses sustained by the United States during and after the Normandy campaign.[131]

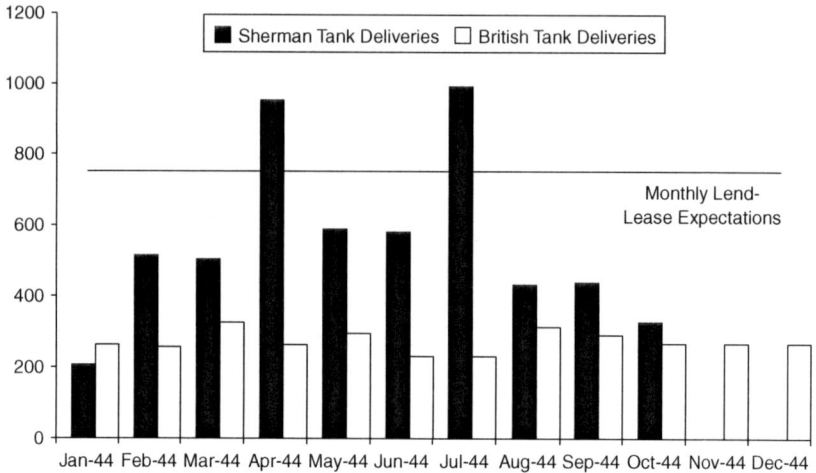

Figure 6.2 Monthly deliveries of Sherman and British front line tanks during 1944, compared to the expected delivery of Sherman tanks under Lend-Lease

Sources: The National Archives, CAB 120/356, 'A.F.V Production' January to December 1944; BT 87/137, 'Assignments from U.S. War Department', by P. J. Grigg, 15 December 1944.

With the situation facing the British authorities at the end of 1944 now reminiscent of 1940, the November 1944 reductions in the Comet programme were immediately reversed. This ensured that enough British tanks were made available to front line units during 1945, albeit with the consequence of delaying the start of a number of civilian programmes.[132] Leyland Motors postponed the conversion of their production facilities to heavy wheeled vehicles for both the army and civilian use, while John Fowler cancelled the transfer of production to agricultural vehicles. Metropolitan-Cammell remained on war production, although capacity destined for work on the Neptune amphibious vehicle was retained for continued Comet production.[133] To increase the number of Firefly tanks, a practical solution was reached early in January 1945. Britain would receive 90 rebuilt Sherman tanks from the United States capable of mounting the 17-pounder gun, in exchange for 90 Sherman tanks already with British units that were unsuitable for conversion.[134]

For the United States, the pressure on front line strength increased at the end of 1944 with the start of the German Ardennes offensive. The US First Army sustained considerable tank losses during the opening phases of the German attack, with battlefield recovery being the only means of providing tank replacements in the short term. Following General Eisenhower's decision to place all American forces in the north under the command of Field Marshal Montgomery, First Army received 300 Sherman tanks from the 21st Army Group reserve, which had previously been denied to them.[135] During February 1945 in response to the shortage of front line tanks, the United States proposed to increase the production of all types of tank, including 10,000 of the new heavy Pershing tank. Upon reviewing the available capacity, these requirements could only be achieved by re-employing former tank firms at a cost and timescale that proved prohibitive. By March 1945, the United States deemed that the end of the war in Europe was close enough to issue cancellation notices to the tank firms, with production ceasing altogether by November.[136] As a final comment on the effect of Lend-Lease upon British industry, wartime Minister Herbert Morrison stated that the sudden removal of this aid programme at the end of the war added to Britain's 'severe economic and financial problems' in supplying the post-war home and export markets.[137]

Conclusion

The British war effort benefited from the strategically secure production facilities and high rate of output provided by North American industry. Britain established an early physical presence in Canada and the United States to take advantage of the British financial and naval resources for the purchasing and shipping of raw materials, equipment and munitions. The introduction of Lend-Lease removed the financial burden from Britain, albeit with the result of giving the United States control over Allied production priorities and restricting the ability of Britain to compete in the post-war marketplace. Ultimately, the increased supply of tanks from the United States meant that British industry focused upon quality tank production and other essential war programmes.

The production of the Valentine tank by the Canadian Pacific Railway Company overcame the shortages of capacity, components and labour to eventually surpass the rate of monthly output achieved by Vickers-Armstrongs in Britain. This production greatly assisted British efforts to provide the Soviet Union with tanks under the supply protocols. The extent of the British tank programme in the United States was limited to the supply of tank components to support the production of tanks in Britain and the Valentine in Canada. The effect that these components had upon British industry was illustrated by the 40 per cent increase in Valentine tank output following the receipt of engines from General Motors.

There was the potential for British armoured units to benefit from a substantial supply of French B1-Bis tanks from the United States, although this was rejected by Britain in favour of pursuing the production of Crusader and Matilda tanks by American industry instead. A British tank programme in the United States failed to materialize due to the uncertainty of British survival during the Battle of Britain, and because the United States justifiably did not want to produce tanks that would not support American plans for rearmament. As a result, Britain placed cash orders for American tanks direct from industry, although not without first inspecting the equipment to ensure the suitability with British General Staff requirements.

Britain considered paying for a small number of American Light tanks by foregoing the supply of a number of aero-engines from the United States. However, this was not possible because these engines were needed for the overall priority given to aircraft production in Britain. The cash orders for American tanks conflicted with the programme of the United States to use the same vehicles for their own armoured formations. The supply of tanks from the United States were superseded by Lend-Lease, while the remainder of the tank contracts and industrial capacity created by the British orders were taken over by the American government at a cost that was discounted or waived.

The supply of aid from the United States and Canada was complemented by the mutual exchange of tank information between the Western Allies, together with the co-ordination and co-operation in respect of planning. Britain received numerous technical and industrial reports during the war, while the American and Canadian authorities gained full access to British tank production and testing facilities and information. This collaboration was highly successful and restrictions were more likely the result of administrative and not security concerns.

Lend-Lease eliminated the financial difficulties and permitted Britain to continue pursuing an offensive strategy in all theatres of war. While Lend-Lease was designed to defend the United States, the promise of large numbers of reliable and battleworthy tanks allowed British industry to concentrate upon quality tank production and other war work. This included an expansion of locomotive production with the result of releasing more Lend-Lease shipping space. The new orders for locomotives with Vulcan Foundry increased the amount of non-military work during the remaining years of war and effectively excluded this firm from any further serious military production. Similarly, Canada and Australia agreed to accept more Lend-Lease tanks to increase the level of standardized equipment on the front line. At home, Canada transferred tank capacity to produce the required 25-pounder armed Sexton self-propelled vehicle, whereas Australia ceased their tank programme altogether and redirected their skilled labour to urgent maritime work and railway wagon production.

The reduction of the British and American tank programmes during 1944 affected front line units with shortages of tanks after the costly Normandy campaign and into 1945. American armoured units received all the Sherman tanks at the end of 1944. This resulted in the complete stoppage of Lend-Lease deliveries to Britain, including the Sherman tank suitable for the vital conversion to the Firefly. For Britain, the effect of the shortages of Sherman tanks into 1945 was reminiscent of the period following the defeat of France, which had ironically been overcome by the large supply of Sherman tanks during 1943.

To keep tank shortages to a minimum, Britain reinstated the full Comet tank programme by reversing the reductions of November 1944. This halted the transfer of these tank firms to civilian and non-tank work and ensured that the tank programme continued later into 1945. Furthermore, to ensure that British units continued to receive the Firefly, British Sherman tanks unsuitable for the 17-pounder conversion were exchanged with reworked American Sherman tanks. A similar plan to reinstate the tank programme in the United States was also considered, although this was too costly and the imminent end to the war in Europe resulted in tank cancellations instead.

Conclusion

This book has reviewed the governmental, industrial and strategic influences upon British tank production from 1934 to 1945, together with comparisons to the other domestic and foreign war production. By reviewing the material held within the different national, local and commercial archives not previously considered by historians, this book adds to the existing commentary and understanding provided by other case studies of a planned economy at war. The main purpose of this book has been to examine how the experience of war affected tank production at individual firms in meeting the priorities of the government and the requirements of the General Staff.

From an overall perspective, this book has arrived at a number of central conclusions in relation to the performance of the British tank programme from rearmament until the end of the war. The British tank programme was rightfully given a lower strategic priority before the war. The policy of quantity production that began in 1936, expanded during 1940, and maintained during 1941 and 1942, successfully introduced a number of new tank firms across a range of civilian industries. The serious problems relating to tank reliability and combat effectiveness were unavoidable because the army required a large and rapid supply of tanks during the first half of the war. This was during a time when aircraft production received the overriding priority and before Britain could benefit from the industrial output of North America. The transfer to quality tank production from 1943 was measured by the greater centralized control of the executive fifth Tank Board, the concentration of effort by fewer tank firms, the higher rate of output for the latest British tank designs, and finally the operational superiority of these tanks on the front line.

The organizational relationship between the 'user' and 'supplier' within the tank programme evolved over the period to meet the expected demands upon industry following the changes in political and strategic outlook. The greater centralized control and technical direction of tank development during rearmament followed the transfer of authority from the Mechanical Warfare Board to the Mechanization Board in 1934 and then again in 1936 under the Director-General of Munitions Production. This last change linked General Staff requirements with the capabilities of industry and upon assuming the responsibilities of the Master-General of the Ordnance in 1938, the Director-General of Munitions Production became the principal authority in supplying the tank programme. This occurred during the policy of 'serious' rearmament that gave the correct priority for industrial capacity to aircraft production and air defence. The tank programme expanded the production of the latest Light tank and introduced the new Infantry and Cruiser tanks to both new and existing firms. Against the limitations of industrial capacity, manpower and design expertise, the development of the Matilda tank at Vulcan Foundry was particularly successful, with a pilot produced after 18 months and the first production tank three years after the original specification.

The centralization of the tank programme expanded during the war with the formation of the Tank Board in June 1940 in an attempt to bring General Staff requirements even closer to the capabilities of industry as directed by the Ministry of Supply. Canada similarly reacted after the defeat of France by creating the Joint Committee on Tank Development to bring together the Department of National Defence and the Department of Munitions and Supply for the greater co-ordination of their tank policy. The difficulties in the operation and effectiveness of the first four Tank Boards were the result of each new Minister of Supply changing the authority, terms of reference and organizational structure until the fifth Tank Board in September 1942. The frequent changes in board membership followed the realities of military promotion, the transfer to 'missions' overseas, and that industry wanted the return of their senior directors. Furthermore, these successive transformations were in response to the changing strategic priorities. The first and second Tank Boards were required to ensure that the tank industry concentrated upon quantity output following the loss of equipment after the defeat of France. The third Tank Board began to introduce the essential modifications to existing tanks while maintaining the mass production of the current programme. Finally, the fourth and the fifth Tank Boards emphasized the qualitative aspects of tank design and introduced the latest tanks into production, while accepting greater numbers of Lend-Lease tanks from the United States.

The fifth Tank Board occurred during the greater centralization of the British war economy by the end of 1942, which had synchronized the relationship between the Secretary of State for War and Minister of Supply, representing the 'user' and 'supplier' respectively. In practical terms, P. J. Grigg and Sir Andrew Duncan formulated tank policy on a joint basis from 1943 onwards. These decisions meant that General Staff requirements and the production forecast for industry were presented to the War Cabinet as a single policy. The implementation of these macro decisions were carried out by the General Staff and Ministry of Supply officials on the executive fifth Tank Board, with the senior members making the micro adjustments to the tank programme on the Armoured Fighting Vehicle Liaison Committee. Ultimately, the arrangement between the General Staff and Ministry of Supply from 1943 achieved the required synthesis between tactical and production planning, which Minister of Production Oliver Lyttelton described was so essential for successful war production.

The General Staff altered the tank programme based upon the experience gained on the battlefield that stressed the need for improved reliability, greater armour protection and increased firepower. Furthermore, Britain, Canada and the United States co-operated and collaborated on the areas of tank design, development and production through an extensive exchange of military personnel, equipment and information. Eventually, British tank production achieved the Allied requirement for operational mobility to fight an offensive war, compared to the heavy German tanks that fought strategically defensive battles with fewer numbers and insufficient range. A key factor of the improved operational capability of British tanks was the decision to mass produce the Meteor tank engine for the Cromwell and Comet tank designs, instead of accepting the prospective Ford V8 from the United States. The increased power provided by the Meteor engine, coupled with the expansion of casting and especially welding within industry, meant that tank assembly during the second half of the war incorporated greater levels of armour protection. While American industry had employed superior welding techniques as early as 1941, unlike Britain and Germany, American tank design did not substantially increase armour protection or firepower until the last year of the war. General Staff requirements for the post-war tank programme included the involvement of a state owned Royal Tank Arsenal for the production of the Centurion tank during peacetime.

One of the most significant changes to the tank programme during 1943 was the increase in reliance upon the United States to supply tanks under Lend-Lease for the majority of General Staff requirements for the remainder of the war. This was an extension of the programme since 1939 that took advantage of the strategically secure production facilities of North America to obtain raw materials, munitions, equipment and tank components. The British cash contracts for tanks from the United States during 1940 helped to fund the enlargement of industrial capacity in some American firms, before these factories began to produce large number of tanks under Lend-Lease. The American policy of refusing to produce foreign tank designs was understandable, although British units in North Africa could have benefited from large-scale deliveries of French B1-Bis tanks from the United States. While British units welcomed American tanks in North Africa during 1942, many vehicles only became operationally effective after the field workshops had rectified the production faults and cannibalized new tanks to reverse the lack of spare parts.

When the tank programme focused upon quality production from 1943, the loss of output caused by the elimination of obsolete tanks was accepted, as more tanks were received from the United States. The large supply of Sherman tanks since 1943 meant that British industry eliminated unsatisfactory tanks from the programme and concentrated upon improving the Cromwell tank, without the pressure to deploy this vehicle prematurely. Eventually Britain became overdependent upon the supply of American tanks as shown at the end of 1944 when Lend-Lease deliveries ceased. This brought about the same threat of quantitative deficiency that had existed following the defeat of France. Both Britain and the United States can be blamed for this predicament because they reduced their front line tank programmes during 1944, under the expectation of an earlier and less costly victory against Germany.

The impact of introducing civilian industry to an emerging and expanding tank programme against the different pressures of rearmament and fighting a world war, have been illustrated through a series of case examples. The new tank firms introduced during rearmament received orders based upon their available capacity. Larger orders were placed when the tank programme expanded to include the latest Infantry and Cruiser types and to reflect the increase in experience gained by each firm. Industry benefited from increased sales and employment, although some firms like English Electric were deliberately excluded from war production despite having the capacity to receive munitions orders, as they supplied the important domestic and export markets. In recognition of the growing threats and capabilities of air power and the heightened political tensions on the Continent, industry started taking air raid precautions as early as April 1938 and continued throughout the war once the bombing had begun. German industry similarly continued to operate against the disruption of Allied bombing, but the necessary precautions and air defences diverted resources away from the front line. In contrast, Canada, the United States and eventually the Soviet Union were able to concentrate production in large facilities away from the threat of enemy bombing.

Senior industrialists from large firms were seconded to the Ministry of Supply as advisors until their role expanded to fulfil Director-General positions to influence the design, development and production of the tank programme. The explicit priority of production was given to aircraft during rearmament until November 1941 when tank production was placed on an equal basis, although, the demand for the Merlin aero-engine delayed the mass production of the Meteor tank engine until the Ministry of Supply took control of the programme from 1943. The geographical locations of the tank firms reflected the greater industrial strength of the Midlands, the North East and North West, with these firms representing the motor, heavy engineering, agricultural and locomotive industries. Industry avoided the full cost of the increase in capacity necessary for the mass production of tanks, although the government ensured that these improved facilities were not wholly subsidized by the taxpayer. German industrial capacity similarly expanded during the course of the war, but too much remained unused or not directed towards war production until late into the war.

While the General Staff sought greater levels of reliability, armour protection and firepower in British tanks, these qualities were not provided by industry in sustainably high numbers to the front line until 1943 with modified or reworked Churchill tanks, by 1944 with the Cromwell tank, and 1945 with the Comet tank. There were a number of reasons to account for these deferments. First, the shortages of labour, materials and components affected the completion of new factories and caused a reduction in monthly output, delaying the transfer of production to a later tank design. Second, the General Staff demand for a high percentage of reliable tanks was incompatible with the policy of quantity production that neglected the supply of spare parts necessary to maintain the completed vehicles. Third, the standard of official inspection within factories only viewed the finished tank instead of the different stages of assembly, such as with aircraft production, therefore permitting faults on the assembly line to be overlooked. Fourth, completed tanks from Britain and the United States were damaged when shipped overseas. Fifth, continuation orders of obsolete or problematic tanks before a suitable replacement was available were necessary. This was because an enforced cancellation would have meant an unacceptable loss of output and a disruption to labour resources during the break in production. Sixth, the production of obsolete Valentine tanks into 1944 was due to the political requirement to meet specific Soviet requests for this tank under the supply protocols. Seventh, the increasing numbers of Lend-Lease tanks from the United States meant that the Cromwell tank was not rushed into service. Finally, when compared to the servicing requirements for British motor cars before and after the war, the reliability of British tanks was actually more impressive when considering the vastly different operational usage.

British tanks delivered to the front line during the second half of the war were supported by a greater supply of spare parts and were very reliable, thus requiring fewer occasions to carry out crew maintenance and possibly contaminate the mechanical components. The transfer of British industry to quality tank production was achieved by the standardization, specialization and simplification of the tank programme. This was similar to that already exercised by the United States and the Soviet Union to achieve extremely high levels of productivity. Similarly, Canadian Pacific Railway produced large numbers of Valentine tanks for the Soviet war effort with an average monthly output that was greater than Vickers-Armstrongs. From 1943 in Britain, the tank industry was concentrated among a smaller number of firms that used custom-built equipment and production techniques for a handful of tank designs that required fewer man-hours to assemble. Similar reductions in tank assembly man-hours made German industry more productive, although these advances were negated by the increase in poor workmanship and mechanical breakdown among the latest and much heavier tanks.

The increased supply of tanks from the United States from 1943 meant that British tank firms concentrated on important tank adaptations like the Sherman Duplex-Drive tank, while others transferred to the essential production of locomotives. The decision to accept more tanks in place of locomotives from the United States increased the amount of Lend-Lease shipping space to meet British requirements. The Canadian and Australian authorities also took advantage of the surplus production of Sherman tanks from the United States during 1943 to change or cancel their domestic tank programmes and transfer capacity to other essential war work. From late 1943, the British government and industry prepared to take advantage of the expected peacetime markets, once the eventual transfer to civilian production occurred with the end of the war.

The archives of industry have provided a further understanding of the factory environment and the different influences upon the tank workers in striving to achieve the required rate of output on the assembly line. Those members of the British public interviewed by Mass Observation that offered an opinion, expressed justifiable concern over the efficiency of industry and for any profiteering occurring from the emergency of war. The profit earned by many British and American firms was based upon a fixed amount or percentage above the variable cost, whereas German firms were encouraged to earn more profit by producing more munitions. Public opinion remained consistent with the changing strategic situation, such as the importance of providing aid to the Soviet Union during 'Tanks for Russia' week and the impact of Lend-Lease upon British fighting ability. Once British tanks became operationally effective on the front line, special praise from the armoured commanders, the General Staff and the Ministry of Supply was displayed within factories. This ensured that the workers received the appropriate credit for their good quality workmanship.

The process of dilution and deskilling to increase the skilled workforce was complemented by the temporary transfer of workers from the Air Ministry and between the tank firms themselves to boost output on a short-term basis. The United States benefited from the greater standard of mechanization in American society to obtain skilled workers, whereas Germany increasingly relied upon slave labour and prisoners of war, with the resulting impact on the quality of munitions being produced. In addition to the call-up of workers for the armed forces in Britain, the level of factory manpower was also affected by the problems relating to the health, poor performance and domestic responsibilities of the workers. Germany attempted to avoid calling-up workers from essential production such as the tank industry, but this could not be sustained against the pressures on the Eastern Front. The introduction of women into British factories compelled firms to provide additional welfare facilities and female conscription permitted firms to operate continuously for seven-days-a-week. However, tank parent firms were reluctant to lose their female administrative staff. The inequality of wages between men and women was greater for those females employed on part-time work and for those deemed to be on 'women's work'. Overall, the war provided many workers with the opportunity to work longer and benefit from overtime so that earnings increased at a faster rate than the rising cost of living.

The expansion of tank welding within factories introduced male and female workers to new skills, but the concentration of fumes and the lack of ventilation meant an increase in absenteeism and additional shifts to maintain the required rate of output. Further pressures on production occurred as a result of factory holidays which were necessary to reduce worker tiredness and the number of industrial accidents. The marked reduction in output for the entire tank programme became noticeable because the forecast consistently failed to take these predictable interruptions into account. A reduction in tank output was also sustained during periods of strike action, although these were random events and had less impact upon the tank programme as a whole. This situation was similar in the United States, while German industry was largely affected by the actions of foreign labourers with some German workers using absenteeism or legal technicalities to carry out occasional strikes.

Overall, British industry achieved the demands of the government to provide the mass production of tanks during the first half of the war, and then successfully transformed to the production of quality tanks for the requirements during the second half. This transition was completed by the centralization of tank policy among the 'user' and 'supplier' branches of government, as part of the greater control of the war economy and war planning generally. Ultimately, the design and development of the British tank programme, supported by North American industry, adapted in accordance with the changing strategic situation that required the latest tanks under production to be operationally mobile and fulfil an offensive role overseas.

Appendix 1 – Tank Specifications and Production Data by Dates of Manufacture

Tank	Max. Weight (Tons)	Main Gun	Max. Armour (mm)	Max. Range (Miles)	Total Output	Production Dates
Britain						
Light Mk VI A/B	5.5	0.50 in	14	130	1,322	1936–40
Cruiser Mk III	14.5	2-pdr	14	90	65	1939
Cruiser Mk I	13	2-pdr	14.	150	125	1939–40
Infantry Mk I	11	0.303 in	60	80	139	1939–40
Cruiser Mk II	14	2-pdr	30	100	170	1939–41
Cruiser Mk IV	14.5	2-pdr	30	90	270	1939–41
Matilda	26.5	2-pdr	78	160	2,908	1939–43
Tetrarch	7.5	2-pdr	14	140	100	1940–2
Covenanter	18	2-pdr	40	100	1,770	1940–3
Crusader	20	2-pdr 6-pdr	66	100	4,917	1940–3
Valentine	18.5	2-pdr 6-pdr 75 mm	65	90	7,041	1940–4
Churchill	38	2-pdr 6-pdr 75 mm 95 mm	102	90	4,276	1941–4
Centaur	28	6-pdr 95 mm	76	165	1,774	1942–4
Cromwell	28	6-pdr 75 mm 95 mm	101	175	2,547	1942–5
Cavalier	26.5	6-pdr	76	165	497	1943–4
Harry Hopkins	8.5	2-pdr	38	125	104	1943–5
Heavy Churchill	40	75 mm 95 mm	152	90	917	1943–5
Sherman DD	32.5	75 mm 76 mm	75	125	693	1944
Sherman Firefly	35	17-pdr	75	125	2,074	1944–5
Challenger	32.5	17-pdr	101	120	192	1944–5
Comet	35	77 mm	101	125	623	1944–5
Centurion Prototype	48	17-pdr	152	60	20	1944–5
Tortoise Pilot	78	32-pdr	229	50	6	1944–7
Canada						
Valentine	18.5	2-pdr	65	90	1,420	1941–3
Grizzly	30	75 mm	75	100	188	1943–4
Sexton SP Gun	25.5	25-pdr	25	145	2,150	1943–5

Tank	Max. Weight (Tons)	Main Gun	Max. Armour (mm)	Max. Range (Miles)	Total Output	Production Dates
Germany						
Panzer Mk I	6	7.92 mm	15	95	1,867	1933–7
Panzer Mk II	10	20 mm	30	120	1,886	1936–42
Panzer Mk III	22	37 mm 50 mm 75 mm	70	100	6,129	1937–43
Panzer Mk IV	23	75 mm	80	125	8,509	1937–45
Tiger	56	88 mm	102	90	1,350	1942–4
Panther	45	75 mm	110	105	6,323	1943–5
King Tiger	67	88 mm	150	100	480	1943–5
United States						
Grant/Lee	29	37 mm & 75 mm	75	160	6,258	1941–2
M3 & M5 Stuart	15	37 mm	51	70	22,743	1941–4
Sherman	32.5	75 mm 76 mm	75	150	44,300	1942–5
Pershing	41	90 mm	102	90	2,202	1944–5

Note: Figures include the production of both standard gun tanks and those models converted to a supporting role.

Sources: The National Archives, Kew, CAB 102/851, 'Brief Particulars of British, American, Russian and German Tanks', October 1944; AVIA 46/188, 'Monthly Deliveries of Infantry and Cruiser Tanks by Firms, 1939–1943', draft official history narrative by D. Hay, after 1950, pp. 269–71; CAB 120/355, 'A.F.V. Production', 1943; CAB 120/356, 'A.F.V. Production', 1944 and 1945; Historical Section, Army Headquarters, Report No. 38, 'Tank Production in Canada', 27 July 1950, p. 2, found in National Defence and the Canadian Forces at www.forces.gc.ca/site/home-accueil-eng.asp, accessed 30 September 2010; P. Chamberlain and C. Ellis, *British and American Tanks of World War Two: The Complete Illustrated History of British, American and Commonwealth Tanks, 1939–1945*, first published 1969 (Wigston: Silverdale Books, 2004); L. Ness, *Jane's World War II Tanks and Fighting Vehicles: The Complete Guide* (London: Harper Collins, 2002), pp. 86–8 & 187.

Appendix 2 – British Tanks Produced by Each Firm

Tank Firm	Light Tanks	Infantry Tanks	Cruiser Tanks
Beyer Peacock		Churchill	
Birmingham Railway		Valentine	Cruiser Mark II
		Churchill	Cromwell
			Challenger
Broom & Wade		Churchill	
Charles Roberts		Churchill	
Crabtree			Cruiser Mark II
Dennis Bros		Churchill	
English Electric			Covenanter
			Centaur
			Cromwell
			Comet
Fodens			Crusader
Gloucester Railway		Churchill	
Harland & Wolff		Matilda	Cruiser Mark I
		Churchill	Centaur
John Fowler	Light Mark VI	Matilda	Centaur
			Cromwell
			Comet
Leyland Motors		Churchill	Covenanter
			Centaur
			Cromwell
			Comet
London Midland Scottish		Matilda	Cruiser Mark IV
			Covenanter
			Centaur
Lysaght			Crusader
M. G. Cars			Crusader
Mechanization & Aero			Cruiser Mark III
			Cruiser Mark IV
			Crusader
			Cavalier
Metropolitan-Cammell	Tetrarch	Valentine	Cruiser Mark II
	Harry Hopkins	Churchill	Cromwell
			Comet
Milners Safe			Crusader
Morris Commercial Cars			Crusader
Morris Industries Exports			Crusader
Newton Chambers		Churchill	
North British Locomotive	Light Mark VI	Matilda	

Tank Firm	Light Tanks	Infantry Tanks	Cruiser Tanks
Ruston & Hornsby	Light Mark VI	Matilda	Cavalier
Ruston-Bucyrus			Crusader
Vauxhall Motors		Churchill	
Vickers-Armstrongs	Light Mark VI	Infantry Mark I	Cruiser Mark I
		Valentine	Cruiser Mark II
Vulcan Foundry	Light Mark VI	Matilda	
West's Gas			Crusader

Sources: TNA, AVIA 46/188, 'Deliveries to 30.6.40', p. 65; 'Monthly Deliveries on Infantry and Cruiser Tanks by Firms, 1939–1943', pp. 269–71; AVIA 22/454, 'Centaur/Cromwell Planning', 9 November 1943; 'Tank Capacity', 28 October 1944.

Notes

Introduction

1   M. M. Postan, *British War Production* (London: HMSO and Longmans, Green, 1952), p. 426.

2   R. M. Ogorkiewicz, *Armour: The Development of Mechanised Forces and Their Equipment* (London: Stevens & Sons, 1960).

3   P. Chamberlain and C. Ellis, *British and American Tanks of World War Two: The Complete Illustrated History of British, American and Commonwealth Tanks, 1939–1945*, first published 1969 (Wigston: Silverdale Books, 2004).

4   D. Fletcher, *The Great Tank Scandal: British Armour in the Second World War, Part 1* (London: HMSO, 1989); D. Fletcher, *The Universal Tank: British Armour in the Second World War, Part 2* (London: HMSO, 1993); P. Beale, *Death by Design: British Tank Development in the Second World War* (Stroud: Sutton Publishing, 1998).

5   J. Buckley, *British Armour in the Normandy Campaign 1944* (London and New York: Frank Cass, 2006).

6   J. P. Harris and F. H. Toase (eds), *Armoured Warfare* (London: B. T. Batsford, 1990); P. Wright, *Tank: The Progress of a Monstrous War Machine* (London: Faber and Faber, 2001); R. M. Citino, *Blitzkrieg to Desert Storm: The Evolution of Operational Warfare* (Lawrence: University of Kansas, 2004).

7   S. Broadberry and P. Howlett, 'The United Kingdom: "Victory at all costs"', in M. Harrison (ed.), *The Economics of World War II: Six Great Powers in International Comparison* (Cambridge: Cambridge University Press, 2000); D. Edgerton, *Warfare State: Britain, 1920–1970* (Cambridge: Cambridge University Press, 2006); G. C. Peden, *Arms, Economics and British Strategy: From Dreadnoughts to Hydrogen Bombs* (Cambridge: Cambridge University Press, 2007); D. Edgerton, *Britain's War Machine: Weapons, Resources and Experts in the Second World War* (London: Allen Lane, 2011).

8   R. Croucher, *Engineers at War, 1939–1945* (London: Merlin Press, 1982); P. Summerfield, *Women Workers in the Second World War: Production and Patriarchy in Conflict* (Beckenham: Croom Helm, 1984); H. Jones, *British Civilians in the Front Line: Air Raids, Productivity and Wartime Culture, 1939–45* (Manchester: Manchester University Press, 2006).

9   A. R. Millett, 'Patterns of Military Innovation in the Interwar Period', in W. Murray and A. R. Millett (eds), *Military Innovation in the Interwar Period* (Cambridge: Cambridge University Press, 1996), pp. 339–42.

10 R. W. Goldsmith, 'The Power of Victory: Munitions Output in World War II', *Military Affairs*, Vol. 10, No. 1 (Spring 1946), p. 72.

11 W. Murray and A. R. Millett, *A War To Be Won: Fighting the Second World War* (Cambridge: Harvard University Press, 2001), p. 408.

12 S. Ritchie, 'A New Audit of War: The Productivity of Britain's Wartime Aircraft Industry Reconsidered', *War & Society*, Vol. 12, No. 1 (May 1994), p. 141.

13   Peden, *Arms, Economics and British Strategy*, p. 187.

14   C. Barnett, *The Audit of War: The Illusion and Reality of Britain as a Great Nation* (London: Macmillan, 1986), p. 304.

15   K. Jefferys, *War and Reform: British Politics during the Second World War* (Manchester: Manchester University Press, 1994), p. 9.

16   J. P. Harris, 'British Armour 1918–1940: Doctrine and Development', in Harris and Toase, *Armoured Warfare*, pp. 49–50; W. Murray, 'Armored Warfare: The British, French, and German Experiences', in Murray and Millett, *Military Innovation in the Interwar Period*, pp. 40–5; Edgerton, *Warfare State*, p. 45.

17   Harris, 'British Armour 1918–1940', pp. 40–2.

18   D. French, *Raising Churchill's Army: The British Army and the War against Germany 1919–1945* (Oxford: Oxford University Press, 2001), pp. 34 & 191–2.

19   B. Bond, *British Military Policy between the Two World Wars* (Oxford: Clarendon Press, 1980), p. 329.

20   R. L. DiNardo and A. Bay, 'Horse-Drawn Transport in the German Army', *Journal of Contemporary History*, Vol. 23, No. 1 (Jan. 1988), pp. 129–42; G. Phillips, 'Scapegoat Arm: Twentieth-Century Cavalry in Anglophone Historiography', *Journal of Military History*, Vol. 71, No. 1 (Jan. 2007), p. 66.

21   M. M. Postan, D. Hay and J. D. Scott, *Design and Development of Weapons: Studies in Government and Industrial Organisation* (London: HMSO and Longmans, Green, 1964), pp. 320–1, 354–5 & 357.

22   Ibid., pp. 328 & 363.

23   W. Hornby, *Factories and Plant: A History of the Second World War* (London: HMSO and Longmans, Green, 1958), pp. 184–6; Postan, *British War Production*, p. 426; R. Jackson, *The Nuffield Story* (London: Muller, 1964), p. 187.

24   L. C. Darbyshire, *The Story of Vauxhall, 1857–1946* (Luton: Vauxhall Motors, 1946), pp. 46–7.

25   Postan et al., *Design and Development of Weapons*, pp. 319–21 & 334.

26   Postan, *British War Production*, p. 189.

27   Buckley, *British Armour in the Normandy Campaign*, pp. 152–3.

28   A. Tooze, *The Wages of Destruction: The Making and Breaking of the Nazi Economy* (London: Allen Lane, 2006), p. 612; French, *Raising Churchill's Army*, pp. 104–5.

29   C. J. Dick, 'The Operational Employment of Soviet Armour in the Great Patriotic War', in Harris and Toase, *Armoured Warfare*, p. 101; C. Bellamy, *Absolute War, Soviet Russia in the Second World War: a modern history* (London: Pan Books, 2007), p. 603.

30   O. Lyttelton, Viscount Chandos, *The Memoirs of Lord Chandos* (London: Bodley Head, 1962), p. 285.

31   J. D. Scott, *Vickers: A Story* (London: Weidenfeld and Nicolson, 1963), p. 287.

32   Peden, *Arms, Economics and British Strategy*, pp. 187–8.

Chapter 1

1   Peden, *Arms, Economics and British Strategy*, p. 98.

2   J. Ferris, 'Treasury Control, the Ten Year Rule and British Service Policies, 1919–1924', *Historical Journal*, Vol. 30, No. 4 (Dec. 1987), pp. 859–73.

3   M. Thomas, 'Rearmament and Economic Recovery in the Late 1930s', *Economic History Review*, New Series, Vol. 36, No. 4 (Nov. 1983), pp. 553–4.

4 Lieutenant-Colonel Sir A. G. Stern, *Tanks 1914–1918: The Log-Book of a Pioneer*, first published 1919 (Uckfield: Naval & Military Press, undated), pp. 71–2.

5 J. P. Harris, *Men, Ideas and Tanks: British Military Thought and Armoured Forces, 1903–1939* (Manchester: Manchester University Press, 1995), pp. 32–3 & 65–72.

6 P. Wright, *Tank: The Progress of a Monstrous War Machine* (London: Faber and Faber, 2001), pp. 77–80.

7 T. Travers, 'Could the Tanks of 1918 Have Been War-Winners for the British Expeditionary Force?', *Journal of Contemporary History*, Vol. 27, No. 3 (Jul. 1992), pp. 396, 398 & 402–3.

8 Peden, *Arms, Economics and British Strategy*, pp. 68 & 94.

9 Harris, *Men, Ideas and Tanks*, pp. 136 & 161–2.

10 P. Fearon, 'The British Airframe Industry and the State, 1918–35', *Economic History Review*, New Series, Vol. 27, No. 2 (May 1974), p. 236.

11 Peden, *Arms, Economics and British Strategy*, pp. 63–6.

12 P. Fearon, 'The Formative Years of the British Aircraft Industry, 1913–1924', *Business History Review*, Vol. 43, No. 4 (Winter, 1969), pp. 487–8.

13 Peden, *Arms, Economics and British Strategy*, p. 68.

14 R. J. Shuster, *German Disarmament after World War I: The Diplomacy of International Arms Inspection 1920–1931* (Abingdon: Routledge, 2006), pp. 2–4.

15 Murray, 'Armored Warfare', p. 7.

16 Ferris, 'Treasury Control', pp. 867 & 876.

17 Peden, *Arms, Economics and British Strategy*, p. 162.

18 Ferris, 'Treasury Control', pp. 863–4, 875, 878 & 881.

19 G. C. Peden, *British Rearmament and the Treasury: 1932–1939* (Edinburgh: Scottish Academic Press, 1979), pp. 174–6; Edgerton, *Warfare State*, pp. 18 & 21–3.

20 Ibid., p. 45n.

21 Fearon, 'British Airframe Industry and the State', p. 237.

22 J. D. Scott and R. Hughes, *The Administration of War Production* (London: HMSO and Longmans, Green, 1955), p. 19.

23 Harris, *Men, Ideas and Tanks*, pp. 241–2.

24 Ibid., pp. 242–4, 258 & 261.

25 Ibid., pp. 284–6.

26 Peden, *British Rearmament and the Treasury*, p. 145.

27 Peden, *Arms, Economics and British Strategy*, p. 123.

28 *The Times*, 2 March 1928; 17 March 1928; 20 March 1928.

29 *The Times*, 9 April 1934; 25 April 1934.

30 The National Archives, WO 194/57, First Report of the Mechanization Board, 1934, 'Preface'.

31 Scott and Hughes, *Administration of War Production*, p. 30.

32 Postan et al., *Design and Development of Weapons*, pp. 238n, 305–6 & 319–20.

33 Peden, *Arms, Economics and British Strategy*, pp. 105–6.

34 Thomas, 'Rearmament and Economic Recovery', p. 554.

35 *The Times*, 15 July 1936.

36 TNA, CAB 24/263, 'War Office Production', 19 June 1936; Brown obituary, *The Times*, 27 February 1968.

37 Peden, *British Rearmament and the Treasury*, pp. 48–50.

38 TNA, WO 32/4585, Office Memo No. 1822: 2. Department of the Director-General of Munitions Production, 10 November 1936.

39 TNA, CAB 24/263, 'War Office Production', 25 June 1936.

40 TNA, WO 32/4196, 'Re-organisation of the Master-General of the Ordnance's Department', 22 November 1937.
41 TNA, WO 32/4196, Brown to Hore-Belisha, 11 November 1937; Scott and Hughes, *Administration of War Production*, p. 28.
42 Ibid., pp. 33–9.
43 Fearon, 'British Airframe Industry and the State', pp. 243–4.
44 Ibid., pp. 246–7.
45 Scott and Hughes, *Administration of War Production*, p. 40; S. Ritchie, *Industry and Air Power: The Expansion of British Aircraft Production, 1935–1941* (London and New York: Routledge, 2007), pp. 44–51.
46 M. Harrison, 'Resource Mobilization for World War II: The U.S.A., U.K., U.S.S.R., and Germany, 1938–1945', *Economic History Review*, New Series, Vol. 41, No. 2 (May 1988), pp. 173–7.
47 Postan et al., *Design and Development of Weapons*, p. 239.
48 TNA, WO 194/57, First Report, 1934, para. 1; Second Report of the Mechanization Board, 1935, para. 1; Third Report of the Mechanization Board, 1936, para. 1.
49 TNA, WO 194/57, First Report, 1934, para. 1.
50 TNA, WO 194/57, Second Report, 1935, para. 1.
51 TNA, WO 194/57, Third Report, 1936, para. 1.
52 TNA, WO 194/57, Fourth Report of the Mechanization Board, 1937, para. 1.
53 TNA, WO 194/57, Fifth Report of the Mechanization Board, 1938, para. 3.
54 Modern Records Centre, AEC, MSS.226/AE/1/1/12, Board and General Meetings, 1935–60, '5284: Reduction in Volume of Output and Number of Employees', 3 May 1938.
55 TNA, WO 194/57, First Report, 1934, para. 7.
56 Ibid.
57 Postan et al., *Design and Development of Weapons*, p. 307.
58 Cambridge University Library, Vickers-Armstrongs, Vickers 755, 'Armour Development', 9 January 1948.
59 A. Isaev, 'Against the T-34 the German Tanks Were Crap', in A. Drabkin and O. Sheremet (eds), *T-34 in Action* (Barnsley: Pen & Sword, 2006), pp. 23–4.
60 TNA, WO 194/57, Second Report, 1935, para. 7.
61 TNA, WO 194/57, Fifth Report, 1938, para. 11.
62 M. Smith 'The Royal Air Force, Air Power and British Foreign Policy, 1932–37', *Journal of Contemporary History*, Vol. 12, No. 1 (Jan. 1977), pp. 153 & 155.
63 J. L. Hughes, 'The Origins of World War II in Europe: British Deterrence Failure and German Expansionism', *Journal of Interdisciplinary History*, Vol. 18, No. 4 (Spring 1988), pp. 856–7 & 889.
64 J. P. D. Dunbabin, 'British Rearmament in the 1930s: A Chronology and Review', *Historical Journal*, Vol. 18, No. 3 (Sept. 1975), p. 609.
65 Edgerton, *Warfare State*, pp. 26–33.
66 Harris, *Men, Ideas and Tanks*, p. 274.
67 Peden, *Arms, Economics and British Strategy*, pp. 153 & 158.
68 Peden, *British Rearmament and the Treasury*, p. 137.
69 G. Till, 'Adopting the Aircraft Carrier: The British, American, and Japanese Case Studies', in Murray and Millett, *Military Innovation in the Interwar Period*, p. 201.
70 W. Murray, 'Strategic Bombing: The British, American, and German experiences', in ibid., pp. 119–20.
71 Ritchie, *Industry and Air Power*, pp. 41–3 & 90–1.

72 CUL, Vickers 744, Tanks, General Correspondence, Memo by Carden, 8 January 1932.
73 CUL, Vickers 744, Wonfor to Vickers' director, Sir Noel Birch, 14 January 1932.
74 CUL, Vickers 744, 'Tank Policy', 21 September 1932.
75 CUL, Vickers 744, Birch to Yapp, 12 April 1933.
76 CUL, Vickers 744, '3-Man Tanks', 30 January 1934.
77 CUL, Vickers 722, 'Notes from Quarterly Reports, Military Armaments, 1934–39', by J. D. Scott, post-war undated; Vickers 744, 'Armoured Fighting Vehicles 1937 to 1959', 7 September 1959.
78 CUL, Vickers 744, Birch to DGMP Brown, 2 March 1938; 'Command Tank', 15 July 1938.
79 Postan, *British War Production*, p. 43.
80 Peden, *British Rearmament and the Treasury*, pp. 173 & 177.
81 Scott and Hughes, *Administration of War Production*, p. 22.
82 Peden, *Arms, Economics and British Strategy*, p. 139.
83 Postan, *British War Production*, p. 7.
84 Postan et al., *Design and Development of Weapons*, p. 318.
85 TNA, WO 194/57, First Report, 1934, para. 18.
86 TNA, WO 194/57, Second Report, 1935, para. 17; Third Report, 1936, para. 19.
87 Harris, *Men, Ideas and Tanks*, p. 301.
88 CUL, Vickers 722, 'Notes from Quarterly Reports', 1934 & 1935.
89 Harris, *Men, Ideas and Tanks*, pp. 273 & 275; CUL, Vickers 722, 'Notes from Quarterly Reports', 1936.
90 Bodleian Library, Oxford, Vulcan Foundry, MS. Marconi 2739, Board Minutes, 1934–40, 24 January and 25 November 1936.
91 Postan, *British War Production*, pp. 419–20; L. C. Darbyshire, *The Story of Vauxhall, 1857–1946* (Luton: Vauxhall Motors, 1946), p. 46.
92 Ritchie, *Industry and Air Power*, pp. 87 & 125.
93 TNA, WO 194/57, Fourth Report, 1937, para. 28; Fifth Report, 1938, para. 33; Sixth and Final Report of the Mechanization Board, 1939 to 1940, para. 18.
94 TNA, WO 194/57, Fifth Report, 1938, para. 33; the Infantry Mark I was called the Matilda originally, although the name is more commonly associated with the later Mark II which will be used hereafter.
95 TNA, WO 194/57, Fifth Report, 1938, para. 33; Harris, *Men, Ideas and Tanks*, p. 278.
96 Ibid., pp. 278–9 & 282.
97 TNA, WO 194/57, Fourth Report, 1937, para. 28; Fifth Report, 1938, para. 33.
98 Peden, *Arms, Economics and British Strategy*, pp. 124–5.
99 W. Philpott and M. S. Alexander, 'The French and the British Field Force: Moral Support or Material Contribution?', *Journal of Military History*, Vol. 71, No. 3 (Jul. 2007), pp. 743–72.
100 TNA, AVIA 46/188, 'Deliveries to 30.6.40', draft official history narrative by D. Hay, after 1950, p. 65.
101 D. French, 'The Mechanization of the British Cavalry between the World Wars', *War in History*, Vol. 10, No. 3 (Jul. 2003), pp. 314–20.
102 J. Jackson, *The Fall of France: The Nazi Invasion of 1940* (Oxford: Oxford University Press, 2003), pp. 13–14.
103 L. Ness, *Jane's World War II Tanks and Fighting Vehicles: The Complete Guide* (London: Harper Collins, 2002), pp. 86–8.
104 Postan, *British War Production*, pp. 34–5.

105   Peden, *Arms, Economics and British Strategy*, pp. 140–1.

106   Ritchie, *Industry and Air Power*, pp. 57–9.

107   N. Nakamura, 'Women, Work and War: Industrial Mobilisation and Demobilisa-
      tion, Coventry and Bolton, 1940–1946' (Ph.D. thesis, University of Warwick, 1984),
      pp. 65–6.

108   Ritchie, *Industry and Air Power*, pp. 59–61.

109   S. H. Friedelbaum, 'The British Iron and Steel Industry: 1929–49', *Journal of Business
      of the University of Chicago*, Vol. 23, No. 2 (Apr. 1950), p. 120.

110   Peden, *British Rearmament and the Treasury*, p. 171.

111   Museum of English Rural Life, Ruston & Hornsby, TR 4RAN/MP1/48, 'Tank
      components for government orders', 8 October and 24 December 1938.

112   CUL, Vickers 722, 'Government Defence Programme', 2 June 1936.

113   MRC, Rover Company, MSS.226/RO/1/1/6, Board Minutes, 1936–43, '6632: Future
      Development Expenditure', 25 May 1939.

114   Peden, *British Rearmament and the Treasury*, pp. 46–7.

115   CUL, Vickers 1225, Directors' Minute Books, 1936–8, '1675: (b) English Steel
      Corporation Limited, Armour Plant Extensions', 17 February 1937.

116   CUL, Vickers 1225, '1578: English Steel, Armour Plant', 16 September 1936.

117   CUL, Vickers 1225, '1805: Government Defence Programme', 16 September 1937.

118   D. Edgerton, 'Public Ownership and the British Arms Industry 1920–50', in
      R. Millward and J. Singleton (eds), *The Political Economy of Nationalisation in
      Britain 1920–1950* (Cambridge: Cambridge University Press, 1995), p. 178.

119   CUL, Vickers 722, 'Summary of Sales from 1931 to 1939', 24 December 1940;
      Ritchie, *Industry and Air Power*, pp. 95–6.

120   CUL, Vickers 722, 'Number of Staff and Workpeople Employed at All Works',
      24 December 1940.

121   BLO, Vulcan Foundry, MS. Marconi 2739, 'Number of Workmen Employed', 1935 to
      1939; Peden, *British Rearmament and the Treasury*, p. 208.

122   Postan et al., *Design and Development of Weapons*, pp. 355 & 357–8.

123   TNA, WO 194/57, Fourth Report, 1937, para. 22; Postan et al., *Design and
      Development of Weapons*, p. 319.

124   TNA, WO 194/57, Fifth Report, 1938, para. 22.

125   BLO, Vulcan Foundry, MS. Marconi 2739, 'Tank A.12. Expressing Satisfaction',
      18 May 1938.

126   TNA, WO 194/57, Fifth Report, 1938, para. 33.

127   BLO, Vulcan Foundry, MS. Marconi 2739, 18 May and 14 June 1938.

128   BLO, Vulcan Foundry, MS. Marconi 2739, January to December 1938.

129   Harris, *Men, Ideas and Tanks*, p. 293.

130   Peden, *British Rearmament and the Treasury*, p. 171.

131   Postan, *British War Production*, p. 12.

132   Peden, *British Rearmament and the Treasury*, p. 93.

133   BLO, English Electric, MS. Marconi 2392, Minutes of Board Meetings, 1937–9, '4:
      Munition Work', 7 April 1938; '2: (a) Munition Work', 5 May 1938.

134   BLO, English Electric, MS. Marconi 2392, '3: (a) Munition Work', 5 July 1938; '3:
      (d) Munition Work', 28 July 1938.

135   BLO, English Electric, MS. Marconi 2392, '7: Sales Report', 6 October 1938.

136   *The Times*, 11 November 1932.

137   Gloucestershire Archives, Gloucester, Gloucester Railway Carriage & Wagon
      Company, D4791/6/18, Directors' Minute Books, 1933–8, '50/38: Air Raid
      Precautions', 7 April 1938.

138 Birmingham Archives and Heritage, Metropolitan-Cammell, MS 99/2006/024, Directors' Minutes, 1935–45, '409: Air Raid Precautions', 19 August 1938.

139 GAG, Gloucester Railway, D4791/6/18, '132/38: Air Raid Precautions', 29 September 1938.

140 MRC, AEC, MSS.226/AE/1/1/12, '5323: Air Raids Precautions Scheme', 3 October 1938.

141 BLO, English Electric, MS. Marconi 2392, '3: Air Raid Precautions', 6 October 1938.

142 GAG, Gloucester Railway, D4791/6/19, Directors' Minute Books, 1939–44, '23: Air Raid Precautions', 9 February 1939; '58: Capital Expenditure', 20 April 1939.

143 GAG, Gloucester Railway, D4791/6/19, '137: Air Raid Precautions', 28 August 1939.

144 CUL, Vickers 1225, '2064: Air Raid Precautions', 19 October 1938; Vickers 1226, Directors' Minute Books, 1939–43, '2648: Air Raid Precautions', 14 May 1941.

145 Ritchie, *Industry and Air Power*, pp. 86–7 & 96.

146 CUL, Vickers 1226, '2146: Air Raid Precautions', 18 January 1939.

147 CUL, Vickers 1226, '2207: Expenditure', 19 April 1939.

148 CUL, Vickers 1226, '2293: Air Raid Precautions', 8 September 1939.

149 MRC, Rover, MSS.226/RO/1/1/6, '6559: Capital Expenditure', 22 November 1938.

150 MRC, Rover, MSS.226/RO/1/1/6, '6899: A.R.P.', 12 December 1940.

Chapter 2

1 J. Stevenson, 'Planner's Moon? The Second World War and the Planning Movement', in H. L. Smith (ed.), *War and Social Change: British Society in the Second World War* (Manchester: Manchester University Press, 1986), pp. 59–60.

2 P. Howlett, '"The Thin End of the Wedge?": Nationalisation and Industrial Structure during the Second World War', in R. Millward and J. Singleton (eds), *The Political Economy of Nationalisation in Britain 1920–1950* (Cambridge: Cambridge University Press, 1995), pp. 237 & 248.

3 Edgerton, *Warfare State*, p. 71.

4 J. P. Harris, 'The War Office and Rearmament, 1935–39' (Ph.D. thesis, King's College London, 1983), pp. 224–5.

5 K. Jefferys, *The Churchill Coalition and Wartime Politics, 1940–1945* (Manchester and New York: Manchester University Press, 1991), p. 64.

6 Ritchie, *Industry and Air Power*, p. 228.

7 J. D. Millett, 'The War Department in World War II', *American Political Science Review*, Vol. 40, No. 5 (Oct. 1946), pp. 863–97.

8 M. G. Carew, *Becoming the Arsenal: The American Industrial Mobilization for World War II, 1938–1942* (Lanham: University Press of America, 2010), p. 177.

9 A. R. Millett, 'The United States Armed Forces in the Second World War', in A. R. Millett and W. Murray (eds), *Military Effectiveness, Volume 3: The Second World War*, new edition, first published 1988 (New York: Cambridge University Press, 2010), pp. 49–50.

10 Ritchie, *Industry and Air Power*, p. 67.

11 Ibid., p. 222.

12 Scott and Hughes, *The Administration of War Production*, p. 218.

13 Ritchie, *Industry and Air Power*, pp. 45, 49–50, 59, 62, 85 & 115.

14 House of Commons, *Parliamentary Debates*, 'Ministry of Supply', vol. 351 col. 1088, 21 September 1939.

15 Duncan obituary, *The Times*, 31 March 1952.

16 TNA, AVIA 22/161, W. A. Robinson to P. J. Grigg, 15 June 1940.
17 TNA, AVIA 22/161, Robinson to Minister, 8 June 1940.
18 TNA, CAB 66/7/25, 'Review of the Strategical Situation on the Assumption That Germany Has Decided to Seek a Decision in 1940', 4 May 1940.
19 TNA, AVIA 22/2642, 'Priority of Production', 14 June 1940.
20 W. K. Hancock and M. M. Gowing, *British War Economy* (London: HMSO, 1949), p. 283.
21 MRC, AEC, MSS.226/AE/1/1/12, Board and General Meetings, 1935–60, '5605: Works Manager's Report', 1 July 1940.
22 TNA, CAB 21/1544, 'Meeting of the Production Council', 25 July 1940.
23 TNA, CAB 21/1544, 'Tank Production', 2 August 1940.
24 TNA, CAB 21/1544, Winston Churchill to Lord Beaverbrook, 9 August 1940.
25 TNA, CAB 65/8/41, 'Priority Policy: Tanks and Aircraft', 16 August 1940.
26 P. Howlett, 'Resource Allocation in Wartime Britain: The Case of Steel, 1939–45', *Journal of Contemporary History*, Vol. 29, No. 3 (Jul. 1994), pp. 523–44.
27 TNA, CAB 21/1544, DGTT to Lieutenant-Colonel Jacob, 6 November 1940.
28 TNA, WO 185/8, Twelfth meeting of the Tank Board, 14 March 1941.
29 TNA, AVIA 46/188, 'Monthly Deliveries of Infantry and Cruiser Tanks by Firms, 1939–1943', draft official history narrative by D. Hay, after 1950, p. 270.
30 TNA, CAB 21/1544, Beaverbrook to Churchill, 4 July 1941.
31 TNA, CAB 21/1544, Bevin to Churchill, 10 July 1941.
32 TNA, BT 168/78, 'Priority of Production Directive', 14 November 1941.
33 T. Jersak, 'Blitzkrieg Revisited: A New Look at Nazi War and Extermination Planning', *Historical Journal*, Vol. 43, No. 2 (Jun. 2000), pp. 566–71.
34 G. L. Weinberg, *A World at Arms: A Global History of World War II*, second edition, first published 2005 (New York: Cambridge University Press, 2008), p. 194.
35 J. E. Förster, 'The Dynamics of Volksgemeinschaft: The Effectiveness of the German Military Establishment in the Second World War', in Millett and Murray, *Military Effectiveness*, p. 196.
36 Ibid., p. 186.
37 TNA, WO 194/57, Sixth and Final Report of the Mechanization Board, 1939 to 1940, 'Preface'.
38 Scott and Hughes, *Administration of War Production*, pp. 221–2; Postan et al., *Design and Development of Weapons*, pp. 331–4; Buckley, *British Armour in the Normandy Campaign*, pp. 164–5.
39 TNA, AVIA 22/161, S. S. Hammersley to Neville Chamberlain, 1 April 1940; Lord Lloyd to Chamberlain, 2 April 1940; Colonel Gretton to Chamberlain, 4 April 1940.
40 Nuffield College Library, Lord Cherwell, CSAC 80.4.81/G.364/18–19, 'Military Co-ordination Committee: Tank Production', statement for meeting on 6 May 1940.
41 TNA, AVIA 22/161, H. J. Wilson to Robinson, 7 April 1940.
42 Jefferys, *Churchill Coalition and Wartime Politics*, p. 61.
43 TNA, AVIA 22/161, Robinson to Minister, 14 May 1940.
44 TNA, AVIA 22/161, Robinson to Grigg, 28 May 1940; Oxford Dictionary of National Biography, 'Roger, Sir Alexander Forbes Proctor', found in www.oxforddnb.com.chain.kent.ac.uk/view/article/47707, accessed 7 October 2009.
45 TNA, WO 185/8, Seventh meeting of the Tank Board, 6 August 1940.
46 TNA, AVIA 22/161, Robinson to Grigg, 28 May 1940.
47 TNA, AVIA 22/161, Burton to Morrison, 28 June 1940; Morrison to J. Reith, 1 July 1940.
48 TNA, WO 185/8, First meeting of the Tank Board, 24 June 1940.

49 TNA, AVIA 22/161, Grigg to Robinson, 20 June 1940.

50 R. Lewin, *Man of Armour: A Study of Lieut-General Vyvyan Pope and the Development of Armoured Warfare* (London: Leo Cooper, 1976), pp. 57–60, 73–5, 95–6, 98–102, 107–22 & 127; Pope obituary, *The Times*, 9 October 1941.

51 Lewin, *Man of Armour*, pp. 45, 108 & 116–17.

52 TNA, WO 185/8, Fourth meeting of the Tank Board, 6 July 1940.

53 C. P. Stacey, *Arms, Men and Governments: The War Policies of Canada, 1939–1945* (Ottawa: Queen's Printer, 1970), pp. 31–2.

54 Library and Archives Canada, RG 24, vol. 2596, file HQS-3352–3, part 1, Colonel J. Ralston to C. Howe, 23 August 1940.

55 LAC, HQS-3352–3, part 1, Howe to Ralston, 27 August 1940.

56 LAC, HQS-3352–3, part 1, Twenty-fifth meeting of the Joint Committee, 11 December 1941.

57 Stacey, *Arms, Men and Governments*, p. 486.

58 LAC, HQS-3352–3, part 1, Lieutenant-General K. Stuart to Howe, 27 December 1941.

59 TNA, AVIA 11/5, 'Tanks', by Lord Weir, 5 November 1940.

60 TNA, AVIA 11/5, Duncan to Churchill, 7 November 1940.

61 J. M. Reid, *James Lithgow, Master of Work* (London: Hutchinson, 1964), pp. 43, 169, 192, 194 & 203.

62 TNA, AVIA 22/1019, Ministry of Supply Memo No. 208, 'Part II – Organisation of the Department of the Controller-General of Mechanical Equipment', 19 February 1941.

63 TNA, AVIA 22/161, W. B. Brown to Grigg, 9 January 1941.

64 TNA, AVIA 22/161, War Office to Ministry of Supply, 14 December 1940.

65 *London Gazette*, 13 April 1934; 6 October 1936; 30 September 1938; 15 November 1940.

66 *London Gazette*, 14 November 1924; 10 October 1933.

67 Ritchie, *Industry and Air Power*, pp. 222, 228–9 & 239.

68 Churchill College Archives, First Viscount Weir, WEIR 20/4, Weir to Beaverbrook, 7 July 1941; Weir to Churchill, 8 July 1941; A. J. P. Taylor, *Beaverbrook* (London: History Book Club, 1972), p. 415.

69 Liddell Hart Centre for Military Archives, Sir Albert Stern, STERN 2/5/79, note by Stern, 9 October 1942.

70 TNA, WO 185/8, Sixth meeting of the Tank Board (Reconstituted), 'Appendix A: A.F.V. Design Procedure', 6 November 1941.

71 Lewin, *Man of Armour*, p. 139; TNA, AVIA 22/161, War Office to Ministry of Supply, 11 November 1941.

72 *London Gazette*, 13 April 1928; 30 September 1930.

73 TNA, PREM 4/87/1, Oliver Lyttelton to Churchill, 27 March 1942, with handwritten comment by Churchill, 29 March 1942.

74 CCA, WEIR 21/1, Weir to Duncan, 28 August 1942.

75 TNA, AVIA 11/27, Ministry of Supply Memo No. 440, 'Tank Board', 2 May 1942.

76 Sir M. Thomas, *Out on a Wing: An autobiography* (London: Michael Joseph, 1964), p. 167; William Rootes obituary, *The Times*, 14 December 1964; Reginald Rootes obituary, *The Times*, 21 December 1977.

77 *The Times*, 12 June 1942.

78 *London Gazette*, 28 March 1941; Weeks obituary, *The Times*, 20 August 1960.

79 *London Gazette*, 19 October 1943; Rowcroft obituary, *The Times*, 28 December 1963.

80 TNA, CAB 66/28/17, 'Reorganisation of the Armoured Fighting Vehicle Division', 28 August 1942.

81   CUL, Vickers-Armstrongs, Vickers 1226, Directors' Minute Books, 1939–43, '2918: Commander E. R. Micklem', 30 September 1942.
82   TNA, PREM 4/87/1, Lyttelton to Churchill, 22 September 1942.
83   BAH, Metropolitan-Cammell, MS 99/2006/024, Directors' Minutes, 1935–45, '712: A. J. Boyd', 21 October 1942.
84   BAH, Metropolitan-Cammell, MS 99/2006/024, '785: A. J. Boyd', 18 August 1943; '793: A. J. Boyd', 17 November 1943.
85   TNA, AVIA 22/161, 'Ministry of Supply Memo No. 662', 15 September 1943.
86   TNA, AVIA 22/161, 'Ministry of Supply Memo No. 694', 15 December 1943.
87   TNA, AVIA 22/161, Ministry of Supply to War Office, 9 January 1943; S. Brooks (ed.), *Montgomery and the Eighth Army* (London: Bodley Head, 1991), p. 398.
88   *London Gazette*, 23 March 1944; TNA, AVIA 22/161, War Office to Ministry of Supply, 6 September 1944; Evetts obituary, *The Times*, 28 August 1958.
89   TNA, AVIA 22/161, Ministry of Supply to War Office, 31 August 1943.
90   Briggs obituary, *The Times*, 6 April 1985.
91   TNA, WO 185/7, First meeting of the A.F.V. Liaison Committee, 20–21 October 1942; WO 185/8, Twentieth meeting of the Tank Board, 26 October 1942.
92   Jefferys, *Churchill Coalition and Wartime Politics*, pp. 61–2.
93   Cmd. 6337, *Office of the Minister of Production* (London: HMSO, 1942); O. Lyttelton, Viscount Chandos, *The Memoirs of Lord Chandos* (London: Bodley Head, 1962), pp. 277–85.
94   P. Howlett, 'New Light through Old Windows: A New Perspective on the British Economy in the Second World War', *Journal of Contemporary History*, Vol. 28, No. 2 (Apr. 1993), p. 370.
95   H. C. Thomson and L. Mayo, *United States Army in World War II, The Technical Services, The Ordnance Department: Procurement and Supply* (Washington: Department of the Army, 1960), reprinted 1968, p. 244.
96   TNA, AVIA 22/454, 'Major Tank and Tank Component Contractors', 11 April 1941.
97   R. Croucher, 'Communist Politics and Shop Stewards in Engineering, 1935–46' (Ph.D. thesis, University of Warwick, 1977), pp. 306–7.
98   Postan et al., *Design and Development of Weapons*, p. 319.
99   TNA, AVIA 22/454, 'Major Tank and Tank Component Contractors', 11 April 1941; 'Tank Capacity', 28 October 1944.
100 British Commercial Vehicle Museum, Leyland Motors, M631 143/5, General Manager's Meetings, 1944–6, 'General', May 1944.
101 BCVM, Leyland Motors, M632 143/5, General Manager's Meetings, 1941–3, 'General', April 1943.
102 Heritage Motor Centre, Sir Miles Thomas, 80/20/1/5 & 6/7, Thomas to Fodens; 80/20/1/7 & 8/7, Thomas to Ruston-Bucyrus; 80/20/1/1 & 2/1, Thomas to West's Gas, all 6 May 1943.
103 TNA, AVIA 22/454, 'Major Tank and Tank Component Contractors', 11 April 1941.
104 Ibid.
105 W. Ashworth, *Contracts and Finance* (London: HMSO and Longmans, Green, 1953), pp. 226–7 & 252.
106 R. J. Overy, 'Great Britain: Cyclops', in D. Reynolds, W. F. Kimball and A. O. Chubarian (eds), *Allies at War: The Soviet, American, and British Experience, 1939–1945* (London: Palgrave Macmillan, 1994), p. 129.
107 M. Kutz, 'Fantasy, Reality, and Modes of Perception in Ludendorff's and Goebbels's Concepts of "Total War"', in R. Chickering, S. Förster and B. Greiner (eds), *A World*

at Total War: Global Conflict and the Politics of Destruction, 1937–1945 (Cambridge: Cambridge University Press, 2005), pp. 202–3.

108 BAH, Metropolitan-Cammell, MS 99/2006/024, '567: Machine Tools for Tanks', 17 July 1940.

109 MRC, Mechanization & Aero, MSS.226/NM/1/1/1, Directors' Meetings, 1935–44, 10 August 1940.

110 GAG, Gloucester Railway Carriage & Wagon Company, D4791/6/19, Directors' Minute Books, 1939–44, '375: Capital Expenditure', 25 October 1940.

111 MRC, Morris Commercial Cars, MSS.226/MC/1/3, Directors' and General Meetings, 22 September 1941, 8 September 1942 and 3 December 1943; Mechanization & Aero, MSS.226/NM/1/1/1, 17 November 1942 and 22 December 1943; Nuffield Exports, MSS.226/NE/1/1/1, Minutes of Directors' Meetings, 1933–48, 21 December 1944.

112 MRC, Morris Commercial, MSS.226/MC/1/3, 28 August and 8 September 1942; Nuffield Exports, MSS.226/NE/1/1/1, 21 December 1944.

113 Staffordshire Record Office, Birmingham Railway Carriage & Wagon Company, D831/1/6/3, Plant and Machinery, 'Agreements to Buy Ministry of Supply Buildings, Plant and Machinery', 19 November 1946.

114 D. Edgerton, 'Public Ownership and the British Arms Industry 1920–50', in Millward and Singleton, *The Political Economy of Nationalisation in Britain*, p. 182.

115 MRC, Mechanization & Aero, MSS.226/NM/1/1/2, Directors' Meetings, 1945–7, 17 April 1945.

116 BCVM, Leyland Motors, M639 143/11, General Manager's Meetings, 1938–40 'Summary Report', September 1939 to June 1940.

117 BCVM, Leyland Motors, M639 143/11, 'Summary Report', June 1940.

118 TNA, AVIA 46/188, 'Monthly Deliveries of Infantry and Cruiser Tanks', pp. 269–70; BCVM, Leyland Motors, M639 143/11, 'Production Issues', August 1940; M632 143/5, 'Mark V', January 1941.

119 TNA, AVIA 46/188, 'Monthly Deliveries of Infantry and Cruiser Tanks', pp. 269–70.

120 CCA, WEIR 20/40, 'Cruiser Tank Mark VI (A.15), Expansion Programme', 7 November 1940.

121 TNA, AVIA 46/188, 'Monthly Deliveries of Infantry and Cruiser Tanks', pp. 269–71.

122 Millett, 'United States Armed Forces in the Second World War', pp. 48–9.

123 J. Zeitlin, 'Flexibility and Mass Production at War: Aircraft Manufacture in Britain, the United States, and Germany, 1939–1945', *Technology and Culture*, Vol. 36, No. 1 (Jan. 1995), pp. 55–6.

124 Thomson and Mayo, *Procurement and Supply*, pp. 228–30 & 233.

125 HMC, Thomas, 80/20/1/5 & 6/4, Tank Engine Mission to USA, 'Production Possibilities of Certain Combat Vehicles', 30 March 1942; Thomson and Mayo, *Procurement and Supply*, p. 242.

126 Ibid., pp. 242 & 249; Zeitlin, 'Flexibility and Mass Production at War', p. 60.

127 See Table 3.1.

128 Zeitlin, 'Flexibility and Mass Production at War', p. 52.

129 R. L. DiNardo, *Germany's Panzer Arm in WWII* (Mechanicsburg: Stackpole Books, 2006), pp. 8, 11 & 143n.

130 MRC, Austin Motors, MSS.226/AU/1/1/2, Board Meetings and AGMs, 1930–42, 'A.R.P. Expenditure for Car Works', 25 January 1939.

131 *The Times*, 17 March 1939; MRC, Austin, MSS.226/AU/1/1/2, 'A.R.P. Expenditure for Car Works', 22 March 1939; Rover, MSS.226/RO/1/1/6, Board Minutes, 1936–43, '6613: Air Raid Precautions', 22 March 1939.

132 Jones, *British Civilians in the Front Line*, pp. 60–2.
133 BCVM, Leyland Motors, M639 143/11, 'Works Defence', September 1939.
134 CUL, Vickers 1226, '2648: Air Raid Precautions', 14 May 1941.
135 CUL, Vickers 1226, '2328: English Steel Corporation, Air Raid Precautions', 26 October 1939.
136 MRC, Austin, MSS.226/AU/1/1/2, 'A.R.P. Expenditure for Car Works', 22 February 1939; 'A.R.P. Tunnel', 25 September 1940; 'Air Raid Precautions', 27 November 1940; Morris Commercial, MSS.226/MC/2/1/6–7, 'Profit and Loss Account', 1939–40; Morris Motors, MSS.226/MO/2/2/6–7, 'Profit and Loss Account', 1939–40; M. G. Cars, MSS.226/MG/2/1/5–6, 'Profit and Loss Account', 1939–40; Nuffield Exports, MSS.226/NE/2/1/5–6, 'Profit and Loss Account', 1939–40; Mechanization & Aero, MSS.226/NM/2/1/5–6, 'Profit and Loss Account', 1939–40; Riley Motors, MSS.226/RI/2/1/2–3, 'Profit and Loss Account', 1939–40.
137 MRC, Morris Motors, MSS.226/MO/2/2/6–10, 'Profit and Loss Account', 1939 to 1940 and 1942 to 1944. 1941 accounts are missing.
138 HMC, Thomas, 80/20/1/1 & 2/1, West's Gas to Thomas, 28 February 1941.
139 MRC, Morris Motors, MSS.226/MO/1/2/1, 'Air Raid Damage to Factories', 23 December 1940.
140 TNA, AVIA 46/188, 'Monthly Deliveries of Infantry and Cruiser Tanks', pp. 269–70.
141 For more detail see Jones, *British Civilians in the Front Line*, 'Roof Spotters'.
142 BCVM, Leyland Motors, M632 143/5, 'Air Raid Warnings', April 1941.
143 J. Eloranta and M. Harrison, 'War and Disintegration, 1914–1950', in S. Broadberry and K. H. O'Rourke (eds), *The Cambridge Economic History of Modern Europe, Volume 2: 1870 to the Present* (New York: Cambridge University Press, 2010), p. 148.
144 Weinberg, *World at Arms*, p. 578.
145 Murray and Millett, *A War To Be Won*, p. 539.
146 Hornby, *Factories and Plant*, p. 35.
147 Tooze, *The Wages of Destruction*, p. 578.
148 M. Harrison, 'The Soviet Union: The Defeated Victor', in Harrison, *The Economics of World War II*, p. 295.
149 Ritchie, 'A New Audit of War', pp. 137–8.
150 BLO, English Electric, MS. Marconi 2393, Minutes of Board Meetings, 1939–41, '4: (a) Dislocation of Works by Enemy Action', 8 February 1940.
151 CCA, WEIR 20/6, 'Dispersal of Factories', by Duncan, 24 December 1940.
152 Ritchie, *Industry and Air Power*, p. 236.
153 Ritchie, 'A New Audit of War', p. 138.
154 CUL, Vickers 723, Dispersal of Factories, 'Basis of Recovery', March 1941.
155 CUL, Vickers 723, 'Dispersal of Manufacture', 19 June 1941.
156 Jones, *British Civilians in the Front Line*, p. 29.
157 Tooze, *Wages of Destruction*, p. 434.
158 A. Speer, *Inside the Third Reich, Memoirs by*, trans. R. and C. Winston, first published 1969 (London: Book Club Associates, 1971), pp. 336–7.

Chapter 3

1 Quoted in Postan et al., *Design and Development of Weapons*, p. 322.

2   Postan, *British War Production*, pp. 190–3; Lieutenant-General Sir R. Weeks, *Organisation and Equipment for War* (Cambridge: Cambridge University Press, 1950), p. 49; French, *Raising Churchill's Army*, p. 107.
3   See Appendix 1.
4   Postan, *British War Production*, p. 190.
5   TNA, AVIA 46/188, 'W.O. Requirements 1936–1940', draft official history narrative by D. Hay, after 1950, p. 44.
6   TNA, AVIA 22/161, 'Draft Suggested Press Notice', late May 1940; W. A. Robinson to P. J. Grigg, 28 May 1940.
7   J. P. Harris, 'British Armour 1918–1940: Doctrine and Development', in Harris and Toase, *Armoured Warfare*, p. 46; French, *Raising Churchill's Army*, p. 98.
8   TNA, WO 185/8, First meeting of the Tank Board, 24 June 1940.
9   TNA, WO 185/8, Third meeting of the Tank Board (Reconstituted), 9 September 1941.
10 TNA, WO 185/8, Tenth meeting of the Tank Board, 17 January 1941.
11 Buckley, *British Armour in the Normandy Campaign*, pp. 144 & 245n.
12 TNA, WO 185/8, Third meeting of the Tank Board (Reconstituted), 9 September 1941.
13 TNA, WO 185/8, Eleventh meeting of the Tank Board, 14 February 1941.
14 TNA, AVIA 46/188, 'Monthly Deliveries of Infantry and Cruiser Tanks', pp. 270–2.
15 TNA, WO 185/8, First meeting of the Tank Board (Reconstituted), 1 August 1941.
16 TNA, WO 32/10521, 'Supply of Tanks to U.S.S.R.', 10 March 1942; CAB 120/357, 'Notes of Points Made in Discussion between Prime Minister and Sir Andrew Duncan', 23 July 1943.
17 TNA, WO 185/8, Sixth meeting of the Tank Board (Reconstituted), 7 November 1941.
18 TNA, WO 185/8, Third meeting of the Tank Board (Reconstituted), 9 September 1941.
19 TNA, CAB 120/355, 'A.F.V. Production', weeks ending 30 January and 21 August 1943.
20 TNA, WO 185/5, 'Directorate of Tank Production', 6 February and 8 March 1941.
21 BAH, Metropolitan-Cammell, MS99/2006/024, Directors' Minutes, 1935–45, '625: Air Raid Damage', 23 April 1941; TNA, WO 185/5, 'Directorate of Tank Production', 6 May and 9 June 1941.
22 TNA, WO 185/5, 'Directorate of Tank Production', 8 July 1941; WO 185/6, 'A.F.V. Output against Target', 29 November 1941.
23 TNA, WO 185/6, 'A.F.V. Output against Target', 16 January and 11 April 1942; CUL, Vickers-Armstrongs, Vickers 717, 'Metropolitan-Cammell Carriage & Wagon Company: Summary of War Production for 5 Years', 6 February 1945.
24 TNA, BT 87/43, Director-General of Army Requirements to Director-General of Programmes, 7 November 1941.
25 See Table 1 in J. Beaumont, *Comrades in Arms: British Aid to Russia 1941–1945* (London: Davis-Poynter, 1980), pp. 58–60 for details of the aid programme to the Soviet Union.
26 TNA, BT 87/43, Permanent Secretary to Minister to DGP, 8 November 1941; CAB 120/355, 'A.F.V. Production', July to December 1943; CAB 120/356, 'A.F.V. Production', January 1944 to April 1945.
27 TNA, AVIA 11/27, 'Tank Board', Memo. No. 440, 2 May 1942.
28 TNA, WO 185/8, Eighteenth meeting of the Tank Board, 4 August 1942.
29 TNA, WO 194/57, Sixth and Final Report of the Mechanization Board, 1939 to 1940, para. 18; AVIA 46/188, 'Number of Cruiser and Infantry Tanks Ordered', p. 56.
30 CUL, Vickers 744, 'Armoured Fighting Vehicles 1937 to 1959', 7 September 1959.
31 SRO, Birmingham Railway Carriage & Wagon Company, D831/4/2/16, 'Order Book for New Work, 1939–1940', pp. 5 & 136.

32 TNA, AVIA 46/188, 'Monthly Deliveries of Infantry and Cruiser Tanks', p. 269.
33 LAC, RG 24, vol. 9377, file 38/TANKS/1, Ministry of Supply to British Purchasing Commission, Ottawa, 7 June 1940.
34 Historical Section, Army Headquarters, Report No. 38, 'Tank Production in Canada', 27 July 1950, p. 2, found in National Defence and the Canadian Forces at www.forces. gc.ca/site/home-accueil-eng.asp, accessed 30 September 2010.
35 BLO, Vulcan Foundry, MS. Marconi 2739, Board Minutes, 1934–40, 'A.12 Tanks', 11 June 1940.
36 TNA, WO 185/8, First meeting of the Tank Board, 24 June 1940.
37 TNA, AVIA 46/188, 'Note on Cost as an Index of Tank Production', p. 284.
38 Ritchie, *Industry and Air Power*, pp. 212 & 227–8.
39 TNA, CAB 66/56/36, 'Supplies from North America in Stage II', 23 October 1944.
40 Hancock and Gowing, *British War Economy*, p. 376n.
41 R. C. D. Allen, 'Mutual Aid between the U.S. and the British Empire, 1941–45', *Journal of the Royal Statistical Society*, Vol. 109, No. 3 (1946), p. 263.
42 Thomson and Mayo, *Procurement and Supply*, p. 256.
43 Ibid., p. 242.
44 TNA, WO 185/8, Eighteenth meeting of the Tank Board, 4 August 1942.
45 TNA, WO 185/7, Fourteenth meeting of the A.F.V. Liaison Committee, 2 February 1943.
46 TNA, WO 32/10521, 'Home Production Programme', 26 November 1942.
47 TNA, CAB 120/355, 'A.F.V. Production', January to December 1943; Cromwell production includes 111 Centaur tanks refitted with the Meteor engine.
48 TNA, WO 32/10521, Military Mission to Moscow to War Office, 19 February 1943.
49 TNA, WO 32/10521, Director of Armoured Fighting Vehicles to DGAR, 27 February 1943.
50 TNA, WO 185/7, Seventeenth meeting of the A.F.V. Liaison Committee, 2 March 1943.
51 TNA, WO 185/7, Twenty-fourth meeting of the A.F.V. Liaison Committee, 11 May 1943.
52 TNA, BT 87/137, 'Tank Policy', Grigg and Duncan, 30 April 1943; Buckley, *British Armour in the Normandy Campaign*, pp. 145–6.
53 'Reply to the Memorandum on Tank Production by the Select Committee on National Expenditure', 2 August 1944, in Cmd. 6865, *War-Time Tank Production* (London: HMSO, 1946), p. 49.
54 G. Macleod Ross, *The Business of Tanks, 1933 to 1945*, in collaboration with Major-General Sir C. Clarke (Ilfracombe: Arthur H. Stockwell, 1976), pp. 330–1; see Figure 12 in Buckley, *British Armour in the Normandy Campaign*, p. 175 for a cross-section of each projectile; the 'sabot' was the Armour-Piercing, Discarding Sabot; the best capped shot was the Armour-Piercing, Capped, Ballistic Capped.
55 TNA, WO 185/6, 'Tank Programme 1944–45', 26 July 1943.
56 TNA, BT 87/137, 'Tank Policy', by Grigg and Duncan, 12 January 1944.
57 NCL, Lord Cherwell, CSAC 80.4.81/G.369/12–15, 'British Tanks now in Production', 21 July 1943.
58 TNA, BT 87/137, 'Tank Policy', 12 January 1944.
59 TNA, CAB 120/356, 'A.F.V. Production', January to December 1944.
60 Postan, *British War Production*, p. 309.
61 TNA, BT 87/137, 'Tank Policy', 12 January 1944.
62 TNA, PREM 3/427/9, 'Tank Production Programme', by Lyttelton, 4 October 1944.
63 W. A. Robotham, *Silver Ghosts & Silver Dawn* (London: Constable, 1970), p. 123.

64 TNA, CAB 120/355, 'A.F.V. Production', week ending 2 January 1943.
65 Postan, *British War Production*, p. 188; Peden, *Arms, Economics and British Strategy*, p. 188.
66 TNA, WO 185/8, Fifth meeting of the Tank Board (Reconstituted), 24 October 1941; Fourteenth meeting of the Tank Board, 4 June 1942.
67 TNA, WO 185/8, Eighteenth meeting of the Tank Board, 4 August 1942.
68 Peden, *Arms, Economics and British Strategy*, pp. 217–19.
69 HMC, Sir Miles Thomas, 80/20/1/1 & 2/6, Ministry of Supply, Director of Contracts to Morris Motors, 24 October 1942.
70 TNA, WO 185/6, 'Conclusions Reached', in Report of the British Tank Engine Mission to the United States, November–December 1942.
71 TNA, WO 185/6, 'Explanatory Comment on Work of and Decisions Reached by Mission', in ibid.
72 TNA, WO 185/8, Twenty-second meeting of the Tank Board, 22 December 1942; Twenty-fourth meeting of the Tank Board, 30 December 1942.
73 HMC, Thomas, 80/20/1/5 & 6/12, Major General G. M. Barnes, Ordnance Department Chief to Thomas, 27 January 1944; 80/20/1/7 & 8/19, Thomas to Weeks, 14 March 1944.
74 HMC, Thomas, 80/20/1/7 & 8/19, Weeks to Thomas, 17 March 1944.
75 Weeks, *Organisation and Equipment for War*, p. 53.
76 MRC, Rover Company, MSS.226/RO/1/1/6, Board Minutes, 1936–43, '7225: Meteor Engine Contract', 4 March 1943.
77 MRC, Rover, MSS.226/RO/1/1/6, '7238: Rolls-Royce Limited', 8 April 1943.
78 TNA, BT 87/137, 'Production Programme for Meteor Engines', 22 November 1943.
79 HMC, Thomas, 80/20/5/35 & 36/9, Thomas to Leyland Motors, 26 July 1943.
80 HMC, Thomas, 80/20/1/1 & 2/2, Thomas to Micklem, 15 May 1944.
81 CAB 120/356, 'A.F.V. Production', January to December 1944.
82 MRC, Rover, MSS.226/RO/1/1/7, Board Minutes, 1943–52, '7443: Meteor Engine Contract', 22 June 1944; HMC, Thomas, 80/20/1/1 & 2/5, Thomas to Morris Motors, 30 June 1944.
83 HMC, Thomas, 80/20/1/3 & 4/21, Director-General of Armoured Fighting Vehicles, C. Gibb to Thomas, 11 May 1945; MRC, Rover, MSS.226/RO/1/1/7, '7619: Meteor Engine Contract', 17 May 1945.
84 HMC, Thomas, 80/20/1/3 & 4/21, Thomas to Gibb, 10 May 1945.
85 TNA, PREM 3/426/2, Churchill to General Ismay, 21 April 1941; CAB 120/52, Churchill to Secretary of State for War, D. Margesson and Minister of Supply Duncan, 23 April 1941.
86 P. Beale, *Death by Design: British Tank Development in the Second World War* (Stroud: Sutton Publishing, 1998), pp. 166–7.
87 Lewin, *Man of Armour*, p. 134.
88 Lieutenant-General Sir G. Martel, *An Outspoken Soldier: His Views and Memoirs* (London: Sifton Praed, 1949), pp. 175–8.
89 TNA, CAB 98/20, First meeting of the Tank Parliament, 5 May 1941.
90 TNA, CAB 102/851, 'Brief Particulars of British, American, Russian and German Tanks', October 1944.
91 Ibid.
92 TNA, WO 185/6, Major-General C. Norman to DAFV, Richardson, 19 December 1942.
93 French, *Raising Churchill's Army*, p. 103.
94 Buckley, *British Armour in the Normandy Campaign*, pp. 148–9.

95   Martel, *An Outspoken Soldier*, pp. 207–8; NCL, Cherwell, CSAC 80.4.81/G.371/7, 'German Pz. Kw. VI', by MI-14, 5 February 1943; CSAC 80.4.81/G.371/8–10, MI-10 to Cherwell, 10 February 1943.
96   Buckley, *British Armour in the Normandy Campaign*, p. 149.
97   TNA, BT 87/137, 'Tank Policy', by Grigg and Duncan, 30 April 1943.
98   TNA, BT 87/137, Duncan to Churchill, 21 December 1944.
99   R. M. Ogorkiewicz, *Armour: The Development of Mechanised Forces and Their Equipment* (London: Stevens & Sons, 1960), pp. 310 & 322; Buckley, *British Armour in the Normandy Campaign*, p. 148.
100 Montgomery to Weeks, 3 April 1944 found in S. Brooks (ed.), *Montgomery and the Battle of Normandy* (Stroud: History Press, 2008), pp. 67–8.
101 HMC, Thomas, 80/20/1/3 & 4/12, Mechanization & Aero to Thomas, 20 July 1945.
102 Ross, *The Business of Tanks,* pp. 330–1.
103 Ibid., p. 71.
104 Hornby, *Factories and Plant*, pp. 282–3.
105 TNA, WO 185/8, Tenth meeting of the Tank Board (Reconstituted), 20 January 1942.
106 TNA, WO 185/8, Forty-second meeting of the Tank Board, 16 August 1944.
107 TNA, WO 185/8, Forty-fifth meeting of the Tank Board, 3 January 1945.
108 Postan et al., *Design and Development of Weapons*, p. 345.
109 TNA, WO 185/5, 'Department of Tank Design – Monthly Report for May 1941'.
110 TNA, WO 185/8, Seventeenth meeting of the Tank Board, 13 June 1941.
111 BCVM, Leyland Motors, M632 143/5, General Manager's Meetings, 1941–3, 'Experimental Welded Hull', June 1942.
112 Ritchie, *Industry and Air Power*, p. 245.
113 BCVM, Leyland Motors, M632 143/5, 'Experimental Welded Hull', September 1942.
114 TNA, WO 185/7, 4th meeting of the A.F.V. Liaison Committee, 10 November 1942.
115 BCVM, Leyland Motors, M632 143/5, 'Experimental Welded Hull', November 1942.
116 TNA, AVIA 11/30, Director-General of Fighting Vehicles Production, A. Boyd to Duncan, 22 June 1943.
117 BCVM, Leyland Motors, M632 143/5, 'Centaur Tank', July 1943.
118 BCVM, Leyland Motors, M632 143/5, 'Cromwell Tank', November 1943.
119 Hornby, *Factories and Plant*, pp. 361–2.
120 BLO, English Electric, MS. Marconi 2724, 'War Diary of the English Electric Company Ltd. March 1938–August 1945', 24 November 1943.
121 BCVM, Leyland Motors, M631 143/5, General Manager's Meetings, 1944–6, 'Plant' and 'Comet Tank', January 1944.
122 BCVM, Leyland Motors, M631 143/5, 'Comet Production', September 1944.
123 BCVM, Leyland Motors, M631 143/5, 'Comet Production', October 1944; 'Comet Tanks', December 1944.
124 Thomson and Mayo, *Procurement and Supply*, p. 247.
125 CCA, First Viscount Weir, WEIR 20/9, Report on visit to American Car and Foundry by Hoare, 29 April 1941.
126 Ibid.
127 HMC, Thomas, 80/20/1/5 & 6/4, Tank Engine Mission to USA, 'Production Possibilities of Certain Combat Vehicles', 30 March 1942.
128 TNA, CAB 65/36/12, War Cabinet, 'Reconstruction Plans', 21 October 1943.
129 P. Adams, 'The Failure of Social Reform: 1918–1920', *Past & Present*, Vol. 24, No. 1 (1963), p. 50; K. O. Morgan, *Consensus and Disunity: The Lloyd George Coalition Government 1918–1922* (Oxford: Clarendon Press, 1979), pp. 22–4.

130 CCA, Ernest Bevin, BEVIN 2/4, 'Demobilisation', by Bevin, 10 December 1943; TNA, CAB 66/44/14, War Cabinet, 'Demobilisation', by Bevin, 14 December 1943.

131 H. L. Smith, 'The Womanpower Problem in Britain during the Second World War', *Historical Journal*, Vol. 27, No. 4 (Dec. 1984), p. 939.

132 617, *Fourteenth Report from the Expenditure Committee: The Motor Vehicle Industry* (London: HMSO, 1975), p. 9; S. Rosevear, 'Regional Policy and the British Motor Vehicle Industry 1945–64: A Study in Selective Intervention and the Economics of Industrial Location' (Ph.D. thesis, University of Bristol, 1998), p. 61.

133 BCVM, Leyland Motors, M632 143/5, 'General', December 1943.

134 BCVM, Leyland Motors, M631 143/5, 'General', February 1944.

135 BCVM, Leyland Motors, M631 143/5, 'General', June 1944.

136 BCVM, Leyland Motors, M631 143/5, 'General', May 1945.

137 TNA, AVIA 22/454, 'Curtailment of Production of Churchill Reworks', 26 May 1945.

138 GAG, Gloucester Railway Carriage & Wagon Company, D4791/6/20, Directors' Minute Books, 1944–8, '1283: Tank Contract', 13 June 1945.

139 TNA, AVIA 22/454, Deputy Director of Contracts to John Fowler, 22 September 1945; Ministry of Supply to Major-General D. Fisher, DGAR, 1 October 1945.

140 TNA, AVIA 22/454, letter to H. Cooper-Thompson, Ministry of Supply, 25 July 1945.

141 C. F. Foss and P. McKenzie, *The Vickers Tanks: From Landships to Challenger* (Wellingborough: Patrick Stephens, 1988), p. 150.

142 Postan, *British War Production*, p. 426.

143 TNA, WO /185/8, Forty-sixth meeting of the Tank Board, 24 April 1945.

144 LAC, RG 24, vol. 9377, file 38/TECH LIA/2/5, '21 Army Group: AFV Technical Report, No. 26', June 1945.

145 TNA, WO 185/129, T. E. Harris, DDGOF to Building Executive, 22 September 1944.

146 TNA, WO 185/129, Micklem to Controller-General of Munitions Production, 22 August 1944.

147 TNA, WO 185/129, War Office to J. K. Eastham, 18 October 1944.

148 TNA, WO 185/129, letter to CGMP, 29 June 1944.

149 TNA, WO 185/129, DDGOF to Building Executive, 22 September 1944.

150 TNA, WO 185/129, Ministry of Supply to Treasury Inter-Service Committee, 29 September 1944.

151 BCVM, Leyland Motors, M631 143/5, 'Ministry of Supply Contracts', April 1945.

152 Postan et al., *Design and Development of Weapons*, p. 352.

153 CUL, Vickers 744, 'Armoured Fighting Vehicles 1937 to 1959', 7 September 1959.

154 P. Howlett, '"The Thin End of the Wedge?": Nationalisation and Industrial Structure during the Second World War', in R. Millward and J. Singleton (eds), *The Political Economy of Nationalisation in Britain 1920–1950* (Cambridge: Cambridge University Press, 1995), pp. 237–47 & 253.

155 S. Bowden, 'The Motor Vehicle Industry', in ibid.

Chapter 4

1 Mass Observation Archive, file 843, 'Opinion about Industrial Output', 21 August 1941, pp. 1–2 & 5.

2 Ibid., pp. 5–8.

3 G. G. Field, *Blood, Sweat, and Toil: Remaking the British Working Class, 1939–1945* (Oxford: Oxford University Press, 2011), pp. 120 & 132–6.

4 Ibid., pp. 119–22.

5 MOA, file 843, pp. 2–5 & 8.

6 A. Calder, *The People's War: Britain 1939–45* (London: Panther Books, 1971), pp. 294–5.

7 SRO, Birmingham Railway Carriage & Wagon Company, D831/1/6/2/M, Minutes of directors' meetings, 1943–4, '6236: Ministry of Supply Rate of Profit', 23 November 1943.

8 Thomson and Mayo, *Procurement and Supply*, pp. 16, 113, 127, 256 & 349.

9 R.-D. Müller, 'Albert Speer and Armaments Policy in Total War', in B. R. Kroener, R.-D. Müller and H. Umbreit (eds), *Germany and the Second World War, Vol. V: Organization and Mobilization of the German Sphere of Power. Part II: Wartime Administration, Economy, and Manpower Resources 1942–1944/5* (Oxford: Clarendon Press, 2003), p. 505.

10 MOA, file 1679, 'Industrial Questionnaire', 13 May 1943, pp. 3–4.

11 B. L. Montgomery, 'Reflections on the Battle', 20–28 March 1943, found in S. Brooks (ed.), *Montgomery and the Eighth Army* (London: Bodley Head, 1991), pp. 186–7.

12 TNA, AVIA 11/30, 'A.F.V. Technical Report No. 15', 2 August 1943, pp. 1–6 & 16–20.

13 MOA, file 613, 'Note on Week's Morale', 18 March 1941.

14 MOA, file 738, 'Second Weekly Report (New Series)', 16 June 1941, pp. 14–17.

15 MOA, file 2229, 'Death of Roosevelt', 13 April 1945.

16 MOA, file 1569, 'Report on Feelings about America and the Americans', 22 January 1943, pp. 21 & 24.

17 H. Rockoff, 'The United States: From Ploughshares to Swords', in Harrison, *The Economics of World War II*, p. 95.

18 Such as Warship Weeks 1941–2, Wings for Victory Weeks in 1943 and Salute the Soldier Weeks in 1944. See Calder, *People's War*, pp. 410–12.

19 MOA, file 714, 'War Weapons' Week: Posters & Bands', 26 May 1941.

20 MOA, file 885, 'Seventeenth Weekly Report (New Series)', 29 September 1941, pp. 2–3.

21 MOA, file 899, 'First Weekly Digest (3rd Series)', 6 October 1941, pp. 1–2.

22 MOA, file 855, 'Thirteenth Weekly Report (New Series)', 1 September 1941.

23 MOA, file 885, 'Seventeenth Weekly Report', p. 1.

24 Hancock and Gowing, *British War Economy*, p. 290; Hornby, *Factories and Plant*, p. 338.

25 J. P. Harris, 'The War Office and Rearmament, 1935–39' (Ph.D. thesis, King's College London, 1983), pp. 137–8.

26 Croucher, 'Communist Politics and Shop Stewards', p. 165.

27 Summerfield, *Women Workers in the Second World War*, pp. 35–6, 55 & 61–2.

28 J. J. T. Sweet, *Iron Arm: The Mechanization of Mussolini's Army, 1920–1940* (Mechanicsburg: Stackpole Books, 2007), p. 14.

29 M. Harrison, 'Resource Mobilization for World War II: The U.S.A., U.K., U.S.S.R., and Germany, 1938–1945', *Economic History Review*, New Series, Vol. 41, No. 2 (May 1988), p. 181.

30 Rockoff, 'The United States: From Ploughshares to Swords', p. 105.

31 W. Abelshauser, 'Germany: Guns, Butter, and Economic Miracles', in Harrison, *Economics of World War II*, pp. 130 & 149; Hancock and Gowing, *British War Economy*, pp. 101–2 & 281.

32 Zeitlin, 'Flexibility and Mass Production at War', pp. 66–71.

33 Peden, *British Rearmament and the Treasury*, pp. 81–2.

34 R. A. C. Parker, 'British Rearmament 1936–9: Treasury, Trade Unions and Skilled Labour', *English Historical Review*, Vol. 96, No. 379 (Apr. 1981), p. 328.

35 CUL, Vickers-Armstrongs, Vickers 722, Craven to Inskip, 19 January 1938.

36 Parker, 'British Rearmament 1936–9', p. 332.

37 P. Inman, *Labour in the Munitions Industries* (London: HMSO and Longmans, Green, 1957), pp. 23–5.

38 TNA, WO 194/57, Third Report of the Mechanization Board, 1936, para. 1.

39 Ritchie, *Industry and Air Power*, pp. 156–7.

40 Peden, *Arms, Economics and British Strategy*, p. 142; Parker, 'British Rearmament 1936–9', pp. 334–6.

41 MRC, AEC, MSS.226/AE/1/1/12, Board and General Meetings, 1935–60, '5441: Labour – Numbers Employed', 5 June 1939.

42 MRC, AEC, MSS.226/AE/1/1/12, '5458: Labour – Numbers Employed – Percentage of Boys', 3 July 1939.

43 BCVM, Leyland Motors, M639 143/11, General Manager's Meetings, 1938–40, 'Headquarters Works', May 1939.

44 BCVM, Leyland Motors, M639 143/11, 'Labour', December 1939.

45 MRC, Morris Motors, MSS.226/MO/1/2/1, Directors' Meetings, 1937–45, 'Staff Reductions due to Wartime Requirements', 18 September 1939.

46 MRC, Rover, MSS.226/RO/1/1/6, Board Minutes, 1936–43, '6678: Rover Factories: (1) Car Production', 20 September 1939.

47 GAG, Gloucester Railway Carriage & Wagon Company, D4791/8/3, Board Meetings, 1939–42, Secretary to Chairman, 12 September 1939.

48 I. F. W. Beckett, *The Amateur Military Tradition: 1558–1945* (Manchester: Manchester University Press, 1991), pp. 266 & 278–9.

49 D. Uziel, *Arming the Luftwaffe: The German Aviation Industry in World War II* (Jefferson: McFarland, 2012), p. 217.

50 M. Balfour, *Propaganda in War, 1939–1945: Organisations, Policies, and Publics in Britain and Germany* (London: Routledge & Kegan Paul, 1979), pp. 407–8.

51 Nakamura, 'Women, Work and War', p. 84.

52 Ibid., p. 84n.

53 HMC, Sir Miles Thomas, 80/20/6/38 & 39/16, Thomas to Ministry of Labour, 10 January 1942; 80/20/1/7 & 8/7, Ruston-Bucyrus to Thomas, 12 February 1942.

54 BCVM, Leyland Motors, M632 143/5, General Manager's Meetings, 1941–3, 'B/X Factory', February 1942.

55 HMC, Thomas, 80/20/1/7 & 8/7, Ruston-Bucyrus to Thomas, 23 December 1942.

56 HMC, Thomas, 80/20/1/7 & 8/7, Ruston-Bucyrus to Ministry of Supply, 1 March 1943.

57 Cmd. 6339, *Committee on Skilled Men in the Services* (London: HMSO, 1942); F. W. Perry, 'Manpower and Organisational Problems in the Expansion of the British and Other Commonwealth Armies during the Two World Wars' (Ph.D. thesis, University of London, 1982), p. 122.

58 B. R. Kroener, 'Management of Human Resources, Deployment of the Population, and Manning the Armed Forces in the Second Half of the War', in Kroener et al., *Germany and the Second World War, Vol. 5: Part II*, pp. 849–55.

59 M. Gowing, 'The Organisation of Manpower in Britain during the Second World War', *Journal of Contemporary History*, Vol. 7, No. 1/2 (Jan.–Apr. 1972), pp. 149–56 & 166.

60 Perry, 'Manpower and Organisational Problems', pp. 125–6.

61 BCVM, Leyland Motors, M631 143/5, General Manager's Meetings, 1944–6, 'Reasons for Leaving', January 1943 to May 1945.

62   BLO, Vulcan Foundry, MS. Marconi 2740, Board Minutes, 1940–5, 12 January 1943 to 12 June 1945.

63   For more details see: Summerfield, *Women Workers in the Second World War*.

64   Calder, *People's War*, pp. 505–6.

65   Weinberg, *A World at Arms*, pp. 405, 471–2, 476, 496 & 755–6.

66   A. S. Milward, *War, Economy and Society, 1939–1945* (London: Allen Lane, 1977), p. 219.

67   CCA, Ernest Bevin, BEVIN 2/3, 'Summary of War Work – Factory Department', June 1942.

68   GAG, Gloucestershire Railway, D4791/6/19, Directors' Minute Books, 1939–44, '410: Employment of Women Workers and Their Welfare Supervisor'; '411: Canteen for Women Workers', 13 December 1940.

69   BAH, Metropolitan-Cammell, MS 99/2006/024, Directors' Minutes, 1935–45, '649: Canteen (Works)'; '650: Women's Lavatory', 27 August 1941.

70   Croucher, *Engineers at War*, pp. 14 & 265–6; Summerfield, *Women Workers in the Second World War*, pp. 101 & 120n.

71   Nakamura, 'Women, Work and War', pp. 85–96.

72   Summerfield, *Women Workers in the Second World War*, pp. 38–42.

73   BCVM, Leyland Motors, M639 143/11, 'Dilution', May 1940; 'Labour', June 1940.

74   BCVM, Leyland Motors, M639 143/11, 'Labour', July 1940.

75   BCVM, Leyland Motors, M632 143/5, 'Labour', April 1942.

76   MOA, file 1009, 'Man-Power and Conscription', 11 December 1941, pp. 1–5.

77   HMC, Thomas, 80/20/6/38 & 39/16, Thomas to Ministry of Labour, 14 July 1942.

78   Mass Observation, *People in Production: An Enquiry into British War Production* (Harmondsworth: Penguin Books, 1942), p. 165.

79   GAG, Gloucester Railway, D4791/8/3, 'Orders Received since Last Meeting', October 1940; TNA, AVIA 46/188, 'Monthly Deliveries of Infantry and Cruiser Tanks, p. 270.

80   MOA, file 1679, 'Industrial Questionnaire', 13 May 1943, p. 1.

81   Ibid., pp. 8–9.

82   V. Douie, *Daughters of Britain* (Oxford: Vincent-Baxter Press, 1949), pp. 98–100.

83   Summerfield, *Women Workers in the Second World War*, pp. 145 & 168–70.

84   W. H. Chafe, *The Unfinished Journey: America Since World War II*, fifth edition (New York: Oxford University Press, 2003), pp. 10–14.

85   BCVM, Leyland Motors, M632 143/5, 'Centaur Tank', April 1943.

86   Field, *Blood, Sweat, and Toil*, p. 141.

87   BCVM, Leyland Motors, M631 143/5, 'B/X Factory', September 1944.

88   Cmd. 6251, *Annual Report of the Chief Inspector of Factories for the Year 1939* (London: HMSO, 1941), p. 6.

89   Cmd. 6992, *Annual Report of the Chief Inspector of Factories for the Year 1945* (London: HMSO, 1946), p. 21.

90   BCVM, Leyland Motors, M631 143/5, 'B/X Factory', December 1944.

91   BCVM, Leyland Motors, M631 143/5, 'Comet Tanks', January 1945.

92   D. A. Reid, 'Playing and Praying', in M. Daunton (ed.), *The Cambridge Urban History of Britain, Volume 3: 1840–1950* (Cambridge: Cambridge University Press, 2000), p. 757; C. Wrigley, *British Trade Unions since 1933* (Cambridge: Cambridge University Press, 2002), p. 9.

93   Croucher, *Engineers at War*, p. 58.

94   House of Commons, *Parliamentary Debates*, 'Workers' Holidays', vol. 361, cols 1358–9, 13 June 1940.

95   TNA, CAB 67/8/7, Production Council, 'Holidays', by Bevin, 30 July 1940.
96   TNA, CAB 65/10/14, War Cabinet, 'Production', 22 November 1940.
97   Croucher, *Engineers at War*, pp. 15 & 78.
98   Jones, *British Civilians in the Front Line*, p. 62.
99   Cmd. 6992, *Annual Report*, 1945, Tables I and II, p. 6.
100   SRO, Birmingham Railway, D831/6/1/2, 'Workmens Accident Book', 1944–9, entries
      from November 1944 to July 1945; Cmd. 6698, *Annual Report of the Chief Inspec-
      tor of Factories for the Year 1944* (London: HMSO, 1946), p. 7; Cmd. 6992, *Annual
      Report*, 1945, pp. 11–12.
101   BLO, Vulcan Foundry, MS. Marconi 2740, weeks ending 19 June to 2 August 1941.
102   TNA, AVIA 46/188, 'Monthly Deliveries of Infantry and Cruiser Tanks', p. 270.
103   Mass Observation, *People in Production*, pp. 179–81.
104   *The Times*, 26 February 1942.
105   TNA, CAB 120/355, Offices of the War Cabinet to Ministry of Supply,
      3 December 1942.
106   TNA, CAB 120/356, M. R. Norman to Ministry of Supply, 11 January 1944.
107   TNA, CAB 120/355, 'A.F.V. Production', weeks ending 12 June to 7 August 1943.
108   TNA, BT 87/137, 'Tank Supply Policy', O. Lyttelton, P. J. Grigg and A. R. Duncan,
      16 April 1943, Appendix IV.
109   CAB 120/355, 'A.F.V Production', weeks ending 8 April to 29 September 1943.
110   Buckley, *British Armour in the Normandy Campaign*, p. 167.
111   TNA, PREM 3/427/9, 'A.F.V. Production', week ending 31 July 1943, with handwrit-
      ten comment by Churchill, 6 August 1943.
112   TNA, PREM 3/427/9, Churchill to Lyttelton and Duncan, 11 August 1943.
113   TNA, PREM 3/427/9, Lyttelton to Churchill, 26 August 1943.
114   TNA, PREM 3/427/9, Churchill to Lyttelton, 2 September 1943.
115   TNA, AVIA 22/454, 'Centaur/Cromwell Planning', 9 November 1943; CAB 120/356,
      'A.F.V. Production', July 1944.
116   BCVM, Leyland Motors, M631 143/5, 'Cromwell Tank', July 1944.
117   Inman, *Labour in the Munitions Industries*, pp. 393–4.
118   J. I. Seidman, *American Labor from Defense to Reconversion* (Chicago: University of
      Chicago Press, 1953), pp. 135 & 150; Milward, *War, Economy and Society*, pp. 241–4.
119   H. Umbreit, 'Towards Continental Dominion', in B. R. Kroener, R.-D. Müller
      and H. Umbreit (eds), *Germany and the Second World War, Vol. V: Organization
      and Mobilization of the German Sphere of Power. Part I: Wartime Administration,
      Economy, and Manpower Resources 1939–1941* (Oxford: Clarendon Press, 2000),
      pp. 201, 229–31 & 379; H. Umbreit, 'German Rule in the Occupied Territories,
      1942–1945', in Kroener et al., *Germany and the Second World War, Vol. 5:
      Part II*, pp. 19–20, 26, 28, 87, 90–1, 129, 166–7 & 245; Tooze, *The Wages of
      Destruction*, p. 414.
120   H. J. Braun, *The German Economy in the Twentieth Century: The German Reich and
      the Federal Republic*, first published 1990 (Abingdon: Routledge, 2011), pp. 123–4.
121   T. Mason, *Nazism, Fascism and the Working Class* (Cambridge: Cambridge Univer-
      sity Press, 1996), p. 236.
122   S. Salter, 'Structures of Consensus and Coercion: Workers' Morale and the
      Maintenance of Work Discipline, 1939–1945', in D. Welch (ed.), *Nazi Propaganda:
      The Power and the Limitations* (Beckenham: Croom Helm, 1983), pp. 102–3 & 111.
123   Croucher, 'Communist Politics and Shop Stewards', pp. 113, 211 & 231.
124   *The Times*, 20 September 1941.

125 *The Times*, 24 September 1941.
126 *The Times*, 23 September 1941; 'Tanks for Russia' newsreel 1941 found in, www.britishpathe.com/ record.php?id=12948, accessed 30 September 2010.
127 TNA, AVIA 11/46, Macmillan to Birmingham Railway; Macmillan to Metropolitan-Cammell, 27 September 1941.
128 TNA, AVIA 11/46, Macmillan to English Electric; Macmillan to Mechanization & Aero, 27 September 1941.
129 TNA, WO 32/10521, 'Tanks Allocated and Shipped to Russia under the Protocol', September 1942; D. Borisenko, Soviet Military Mission to Brigadier R. Firebrace, Russian Liaison Group, 22 March 1943.
130 *The Times*, 31 October 1941; BLO, Vulcan Foundry MS. Marconi 2740, Board Minutes, 12 November 1941.
131 Croucher, 'Communist Politics and Shop Stewards', p. 335.
132 Field, *Blood, Sweat, and Toil*, p. 149.
133 Inman, *Labour in the Munitions Industries*, p. 398.
134 TNA, CAB 120/355, 'A.F.V. Production', weeks ending 5, 12 and 19 December 1942.
135 TNA, AVIA 46/188, 'Monthly Deliveries of Infantry and Cruiser Tanks', p. 271.
136 SRO, Birmingham Railway, D831/1/6/2/M, '6237: Unofficial Works Strike', 23 November 1943.
137 BCVM, Leyland Motors, M632 143/5, 'Cromwell Tank', November 1943.
138 TNA, CAB 120/355, 'A.F.V. Production', weeks ending 23 and 30 October 1943.
139 TNA, CAB 120/355, 'A.F.V. Production', September to November 1943.
140 BCVM, Leyland Motors, M632 143/5, 'Cromwell Tank', November 1943.
141 Inman, *Labour in the Munitions Industries*, p. 393.
142 Croucher, *Engineers at War*, pp. 241 & 308–9.

Chapter 5

1 Murray and Millett, *A War To Be Won*, p. 408.
2 J. Zeitlin, 'Americanisation and Its Limits: The Reconstruction of Britain's Engineering Industries, 1945–1955', in N. Whiteside and R. Salais (eds), *Governance, Industry and Labour Markets in Britain and France: The Modernising State in the Mid-Twentieth Century* (London: Routledge, 1998), p. 99.
3 Milward, *War, Economy and Society*, p. 29; M. Harrison, 'The Economics of World War II: An Overview', in Harrison, *The Economics of World War II*, pp. 21–2 & 24.
4 Zeitlin, 'Flexibility and Mass Production at War', pp. 48–9.
5 TNA, AVIA 46/188, 'Monthly Deliveries of Infantry and Cruiser Tanks, pp. 270–1; BCVM, Leyland Motors, M632 143/5, General Manager's Meetings, 1941–3, reports for June 1941 to September 1943.
6 BCVM, Leyland Motors, M632 143/5, 'Churchill', March 1943.
7 Ritchie, *Industry and Air Power*, p. 241.
8 HMC, Sir Miles Thomas, 80/20/1/1 & 2/1, West's Gas to Thomas, 14 May 1942; 80/20/1/7 & 8/8, Milners Safe to Thomas, 19 May 1942.
9 HMC, Thomas, 80/20/1/1 & 2/1, Thomas to West's Gas; 80/20/1/5 & 6/7, Thomas to Fodens, both 8 June 1942.
10 CCA, First Viscount Weir, WEIR 20/9, Report on visit to Montreal Locomotive Works by Hoare, 21 April 1941.

11 Thomson and Mayo, *Procurement and Supply*, pp. 230 & 246.
12 Ibid., p. 238.
13 French, *Raising Churchill's Army*, pp. 97–100.
14 NCL, Lord Cherwell, CSAC 80.4.81/G.368/4, Special Supplement to A.F.V. Technical Report No. 12, Fighting Efficiency, 'British Tanks in M.E.', 6 February 1943.
15 Fletcher, *Great Tank Scandal*, pp. 85–6.
16 P. Warner, *Auchinleck: The Lonely Soldier*, first published 1981 (Barnsley: Pen & Sword, 2006), p. 116.
17 J. Fennell, *Combat and Morale in the North African Campaign: The Eighth Army and the Path to El Alamein* (Cambridge: Cambridge University Press, 2011), pp. 73–6.
18 HMC, Thomas, 80/20/1/1 & 2/18, Thomas to Martel, 20 February 1942.
19 HMC, Thomas, 80/20/1/1 & 2/18, Martel to Thomas, 23 February 1942.
20 HMC, Thomas, 80/20/1/1 & 2/18, Thomas to Martel, 26 February 1942.
21 TNA, WO 185/8, Seventeenth meeting of the Tank Board, 9 July 1942.
22 TNA, WO 185/6, Auchinleck to War Office, 30 June 1942.
23 HMC, Thomas, 80/20/1/5 & 6/4, 'AFV Comparative Reliability Chart (1000 Mile Basis)', 12 July 1942.
24 House of Commons, *Parliamentary Debates*, 'Central Direction of the War', vol. 381, cols 224–476, 1 July 1942; House of Lords, *Parliamentary Debates*, 'Conduct of the War', vol. 123, cols 619–90, 2 July 1942.
25 HMC, Thomas, 80/20/1/1 & 2/1, Thomas to West's Gas; 80/20/1/5 & 6/7, Thomas to Fodens; 80/20/1/7 & 8/7, Thomas to Ruston-Bucyrus, all 6 July 1942.
26 Fletcher, *Great Tank Scandal*, p. 111.
27 NCL, Cherwell, CSAC 80.4.81/G.368/5, Special Supplement, 'Grant and Sherman', 6 February 1943.
28 LAC, RG 24, vol. 9363, file 38/ARM VEH/10, Ordnance Consulting Officer for India to Master-General of the Ordnance in India, 28 July 1942.
29 Thomson and Mayo, *Procurement and Supply*, p. 255.
30 Fennell, *Combat and Morale in the North African Campaign*, pp. 67–9.
31 Thomson and Mayo, *Procurement and Supply*, p. 252.
32 NCL, Cherwell, CSAC 80.4.81/G.368/5, Special Supplement, 'Grant and Sherman', 6 February 1943.
33 NCL, Cherwell, CSAC 80.4.81/G.368/8, Special Supplement, 'American Tanks: Defects on Arrival', 2 February 1943.
34 NCL, Cherwell, CSAC 80.4.81/G.368/9–10, Special Supplement, Technician to GMC, 20 January 1943.
35 NCL, Cherwell, CSAC 80.4.81/G.368/5, Special Supplement, 'Grant and Sherman', 6 February 1943.
36 NCL, Cherwell, CSAC 80.4.81/G.368/6, Special Supplement, 'General Stuart', 6 February 1943.
37 HMC, Thomas, 80/20/1/7 & 8/19, Weeks to Thomas, 20 July 1942.
38 HMC, Thomas, 80/20/1/1 & 2/1, Thomas to West's Gas; 80/20/1/5 & 6/7, Thomas to Fodens; 80/20/1/7 & 8/7, Thomas to Ruston-Bucyrus, all 10 August 1942.
39 HMC, Thomas, 80/20/1/7 & 8/19, Weeks to Thomas, 20 July 1942.
40 HMC, Thomas, 80/20/1/7 & 8/15, Thomas to Director-General of Armoured Fighting Vehicles, C. Gibb, 10 March 1944.
41 Ritchie, 'A New Audit of War', p. 135.
42 TNA, WO 185/8, Seventeenth meeting of the Tank Board, 9 July 1942.
43 TNA, WO 185/8, Eighteenth meeting of the Tank Board, 4 August 1942.

44 TNA, AVIA 22/161, Ministry of Supply Memo No. 527, 'Organisation for the Provision of Armoured Fighting Vehicles', 9 October 1942; Cmd. 6865, *War-Time Tank Production* (London: HMSO, 1946), Appendix A, pp. 19–20.

45 TNA, AVIA 46/188, 'Numerical Strength of Tank Department', p. 114.

46 Postan et al., *Design and Development of Weapons*, p. 352; Edgerton, *Warfare State*, p. 81; TNA, WO 185/8, Thirty-sixth meeting of the Tank Board, 22 November 1943.

47 NCL, Cherwell, CSAC 80.4.81/G.368/5, Special Supplement, 'Crusader', 6 February 1943.

48 HMC, Thomas, 80/20/1/1 & 2/8, Mechanization & Aero to Thomas, 'Assembly and Machining Time in Man Hours', 3 January 1944.

49 TNA, AVIA 11/24, Duncan to Winston Churchill, 9 November 1942; AVIA 46/188, 'Monthly Deliveries of Infantry and Cruiser Tanks', p. 271.

50 Weeks, *Organisation and Equipment for War*, p. 90.

51 DiNardo, *Germany's Panzer Arm in WWII*, pp. 11, 14–15, 20–1, 112–13 & 124.

52 TNA, CAB 98/20, Second meeting of the Tank Parliament, 13 May 1941.

53 TNA, WO 185/8, Eighteenth meeting of the Tank Board, 11 July 1941.

54 NCL, Cherwell, CSAC 80.4.81/G.367/19–22, Harriman to Under Secretary of War, R. P. Patterson, 13 July 1942.

55 TNA, WO 185/8, Ninth meeting of the Tank Board (Reconstituted), 8 January 1942.

56 TNA, WO 185/7, Second meeting of the A.F.V. Liaison Committee, 27 October 1942.

57 MRC, Mechanization & Aero, MSS.226/NM/2/1/5–10, 'Trading Account', 1939–44.

58 Ritchie, 'A New Audit of War', pp. 128–9.

59 TNA, PREM 3/426/16, 'Tank Return for the United Kingdom', 27 June 1941.

60 TNA, PREM 3/426/4, Churchill to Margesson and Beaverbrook, 11 July 1941.

61 Jefferys, *Churchill Coalition and Wartime Politics*, pp. 37, 47, 55, 93–4 & 108n; A. Danchev, '"Dilly-Dally", or Having the Last Word: Field Marshal Sir John Dill and Prime Minister Winston Churchill', *Journal of Contemporary History*, Vol. 22, No. 1 (Jan. 1987), p. 28.

62 TNA, PREM 3/426/4, Margesson to Churchill, 15 July 1941.

63 TNA, PREM 3/426/16, 'Tank Return for the United Kingdom', 21 September 1941.

64 TNA, CAB 120/355, 'State of Readiness of Operational Tanks', 17 September and 26 November 1942

65 TNA, CAB 120/355, 'Summary of Tank State of Readiness', 25 March 1943.

66 Zeitlin, 'Flexibility and Mass Production at War', pp. 53–4; Ritchie, 'A New Audit of War', pp. 139–40.

67 R. Lloyd-Jones and M. J. Lewis, *Alfred Herbert Ltd and the British Machine Tool Industry, 1887–1983* (Aldershot: Ashgate Publishing, 2006), p. 160.

68 French, *Raising Churchill's Army*, pp. 102 & 107; Buckley, *British Armour in the Normandy Campaign*, pp. 105–6.

69 TNA, CAB 120/357, 'Notes of Points Made in Discussion between Prime Minister and Sir Andrew Duncan', 23 July 1943; CAB 120/356, 'A.F.V. Production', May 1944.

70 BLO, English Electric, MS. Marconi 2724, 'War Diary of the English Electric Company Ltd. March 1938 – August 1945', 10 December 1940 and 21 March 1941; BCVM, Leyland Motors, M632 143/5, 'Comparative Statement of Orders Received', April 1941.

71 TNA, WO 185/8, Sixteenth meeting of the Tank Board, 23 May 1941.

72 HMC, Thomas, 80/20/6/38 & 39/16, Thomas to Ministry of Labour, 26 August 1942.

73 TNA, WO 185/8, First meeting of the Tank Board (Reconstituted), 1 August 1941.

74 BCVM, Leyland Motors, M632 143/5, 'Mark V', August 1941; TNA, AVIA 46/188, 'Monthly Deliveries of Infantry and Cruiser Tanks', p. 271.

75 TNA, WO 185/8, Tenth meeting of the Tank Board (Reconstituted), 20 January 1942.

76 TNA, WO 185/8, Weeks to Burton, 21 January 1942.

77 TNA, WO 185/8, Burton to Bartlett, 22 January 1942.

78 TNA, WO 185/8, Eleventh meeting of the Tank Board (Reconstituted), 11 February 1942.

79 TNA, WO 185/8, Twelfth meeting of the Tank Board (Reconstituted), 17 February 1942.

80 TNA, WO 185/8, Thirteenth meeting of the Tank Board, 7 May 1942.

81 TNA, CAB 121/261, 'Tank Production by Vauxhall Group', by Grigg and Duncan, 7 August 1942.

82 TNA, CAB 121/261, Defence Committee (Operations), 11 August 1942.

83 TNA, WO 185/7, Eighth meeting of the A.F.V. Liaison Committee, 8 December 1942.

84 TNA, CAB 121/261, 'Tank Production by Vauxhall Group', by Grigg and Duncan, 20 January 1943.

85 TNA, CAB 65/33/12, War Cabinet, 'Tank Production', 20 January 1943.

86 TNA, WO 185/8, Twenty-fifth meeting of the Tank Board, 25 January 1943.

87 BCVM, Leyland Motors, M632 143/5, 'Covenanter Tank', February 1942.

88 BCVM, Leyland Motors, M632 143/5, 'Covenanter Tank', August and November 1942.

89 TNA, AVIA 46/188, 'Monthly Deliveries of Infantry and Cruiser Tanks', p. 271.

90 Ritchie, *Industry and Air Power*, p. 248.

91 J. E. Förster, 'The Dynamics of Volksgemeinschaft: The Effectiveness of the German Military Establishment in the Second World War', in Millett and Murray, *Military Effectiveness*, p. 186.

92 Murray and Millett, *A War To Be Won*, pp. 240, 257, 590 & 598.

93 LAC, RG 24, vol. 2626 part 1, file HQS-3352–37–6-1, 'North African Theatre of Operations – A.F.V. Technical Report No. 1', 26 March 1943.

94 TNA, AVIA 11/30, 'A.F.V. Technical Report No. 15', Appendix E, 2 August 1943.

95 HMC, Thomas, 80/20/5/37/1, Weeks to C. J. Bartlett, Vauxhall Motors, 18 June 1943.

96 'Reply to the Memorandum on Tank Production by the Select Committee on National Expenditure', 2 August 1944, in Cmd. 6865, *War-Time Tank Production*, p. 49.

97 LAC, RG 24, vol. 9377, file 38/TECH LIA/2/2, '21 Army Group: AFV Technical Report and Reply, No. 14', para. 14, 30 August 1944.

98 LAC, RG 24, vol. 9377, file 38/TECH LIA/2/3, '21 Army Group: AFV Technical Report and Reply, No. 19', para. 26, 9 December 1944.

99 CCA, Sir Percy James Grigg, PJGG/9/8/11, Montgomery to Lieutenant-General Miles Dempsey, 25 June 1944.

100 Montgomery to Major-General F. de Guingand, 24 June 1944, found in French, *Raising Churchill's Army*, p. 96.

101 Buckley, *British Armour in the Normandy Campaign*, p. 120.

102 'Reply to the memorandum', in Cmd. 6865, *War-Time Tank Production*, p. 48.

103 BCVM, Leyland Motors, M631 143/5, General Manager's Meetings, 1944–6, 'General', July 1944.

104 SRO, Birmingham Railway Carriage & Wagon Company, D831/1/6/2/M, Routine Correspondence and Letters, Verney to Briggs, 6 September 1944.
105 SRO, Birmingham Railway, D831/4/2/20, Order book for new work, 1944–5, 21 April and 12 August 1944; D831/4/2/21, Order book for new work, 1945–6, 20 January 1945.
106 LAC, 38/TECH LIA/2/3, '21 Army Group: AFV Technical Report and Reply, No. 17', para. 24, 15 November 1944.
107 'General Summary of Routine Maintenance', in *Churchill III and IV Instruction Book*, July 1942; 'Lubrication Chart', in *Valentine X: Service Instruction Book*, December 1943.
108 'Lubrication Chart', in *Handbook for the Cromwell VII*, January 1945.
109 'After Sales Service', in *The New Austin Ten* (Birmingham: J. C. Ltd, 1939).
110 'Maintenance Summary', in *Riley Instruction Book for the 100 H.P. 2½ Litre Model* (Oxford: Nuffield Press, undated), approximately 1950.
111 LAC, 38/TECH LIA/2/3, 'AFV Technical Report', No. 17, para. 24, 15 November 1944.
112 TNA, WO 185/6, 'Memorandum on British Armour: No. 2', by Montgomery, 21 February 1945.
113 P. Beale, *Death by Design: British Tank Development in the Second World War* (Stroud: Sutton Publishing, 1998), p. 203.
114 Martel, *An Outspoken Soldier*, p. 283.
115 French, *Raising Churchill's Army*, p. 263.
116 Unreferenced quotation dated 19 March 1945 in W. W. Stout, *'Tanks Are Mighty Fine Things'* (Detroit: Chrysler Corporation, 1946), pp. 826.
117 TNA, AVIA 22/454, 'Centaur/Cromwell Planning', 9 November 1943; 'Tank Capacity', 28 October 1944.
118 Ritchie, 'A New Audit of War', p. 140.
119 TNA, AVIA 22/454, 'Centaur/Cromwell Planning', 9 November 1943; 'Tank Capacity', 28 October 1944.
120 HMC, Thomas, 80/20/1/1 & 2/8, Mechanization & Aero to Thomas, 17 December 1943.
121 BCVM, Leyland Motors, M631 143/5, 'Ministry of Supply Contracts', Cromwell material shortages: January to April, June, August, November and December 1944; Comet material shortages: September and October 1944 and April 1945.
122 BCVM, Leyland Motors, M631 143/5, 'General', October 1944.
123 Ritchie, 'A New Audit of War', pp. 127 & 135.
124 Ritchie, *Industry and Air Power*, pp. 243–4.
125 BCVM, Leyland Motors, M632 143/5, 'B/X Factory', July 1942; HMC, Thomas, 80/20/1/1 & 2/8, Mechanization & Aero to Thomas, 'Assembly and Machining Time in Man Hours', 3 January 1944.
126 Postan, *British War Production*, p. 171n.
127 BCVM, Leyland Motors, M632 143/5, 'Cromwell Tank', November 1943.
128 R. Overy, *War and Economy in the Third Reich* (New York: Oxford University Press, 2002), p. 369.
129 Buckley, *British Armour in the Normandy Campaign*, p. 36.
130 E. Belfield and H. Essame, *The Battle for Normandy* (London: Batsford, 1965), p. 145.
131 BCVM, Leyland Motors, M631 143/5, 'General', August 1944.
132 DiNardo, *Germany's Panzer Arm in WWII*, p. 20.
133 BCVM, Leyland Motors, M631 143/5, 'General', July 1944.

Chapter 6

1 Thomson and Mayo, *Procurement and Supply*, p. 242.
2 Historical Section, 'Tank Production in Canada', p. 1.
3 Hancock and Gowing, *British War Economy*, pp. 105, 195n, 229 & 382; Stacey, *Arms, Men and Governments*, pp. 490–1.
4 Rockoff, 'The United States: From Ploughshares to Swords', p. 94.
5 TNA, CAB 68/2/39, 'Third Monthly Report by the Minister of Supply', 13 November 1939; CAB 68/3/29, 'Fourth', 18 December 1939; CAB 68/4/27, 'Fifth' 17 January 1940; CAB 68/5/14, 'Sixth', 17 February 1940; CAB 68/5/51, 'Seventh', 23 March 1940; CAB 68/6/7, 'Eighth', 20 April 1940; CAB 68/6/34, 'Ninth', 23 May 1940.
6 Thomson and Mayo, *Procurement and Supply*, p. 10.
7 Historical Section, 'Tank Production in Canada', pp. 1–2.
8 LAC, RG 24, vol. 9377, file 38/TANKS/1, Canadian Military Headquarters, London to Department of National Defence, Ottawa, 20 December 1939.
9 LAC, 38/TANKS/1, CMH to DND, 6 January 1940.
10 LAC, 38/TANKS/1, 'Record of a Meeting Held at the Ministry of Supply', 21 March 1940.
11 LAC, 38/TANKS/1, CMH to DND, 5 April 1940.
12 Chamberlain and Ellis, *British and American Tanks of World War Two*, pp. 66–7.
13 LAC, 38/TANKS/1, Crawford to British Supply Board, Ottawa, 22 May 1940.
14 LAC, 38/TANKS/1, Ministry of Supply to British Purchasing Commission, 7 June 1940.
15 Historical Section, 'Tank Production in Canada', p. 2.
16 Quoted in C. P. Stacey, *Six Years of War: The Army in Canada, Britain and the Pacific, Volume I* (Ottawa: Queen's Printer, 1955), reprinted 1956, p. 90.
17 LAC, 38/TANKS/1, Department of Munitions and Supply to CMH, 10 June 1940.
18 LAC, 38/TANKS/1, CMH to DND, 14 June 1940; Vickers-Armstrongs to CMH, 15 June 1940; CMH to Vickers-Armstrongs, 18 June 1940.
19 LAC, RG 24, vol. 2596 part 1, file HQS-3352–3, vol. 1, C. D. Howe to Colonel J. L. Ralston, Minister of National Defence, 27 August 1940.
20 TNA, AVIA 46/188, 'Monthly Deliveries of Infantry and Cruiser Tanks, pp. 269–71.
21 LAC, RG 24, vol. 2596 part 1, file HQS-3352–4, Major-General H. Crerar to Minister, 19 September 1940.
22 LAC, HQS-3352–4, tank meeting in Washington, 20 September 1940.
23 LAC, HQS-3352–4, Ralston to Crerar, 26 September 1940.
24 LAC, HQS-3352–3, vol. 1, Sixth meeting of the Joint Committee on Tank Development, 24 January 1941.
25 LAC, HQS-3352–3, vol. 1, Eighth meeting of the Joint Committee, 18 February 1941.
26 LAC, HQS-3352–3, vol. 1, Eleventh meeting of the Joint Committee, 1 May 1941; Fourteenth meeting of the Joint Committee, 29 May 1941.
27 CUL, Vickers-Armstrongs, Vickers 744, 'Armoured Fighting Vehicles 1937 to 1959', 7 September 1959.
28 LAC, HQS-3352–3, vol. 1, Department of Munitions and Supply to Master-General of the Ordnance, 4 February 1941; Historical Section, 'Tank Production', pp. 3–5.
29 Ibid., p. 5; House of Commons, *Parliamentary Debates*, 'Russia (British Empire War Assistance)', vol. 421, cols 2516–19, 16 April 1946.
30 TNA, WO 32/10521, Major-General Richardson to Major-General Watson, 23 June 1942.

31 TNA, AVIA 46/188, 'Monthly Deliveries of Infantry and Cruiser Tanks', pp. 269–71.
32 Stacey, *Arms, Men and Governments*, p. 488.
33 TNA, AVIA 38/102, Memo from BPC, 1 June 1940.
34 CCA, First Viscount Weir, WEIR 20/9, Report on visit to American Car and Foundry, by Hoare, 29 April 1941.
35 TNA, WO 185/8, Fifteenth meeting of the Tank Board, 16 May 1941.
36 TNA, AVIA 46/188, 'Monthly deliveries of Infantry and Cruiser Tanks', pp. 269–70.
37 LAC, RG 24, vol. 2615, file HQS-3352–25–1, 'Minutes of British Tank Components Meeting', weekly from 10 July to 14 August 1942.
38 TNA, BT 87/29, 'Tank Programme in the United States of America', 15 June 1940.
39 Liddell Hart Centre for Military Archives, Sir Albert Stern, STERN 2/16, 'Details of the French Tank (Char "B")', 2 November 1939.
40 J. Jackson, *The Fall of France: The Nazi Invasion of 1940* (Oxford: Oxford University Press, 2003), pp. 14–15.
41 TNA, WO 185/8, Second meeting of the Tank Board, 26 June 1940.
42 TNA, AVIA 38/102, 'Minutes of Meeting in New York: Tanks – Cruiser', 18 August 1940.
43 CCA, WEIR 20/42, Report on Mission to the United States by Pakenham-Walsh, October 1940.
44 D. Edgerton, *Britain's War Machine: Weapons, Resources and Experts in the Second World War* (London: Allen Lane, 2011), pp. 80–1.
45 Thomson and Mayo, *Procurement and Supply*, p. 227.
46 Ibid., p. 10.
47 TNA, AVIA 38/102, Purvis to M. Greenly, BPC Ottawa, 11 May 1940.
48 TNA, AVIA 38/102, BPC to J. Monnet, 13 June 1940.
49 Stout, *'Tanks Are Mighty Fine Things'*, pp. 5–7.
50 TNA, AVIA 38/42, Vice-Chief of the Imperial General Staff to Pakenham-Walsh, 21 August 1940.
51 CCA, WEIR 20/42, Report by Pakenham-Walsh, October 1940.
52 Chamberlain and Ellis, *British and American Tanks of World War Two*, p. 112.
53 TNA, AVIA 38/42, 'Launching of the Tank Programme', Appendix V (A): Principal tank contracts placed by British Supply Mission, dated after 1945.
54 Thomson and Mayo, *Procurement and Supply*, p. 254.
55 C. M. Green, H. C. Thomson and P. C. Roots, *United States Army in World War II, The Technical Services, The Ordnance Department: Planning Munitions for War* (Washington: Department of the Army, 1955), reprinted 1970, pp. 75–6.
56 E. R. Stettinius, Jr, *Lend-Lease: Weapon for Victory* (New York: Macmillan, 1944), p. 94.
57 TNA, AVIA 38/42, 'Launching of the Tank Programme', Appendix V (B): Recoveries from United States Government on Sale of Material, after 1945.
58 Ibid., Appendix V (C): Recoveries from Sale of Capital Facilities, after 1945.
59 TNA, AVIA 38/102, 'Minutes of Meeting in Washington: Tanks – M2A4', 3 October 1940.
60 TNA, AVIA 38/102, BPC to North American Supplies Committee, London, 27 October 1940.
61 TNA, AVIA 38/102, North American Supplies Committee to BPC, 31 October 1940.
62 TNA, CAB 115/88, Telegram from Consul General in New York, 31 January 1941.
63 CCA, WEIR 20/9, Report on visit to Baldwin Locomotive Works, by Hoare, 24 April 1941.
64 TNA, AVIA 38/137, BPC to British Raw Materials Mission, Washington, 1 July 1941.

65 LAC, HQS-3352-4, Second meeting of the Joint Committee, 14 September 1940.
66 LAC, RG 24, vol. 2615, file HQS-3352-25, telegram to Military Attaché, Washington, 19 February 1941.
67 LAC, HQS-3352-25, 'Minutes of a Meeting at the Mount Stephen Club, Montreal', 28 February 1941.
68 LAC, RG 24, vol. 9370, file 38/COMM AFV/1, CMH to Ministry of Supply, 26 August 1941.
69 LAC, 38/COMM AFV/1, Tank Board chairman, G. D. Burton to CMH, 9 September 1941.
70 LAC, RG 24, vol. 9370, file 38/COM AFV/2, 30 September 1941 to 3 April 1943; LAC, RG 24, vol. 9370, file 38/COM AFV/2/2, 17 April to 4 December 1943.
71 *The Times*, 28 July 1941.
72 TNA, PREM 4/87/1, 'Tank Board Composition', 23 September 1943; WO 185/8, Thirty-sixth meeting of the Tank Board, 22 November 1943.
73 Green et al., *Planning Munitions for War*, pp. 268–9.
74 A. Danchev, 'Dill', in J. Keegan (ed.), *Churchill's Generals* (New York: Grove Weidenfeld, 1991), pp. 60–8.
75 Green et al., *Planning Munitions for War*, p. 269.
76 TNA, CAB 111/28, Foreign Office to Moscow, 7 September 1942; WO 32/10521, P. Soloviev, Soviet Trade Delegation to Brigadier R. Firebrace, Russian Liaison Group, 9 November 1944; Firebrace to Lieutenant-General A. F. Vasiliev, Soviet Military Mission, 1 February 1945.
77 Green et al., *Planning Munitions for War*, p. 274.
78 Ibid., p. 270; A. R. Lewis, 'The Failure of Allied Planning and Doctrine for Operation Overlord: The Case of Minefield and Obstacle Clearance', *Journal of Military History*, Vol. 62, No. 4 (Oct. 1998), pp. 787–807.
79 Green et al., *Planning Munitions for War*, p. 272; B. H. Reid, 'The Attack by Illumination: The Strange Case of Canal Defence Lights', *RUSI Journal*, Vol. 128, No. 4 (1983), pp. 44–9.
80 Green et al., *Planning Munitions for War*, p. 270.
81 LAC, RG 24, vol. 9363, file 38/ARM VEH/10, CMH to DND, 2 September 1943.
82 Zeitlin, 'Flexibility and Mass Production at War', p. 61.
83 Green et al., *Planning Munitions for War*, p. 271.
84 Hancock and Gowing, *British War Economy*, p. 246; W. S. Churchill, *The Second World War, Volume II: Their Finest Hour* (London: Cassell, 1949), p. 503; Broadberry and Howlett, 'The United Kingdom: "Victory at all costs"', p. 53.
85 Stacey, *Arms, Men and Governments*, pp. 49 & 172.
86 CCA, WEIR 20/42, Report by Pakenham-Walsh, October 1940.
87 TNA, AVIA 46/188, 'Monthly Deliveries of Infantry and Cruiser Tanks', pp. 269–70; Thomson and Mayo, *Procurement and Supply*, p. 263.
88 Ibid., pp. 231–3.
89 Ibid., p. 255.
90 Ibid., p. 253.
91 Field Marshal Sir W. Slim, *Defeat into Victory*, second edition (London: Cassell, 1956), pp. 230, 288 & 479–80.
92 National Archives of Australia, A816, 45/302/161, File No. 1, Minister for the Army, F. M. Forde to Prime Minister, J Curtin, 7 January 1942.
93 D. P. Mellor, *Australia in the War of 1939–1945, Volume V: The Role of Science and Industry* (Canberra: Australian War Memorial, 1958), pp. 301–22.

94 NAA, A816, 45/302/161, 'Notes on Tanks Being Supplied from Overseas', April 1942.
95 NAA, A816, 45/302/161, Director Armoured Fighting Vehicle Production, A. R. Code to Ministry of Munitions, 25 February 1943.
96 NAA, A816, 45/302/184, File No. 2, Australian Tank Production, by Colonel G. A. Green, 17 May 1943, 'Survey of Tanks Received from Overseas and Tanks on Issue', p. 16.
97 NCL, Lord Cherwell, CSAC 80.4.81/G.368/48–52, Harriman to Churchill, 25 May 1943.
98 Historical Section, 'Tank Production in Canada', pp. 11–13.
99 NCL, Cherwell, CSAC 80.4.81/G.369/9, Harriman to Cherwell, 21 July 1943.
100 TNA, WO 185/6, Director-General of Artillery to CAFV Micklem, 30 July 1943.
101 TNA, WO 185/6, Micklem to DCIGS Weeks, 13 August 1943; Specification of the Comet tank, 20 December 1943.
102 Thomson and Mayo, *Procurement and Supply*, pp. 222–3 & 231.
103 Ross, *The Business of Tanks*, pp. 41 & 311.
104 Ibid., pp. 284–8.
105 O. N. Bradley, *A Soldier's Story of the Allied Campaigns from Tunis to the Elbe* (London: Eyre & Spottiswoode, 1951), pp. 322–3.
106 Thomson and Mayo, *Procurement and Supply*, pp. 242 & 263.
107 TNA, AVIA 46/188, 'Monthly Deliveries of Infantry and Cruiser Tanks', p. 271; CAB 120/355, 'A.F.V. Production', 1943; CAB 120/356, 'A.F.V. Production', 1944.
108 TNA, AVIA 22/454, 'Medium Tanks', 5 February 1944; BT 87/137, 'Assignments from U.S. War Department', by P. J. Grigg, 15 December 1944.
109 TNA, AVIA 46/188, 'Monthly Deliveries of Infantry and Cruiser Tanks', p. 271; CAB 120/355, 'A.F.V. Production', 1943; CAB 120/356, 'A.F.V. Production', 1944.
110 'Reply to the Memorandum on Tank Production by the Select Committee on National Expenditure', 2 August 1944, in Cmd. 6865, *War-Time Tank Production* (London: HMSO, 1946), p. 50.
111 TNA, PREM 3/426/15, Lyttelton to Churchill, 28 August 1942.
112 Ibid.
113 TNA, PREM 3/426/15, Lyttelton to Churchill, 8 September 1942.
114 TNA, PREM 3/426/15, Churchill to Lyttelton, 13 September 1942.
115 Peden, *Arms, Economics and British Strategy*, p. 190.
116 TNA, AVIA 46/188, 'Monthly Deliveries of Infantry and Cruiser Tanks', p. 271; AVIA 22/454, 'Tank Capacity', 28 October 1944.
117 TNA, CAB 66/31/48, 'Report by the Minister of Production on his visit to America', 9 December 1942, Appendix C.
118 Tooze, *The Wages of Destruction*, p. 567.
119 BLO, Vulcan Foundry, MS. Marconi 2740, Board Minutes, 1940–2, 11 May and 13 July 1943.
120 BLO, Vulcan Foundry, MS. Marconi 2740, 12 January and 8 June 1943.
121 BLO, Vulcan Foundry, MS. Marconi 2740, 12 February 1945.
122 NAA, A816, 45/302/184, 'Review of Australian Tank Production Policy', 12 July 1943; General D. MacArthur to Curtin, 14 August 1943.
123 NAA, A816, 45/302/184, Curtin to MacArthur, 10 June 1944; War Cabinet, 'Australian Tank Policy', 5 January 1945.
124 NAA, A816, 45/302/184, Curtin to MacArthur, 31 January 1945; Defence Committee, 'Australian Tank Policy', 25 January 1946.

125 TNA, AVIA 22/454, 'Curtailment of Production of Cromwell, Comet, Challenger & S.P.2', 14 November 1944.

126 TNA, PREM 3/427/9, 'Tank Production in 1945', 6 October 1944.

127 TNA, BT 87/137, British Army Staff and British Supply Mission, Washington to Ministry of Supply and War Office, 6 December 1944.

128 Thomson and Mayo, *Procurement and Supply*, pp. 256–7.

129 TNA, BT 87/137, 'Assignments from U.S. War Department', by Grigg, 15 December 1944.

130 'Reply to the Memorandum', in Cmd. 6865, *War-Time Tank Production*, p. 50.

131 TNA, BT 87/137, BAS and BSM to Ministry of Supply and War Office, 6 December 1944.

132 TNA, AVIA 22/454, 'Amendment', Director-General of Armoured Fighting Vehicles, C. Gibb to Regional Controllers, 15 December 1944.

133 TNA, BT 87/137, 'Assignments from United States War Department – Reactions on United Kingdom Production Plans', by Minister of Supply Duncan, 23 December 1944.

134 TNA, CAB 120/358, 'Record of Decisions Taken at Meeting Held on 20 January 1945', 22 January 1945.

135 L. Mayo, *United States Army in World War II, The Technical Services, The Ordnance Department: On Beachhead and Battlefront* (Washington: Department of the Army, 1968), reprinted 1971, p. 312.

136 Thomson and Mayo, *Procurement and Supply*, p. 259.

137 H. Morrison, *Government and Parliament: A Survey from the Inside*, first published 1954 (London: Oxford University Press, 1956), pp. 288–9.

Bibliography

Unpublished national archives

National Archives, Kew

AVIA   11/5, 11/24, 11/27, 11/30, 11/46, 22/161, 22/454, 22/1019, 22/2642, 38/42, 38/102, 38/137, 46/188

BT   87/29, 87/43, 87/137, 168/78

CAB   21/1544, 24/263, 24/272, 65/8/41, 65/10/14, 65/33/12, 65/36/12, 66/7/25, 66/28/17, 66/31/48, 66/44/14, 66/56/36, 67/8/7, 68/2/39, 68/3/29, 68/4/27, 68/5/14, 68/5/51, 68/6/7, 68/6/34, 98/20, 102/851, 111/28, 115/88, 120/52, 120/355, 120/356, 120/357, 120/358, 121/261

PREM   3/426/2, 3/426/4, 3/426/15, 3/426/16, 3/427/9, 4/87/1

WO   32/4196, 32/4585, 32/10521, 185/5, 185/6, 185/7, 185/8, 185/129, 194/57

Library and Archives Canada, Ottawa

2596   HQS-3352–3, HQS-3352–4

2615   HQS-3352–25, HQS-3352–25–1

2626   HQS-3352–37-6-1

9363   38/ARM VEH/10

9370   38/COMM AFV/1, 38/COM AFV/2, 38/COM AFV/2/2

9377   38/TANKS/1, 38/TECH LIA/2/2, 38/TECH LIA/2/3, 38/TECH LIA/2/5

National Defence and the Canadian Forces

www.forces.gc.ca/site/home-accueil-eng.asp, accessed 30 September 2010
   Historical Section, Army Headquarters, Report No. 38

National Archives of Australia, Canberra

A816   45/302/161, 45/302/184

Unpublished university archives

Bodleian Library, Department of Special Collections and Western Manuscripts, Oxford

English Electric
   MS. Marconi 2392, 2393, 2724

Vulcan Foundry
    MS. Marconi 2739, 2740

Cambridge University Library, Manuscripts Department

Vickers-Armstrongs
    Vickers 717, 722, 723, 744, 755, 1225, 1226

Churchill College Archives, University of Cambridge

Ernest Bevin
    BEVIN 2/3, 2/4
Sir Percy James Grigg
    PJGG 9/8/11
First Viscount Weir
    WEIR 20/4, 20/6, 20/9, 20/40, 20/42, 21/1

Liddell Hart Centre for Military Archives, King's College London

Sir Albert Stern
    STERN 2/5/79, 2/16

Mass Observation Archive, University of Sussex

File   613, 714, 738, 843, 855, 885, 899, 1009, 1569, 1679, 2229

Modern Records Centre, University of Warwick

Associated Equipment Company
    MSS.226/AE/1/1/12
Austin Motor Company
    MSS.226/AU/1/1/2
M. G. Cars
    MSS.226/MG/2/1/5–6
Morris Commercial Cars
    MSS.226/MC/1/3, MC/2/1/6–7
Morris Motors
    MSS.226/MO/1/2/1, MO/2/2/6–10
Nuffield Exports
    MSS.226/NE/1/1/1, NE/2/1/5–6
Mechanization & Aero
    MSS.226/NM/1/1/1, NM/1/1/2, NM/2/1/5–10
Riley Motors
    MSS.226/RI/2/1/2–3
Rover Company
    MSS.226/RO/1/1/6, RO/1/1/7

Museum of English Rural Life, University of Reading

Ruston & Hornsby
    TR 4RAN/MP1/48

Nuffield College Library, Oxford

Lord Cherwell
    CSAC 80.4.81/G.364, G.367, G.368, G.369, G.371

Unpublished local and county archives

Birmingham Archives and Heritage Service, Birmingham Central Library

Metropolitan-Cammell
    MS 99/2006/024

Gloucestershire Archives, Gloucester

Gloucester Railway Carriage & Wagon Company
    D4791/6/18, D4791/6/19, D4791/6/20, D4791/8/3

Staffordshire Record Office, Stafford

Birmingham Railway Carriage & Wagon Company
    D831/1/6/2/M, D831/1/6/3, D831/4/2/16, D831/4/2/20, D831/4/2/21, D831/6/1/2

Unpublished motor vehicle museum archives

British Commercial Vehicle Museum, Leyland

Leyland Motors
    M631 143/5, M632 143/5, M639 143/11

Heritage Motor Centre Motor Museum, Gaydon

Sir Miles Thomas
    80/20/1/1 & 2, 80/20/1/3 & 4, 80/20/1/5 & 6, 80/20/1/7 & 8, 80/20/5/35 & 36,
80/20/5/37, 80/20/6/38 & 39

Published official sources

617, *Fourteenth Report from the Expenditure Committee: The Motor Vehicle Industry*
    (London: HMSO, 1975).

Cmd. 6251, *Annual Report of the Chief Inspector of Factories for the Year 1939* (London: HMSO, 1941).

Cmd. 6337, *Office of the Minister of Production* (London: HMSO, 1942).

Cmd. 6339, *Committee on Skilled Men in the Services* (London: HMSO, 1942).

Cmd. 6698, *Annual Report of the Chief Inspector of Factories for the Year 1944* (London: HMSO, 1946).

Cmd. 6865, *War-Time Tank Production* (London: HMSO, 1946).

Cmd. 6992, *Annual Report of the Chief Inspector of Factories for the Year 1945* (London: HMSO, 1946).

House of Commons, *Parliamentary Debates*.

House of Lords, *Parliamentary Debates*.

Mass Observation, *People in Production: An Enquiry into British War Production* (Harmondsworth: Penguin Books, 1942).

Newspapers

London Gazette
The Times

World wide web

Oxford Dictionary of National Biography

www.oxforddnb.com, accessed 7 October 2009
Sir Alexander Forbes Proctor Roger

Pathé

www.britishpathe.com, accessed 30 September 2010

Published Tank instruction handbooks

Churchill III and IV Instruction Book, 1942.
Handbook for the Cromwell VII, 1945.
Valentine X: Service Instruction Book, 1943.

Published primary sources

Bradley, O. N., *A Soldier's Story of the Allied Campaigns from Tunis to the Elbe* (London: Eyre and Spottiswoode, 1951).

Brooks, S. (ed.), *Montgomery and the Battle of Normandy* (Stroud: History Press, 2008).

— (ed.), *Montgomery and the Eighth Army* (London: Bodley Head, 1991).

Churchill, W. S., *The Second World War, Volume II: Their Finest Hour* (London: Cassell, 1949).

Lyttelton, O., Viscount Chandos, *The Memoirs of Lord Chandos* (London: Bodley Head, 1962).

Martel, Lieutenant-General Sir G., *An Outspoken Soldier: His Views and Memoirs* (London: Sifton Praed, 1949).

Morrison, H., *Government and Parliament: A Survey from the Inside*, first published 1954 (London: Oxford University Press, 1956).

Robotham, W. A., *Silver Ghosts & Silver Dawn* (London: Constable, 1970).

Slim, Field Marshal Sir W., *Defeat into Victory*, 2nd edition (London: Cassell, 1956).

Speer, A., *Inside the Third Reich, Memoirs by*, trans. R. and C. Winston, first published 1969 (London: Book Club Associates, 1971).

Stern, Lieutenant-Colonel Sir A. G., *Tanks 1914–1918: The Log-Book of a Pioneer*, first published 1919 (Uckfield: Naval & Military Press, undated).

Stettinius, Jr, E. R., *Lend-Lease: Weapon for Victory* (New York: Macmillan, 1944).

Thomas, Sir M., *Out on a Wing: An Autobiography* (London: Michael Joseph, 1964).

Weeks, Lieutenant-General Sir R., *Organisation and Equipment for War* (Cambridge: Cambridge University Press, 1950).

Published manufacturer's histories and handbooks

Darbyshire, L. C., *The Story of Vauxhall, 1857–1946* (Luton: Vauxhall Motors, 1946).

Jackson, R., *The Nuffield Story* (London: Muller, 1964).

The New Austin Ten (Birmingham: J. C. Ltd., 1939).

Riley Instruction Book for the 100 H.P. 2½ Litre Model (Oxford: Nuffield Press, undated), approximately 1950.

Scott, J. D., *Vickers: A Story* (London: Weidenfeld and Nicolson, 1963).

Stout, W. W., *'Tanks Are Mighty Fine Things'* (Detroit: Chrysler Corporation, 1946).

Official histories

Australia

Mellor, D. P., *Australia in the War of 1939–1945, Volume V: The Role of Science and Industry* (Canberra: Australian War Memorial, 1958).

Britain

Ashworth, W., *Contracts and Finance* (London: HMSO and Longmans, Green, 1953).

Hancock, W. K., and Gowing, M. M., *British War Economy* (London: HMSO, 1949).

Hornby, W., *Factories and Plant: A History of the Second World War* (London: HMSO and Longmans, Green, 1958).

Inman, P., *Labour in the Munitions Industries* (London: HMSO and Longmans, Green, 1957).

Postan, M. M., *British War Production* (London: HMSO and Longmans, Green, 1952).

Postan, M. M., Hay, D., and Scott, J. D., *Design and Development of Weapons: Studies in Government and Industrial Organisation* (London: HMSO and Longmans, Green, 1964).

Scott, J. D., and Hughes, R., *The Administration of War Production* (London: HMSO and Longmans, Green, 1955).

Canada

Stacey, C. P., *Arms, Men and Governments: The War Policies of Canada, 1939–1945* (Ottawa: Queen's Printer, 1970).
—, *Six Years of War: The Army in Canada, Britain and the Pacific, Volume I*, first published 1955 (Ottawa: Queen's Printer, 1956).

United States

Green, C. M., Thomson, H. C., and Roots, P. C., *United States Army in World War II, The Technical Services, The Ordnance Department: Planning Munitions for War* (Washington: Department of the Army, 1955), reprinted 1970.
Mayo, L., *United States Army in World War II, The Technical Services, The Ordnance Department: On Beachhead and Battlefront* (Washington: Department of the Army, 1968), reprinted 1971.
Thomson, H. C., and Mayo, L., *United States Army in World War II, The Technical Services, The Ordnance Department: Procurement and Supply* (Washington: Department of the Army, 1960), reprinted 1968.

Published secondary sources

Balfour, M., *Propaganda in War, 1939–1945: Organisations, Policies, and Publics in Britain and Germany* (London: Routledge & Kegan Paul, 1979).
Barnett, C., *The Audit of War: The Illusion and Reality of Britain as a Great Nation* (London: Macmillan, 1986).
Beale, P., *Death by Design: British Tank Development in the Second World War* (Stroud: Sutton Publishing, 1998).
Beaumont, J., *Comrades in Arms: British Aid to Russia 1941–1945* (London: Davis-Poynter, 1980).
Beckett, I. F. W., *The Amateur Military Tradition: 1558–1945* (Manchester: Manchester University Press, 1991).
Belfield, E., and Essame, H., *The Battle for Normandy* (London: Batsford, 1965).
Bellamy, C., *Absolute War, Soviet Russia in the Second World War: A Modern History* (London: Pan Books, 2007).
Bond, B., *British Military Policy between the Two World Wars* (Oxford: Clarendon Press, 1980).
Braun, H. J., *The German Economy in the Twentieth Century: The German Reich and the Federal Republic*, first published 1990 (Abingdon: Routledge, 2011).
Broadberry, S., and O'Rourke, K. H. (eds), *The Cambridge Economic History of Modern Europe: Volume 2, 1870 to the Present* (New York: Cambridge University Press, 2010).
Buckley, J., *British Armour in the Normandy Campaign 1944* (London and New York: Frank Cass, 2006).
Calder, A., *The People's War: Britain 1939–45* (London: Panther Books, 1971).
Carew, M. G., *Becoming the Arsenal: The American Industrial Mobilization for World War II, 1938–1942* (Lanham: University Press of America, 2010).
Chafe, W. H., *The Unfinished Journey: America Since World War II*, 5th edition (New York: Oxford University Press, 2003).

Chamberlain, P., and Ellis, C., *British and American Tanks of World War Two: The Complete Illustrated History of British, American and Commonwealth Tanks, 1939–1945,* first published 1969 (Wigston: Silverdale Books, 2004).

Chickering, R., Förster, S., and Greiner, B. (eds), *A World at Total War: Global Conflict and the Politics of Destruction, 1937–1945* (Cambridge: Cambridge University Press, 2005).

Citino, R. M., *Blitzkrieg to Desert Storm: The Evolution of Operational Warfare* (Lawrence: University of Kansas, 2004).

Croucher, R., *Engineers at War, 1939–1945* (London: Merlin Press, 1982).

Daunton, M. (ed.), *The Cambridge Urban History of Britain, Volume 3: 1840–1950* (Cambridge: Cambridge University Press, 2000).

DiNardo, R. L., *Germany's Panzer Arm in WWII* (Mechanicsburg: Stackpole Books, 2006).

Douie, V., *Daughters of Britain* (Oxford: Vincent-Baxter Press, 1949).

Drabkin, A., and Sheremet, O. (eds), *T-34 in Action* (Barnsley: Pen & Sword, 2006).

Edgerton, D., *Britain's War Machine: Weapons, Resources and Experts in the Second World War* (London: Allen Lane, 2011).

—, *Warfare State: Britain, 1920–1970* (Cambridge: Cambridge University Press, 2006).

Fennell, J., *Combat and Morale in the North African Campaign: The Eighth Army and the Path to El Alamein* (Cambridge: Cambridge University Press, 2011).

Field, G. G., *Blood, Sweat, and Toil: Remaking the British Working Class, 1939–1945* (Oxford: Oxford University Press, 2011).

Fletcher, D., *The Great Tank Scandal: British Armour in the Second World War, Part 1* (London: HMSO, 1989).

—, *The Universal Tank: British Armour in the Second World War, Part 2* (London: HMSO, 1993).

Foss, C. F., and McKenzie, P., *The Vickers Tanks: From Landships to Challenger* (Wellingborough: Patrick Stephens, 1988).

French, D., *Raising Churchill's Army: The British Army and the War against Germany 1919–1945* (Oxford: Oxford University Press, 2001).

Harris, J. P., *Men, Ideas and Tanks: British Military Thought and Armoured Forces, 1903–1939* (Manchester: Manchester University Press, 1995).

Harris, J. P., and Toase, F. H. (eds), *Armoured Warfare* (London: B. T. Batsford, 1990).

Harrison, M. (ed.), *The Economics of World War II: Six Great Powers in International Comparison* (Cambridge: Cambridge University Press, 2000).

Jackson, J., *The Fall of France: The Nazi Invasion of 1940* (Oxford: Oxford University Press, 2003).

Jefferys, K., *The Churchill Coalition and Wartime Politics, 1940–1945* (Manchester and New York: Manchester University Press, 1991).

—, *War and Reform: British Politics during the Second World War* (Manchester: Manchester University Press, 1994).

Jones, H., *British Civilians in the Front Line: Air Raids, Productivity and Wartime Culture, 1939–45* (Manchester: Manchester University Press, 2006).

Keegan, J. (ed.), *Churchill's Generals* (New York: Grove Weidenfeld, 1991).

Kroener, B. R., Müller, R.-D., and Umbreit, H. (eds), *Germany and the Second World War, Vol. V: Organization and Mobilization of the German Sphere of Power. Part I: Wartime Administration, Economy, and Manpower Resources 1939–1941* (Oxford: Clarendon Press, 2000).

— (eds), *Germany and the Second World War, Vol. V: Organization and Mobilization of the German Sphere of Power. Part II: Wartime Administration, Economy, and Manpower Resources 1942–1944/5* (Oxford: Clarendon Press, 2003).

Lewin, R., *Man of Armour: A Study of Lieut-General Vyvyan Pope and the Development of Armoured Warfare* (London: Leo Cooper, 1976).

Lloyd-Jones, R., and Lewis, M. J., *Alfred Herbert Ltd and the British Machine Tool Industry, 1887–1983* (Aldershot: Ashgate Publishing, 2006).

Macleod Ross, G., *The Business of Tanks, 1933 to 1945*, in collaboration with Major-General Sir C. Clarke (Ilfracombe: Arthur H. Stockwell, 1976).

Mason, T., *Nazism, Fascism and the Working Class* (Cambridge: Cambridge University Press, 1996).

Millett, A. R., and Murray, W. (eds), *Military Effectiveness, Volume 3: The Second World War*, new edition, first published 1988 (New York: Cambridge University Press, 2010).

Millward, R., and Singleton, J. (eds), *The Political Economy of Nationalisation in Britain 1920–1950* (Cambridge: Cambridge University Press, 1995).

Milward, A. S., *War, Economy and Society: 1939–1945* (London: Allen Lane, 1977).

Morgan, K. O., *Consensus and Disunity: The Lloyd George Coalition Government 1918–1922* (Oxford: Clarendon Press, 1979).

Murray, W., and Millett, A. R., *A War To Be Won: Fighting the Second World War* (Cambridge: Harvard University Press, 2001).

— (eds), *Military Innovation in the Interwar Period* (Cambridge: Cambridge University Press, 1996).

Ness, L., *Jane's World War II Tanks and Fighting Vehicles: The Complete Guide* (London: Harper Collins, 2002).

Ogorkiewicz, R. M., *Armour: The Development of Mechanised Forces and Their Equipment* (London: Stevens & Sons, 1960).

Overy, R., *War and Economy in the Third Reich* (New York: Oxford University Press, 2002).

Peden, G. C., *Arms, Economics and British Strategy: From Dreadnoughts to Hydrogen Bombs* (Cambridge: Cambridge University Press, 2007).

— *British Rearmament and the Treasury: 1932–1939* (Edinburgh: Scottish Academic Press, 1979).

Reid, J. M., *James Lithgow, Master of Work* (London: Hutchinson, 1964).

Reynolds, D., Kimball, W. F., and Chubarian, A. O. (eds), *Allies at War: The Soviet, American, and British Experience, 1939–1945* (London: Palgrave Macmillan, 1994).

Ritchie, S., *Industry and Air Power: The Expansion of British Aircraft Production, 1935–1941* (London and New York: Routledge, 2007).

Seidman, J. I., *American Labor from Defense to Reconversion* (Chicago: University of Chicago Press, 1953).

Shuster, R. J., *German Disarmament after World War I: The Diplomacy of International Arms Inspection 1920–1931* (Abingdon: Routledge, 2006).

Smith, H. L. (ed.), *War and Social Change: British Society in the Second World War* (Manchester: Manchester University Press, 1986).

Summerfield, P., *Women Workers in the Second World War: Production and Patriarchy in Conflict* (Beckenham: Croom Helm, 1984).

Sweet, J. J. T., *Iron Arm: The Mechanization of Mussolini's Army, 1920–1940* (Mechanicsburg: Stackpole Books, 2007).

Taylor, A. J. P., *Beaverbrook* (London: History Book Club, 1972).

Tooze, A., *The Wages of Destruction: The Making and Breaking of the Nazi Economy* (London: Allen Lane, 2006).

Uziel, D., *Arming the Luftwaffe: The German Aviation Industry in World War II* (Jefferson: McFarland, 2012).

Warner, P., *Auchinleck: The Lonely Soldier*, first published 1981 (Barnsley: Pen & Sword, 2006).

Weinberg, G. L., *A World at Arms: A Global History of World War II*, 2nd edition, first published 2005 (New York: Cambridge University Press, 2008).

Welch, D. (ed.), *Nazi Propaganda: The Power and the Limitations* (Beckenham: Croom Helm, 1983).

Whiteside, N., and Salais, R. (eds), *Governance, Industry and Labour Markets in Britain and France: The Modernising State in the Mid-Twentieth Century* (London: Routledge, 1998).

Wright, P., *Tank: The Progress of a Monstrous War Machine* (London: Faber and Faber, 2001).

Wrigley, C., *British Trade Unions since 1933* (Cambridge: Cambridge University Press, 2002).

Published articles

Adams, P., 'The Failure of Social Reform: 1918–1920', *Past & Present*, Vol. 24, No. 1 (1963), pp. 43–64.

Allen, R. C. D., 'Mutual Aid between the U.S. and the British Empire, 1941–45', *Journal of the Royal Statistical Society*, Vol. 109, No. 3 (1946), pp. 243–77.

Danchev, A., '"Dilly-Dally", or Having the Last Word: Field Marshal Sir John Dill and Prime Minister Winston Churchill', *Journal of Contemporary History*, Vol. 22, No. 1 (Jan. 1987), pp. 21–44.

DiNardo, R. L., and Bay, A., 'Horse-Drawn Transport in the German Army', *Journal of Contemporary History*, Vol. 23, No. 1 (Jan. 1988), pp. 129–42.

Dunbabin, J. P. D., 'British Rearmament in the 1930s: A Chronology and Review', *Historical Journal*, Vol. 18, No. 3 (Sept. 1975), pp. 587–609.

Fearon, P., 'The British Airframe Industry and the State, 1918–35', *Economic History Review*, New Series, Vol. 27, No. 2 (May 1974), pp. 236–51.

—, 'The Formative Years of the British Aircraft Industry, 1913–1924', *Business History Review*, Vol. 43, No. 4 (Winter 1969), pp. 476–95.

Ferris, J., 'Treasury Control, the Ten Year Rule and British Service Policies, 1919–1924', *Historical Journal*, Vol. 30, No. 4 (Dec. 1987), pp. 859–83.

French, D., 'The Mechanization of the British Cavalry between the World Wars', *War in History*, Vol. 10, No. 3 (Jul. 2003), pp. 296–320.

Friedelbaum, S. H., 'The British Iron and Steel Industry: 1929–49', *Journal of Business of the University of Chicago*, Vol. 23, No. 2 (Apr. 1950), pp. 117–32.

Goldsmith, R. W., 'The Power of Victory: Munitions Output in World War II', *Military Affairs*, Vol. 10, No. 1 (Spring 1946), pp. 69–80.

Gowing, M., 'The Organisation of Manpower in Britain during the Second World War', *Journal of Contemporary History*, Vol. 7, No. 1/2 (Jan.–Apr. 1972), pp. 147–67.

Harrison, M., 'Resource Mobilization for World War II: The U.S.A., U.K., U.S.S.R., and Germany, 1938–1945', *Economic History Review*, New Series, Vol. 41, No. 2 (May 1988), pp. 171–92.

Howlett, P., 'New Light through Old Windows: A New Perspective on the British Economy in the Second World War', *Journal of Contemporary History*, Vol. 28, No. 2 (Apr. 1993), pp. 361–79.

—, 'Resource Allocation in Wartime Britain: The Case of Steel, 1939–45', *Journal of Contemporary History*, Vol. 29, No. 3 (Jul. 1994), pp. 523–44.

Hughes, J. L., 'The Origins of World War II in Europe: British Deterrence Failure and German Expansionism', *Journal of Interdisciplinary History*, Vol. 18, No. 4 (Spring 1988), pp. 851–91.

Jersak, T., 'Blitzkrieg Revisited: A New Look at Nazi War and Extermination Planning',
    Historical Journal, Vol. 43, No. 2 (Jun. 2000), pp. 565–82.
Lewis, A. R., 'The Failure of Allied Planning and Doctrine for Operation Overlord: The
    Case of Minefield and Obstacle Clearance', *Journal of Military History*, Vol. 62, No. 4
    (Oct. 1998), pp. 787–807.
Millett, J. D., 'The War Department in World War II', *American Political Science Review*,
    Vol. 40, No. 5 (Oct. 1946), pp. 863–97.
Parker, R. A. C., 'British Rearmament 1936–9: Treasury, Trade Unions and Skilled Labour',
    English Historical Review, Vol. 96, No. 379 (Apr. 1981), pp. 306–43.
Phillips, G., 'Scapegoat Arm: Twentieth-Century Cavalry in Anglophone Historiography',
    Journal of Military History, Vol. 71, No. 1 (Jan. 2007), pp. 37–74.
Philpott, W., and Alexander, M. S., 'The French and the British Field Force: Moral Support
    or Material Contribution?', *Journal of Military History*, Vol. 71, No. 3 (Jul. 2007),
    pp. 743–72.
Reid, B. H., 'The Attack by Illumination: The Strange Case of Canal Defence Lights', *RUSI
    Journal*, Vol. 128, No. 4 (1983), pp. 44–9.
Ritchie, S., 'A New Audit of War: The Productivity of Britain's Wartime Aircraft Industry
    Reconsidered', *War & Society*, Vol. 12, No. 1 (May 1994), pp. 125–47.
Smith, H. L., 'The Womanpower Problem in Britain during the Second World War',
    Historical Journal, Vol. 27, No. 4 (Dec. 1984), pp. 925–45.
Smith, M., 'The Royal Air Force, Air Power and British Foreign Policy, 1932–37', *Journal of
    Contemporary History*, Vol. 12, No. 1 (Jan. 1977), pp. 153–74.
Thomas, M., 'Rearmament and Economic Recovery in the Late 1930s', *Economic History
    Review*, New Series, Vol. 36, No. 4 (Nov. 1983), pp. 552–79.
Travers, T., 'Could the Tanks of 1918 Have Been War-Winners for the British
    Expeditionary Force?', *Journal of Contemporary History*, Vol. 27, No. 3 (Jul. 1992),
    pp. 389–406.
Zeitlin, J., 'Flexibility and Mass Production at War: Aircraft Manufacture in Britain, the
    United States, and Germany, 1939–1945', *Technology and Culture*, Vol. 36, No. 1 (Jan.
    1995), pp. 46–79.

Ph.D. theses

Croucher, R., 'Communist Politics and Shop Stewards in Engineering, 1935–46' (Ph.D.
    thesis, University of Warwick, 1977).
Harris, J. P., 'The War Office and Rearmament, 1935–39' (Ph.D. thesis, King's College
    London, 1983).
Nakamura, N., 'Women, Work and War: Industrial Mobilisation and Demobilisation,
    Coventry and Bolton, 1940–1946' (Ph.D. thesis, University of Warwick, 1984).
Perry, F. W., 'Manpower and Organisational Problems in the Expansion of the British and
    Other Commonwealth Armies during the Two World Wars' (Ph.D. thesis, University
    of London, 1982).
Rosevear, S., 'Regional Policy and the British Motor Vehicle Industry 1945–64: A Study
    in Selective Intervention and the Economics of Industrial Location' (Ph.D. thesis,
    University of Bristol, 1998).

Index